4/02

Understanding Shyness

WITHDRAWN

Also by W. Ray Crozier

Cognitive Processes in the Perception of Art (editor with A. J. Chapman)

Decision Making: Cognitive Models and Explanations (editor with
   R. H. Ranyard and O. Svenson)

Individual Learners: Personality Differences in Education

International Handbook of Social Anxiety (editor with L. E. Alden)

Manufactured Pleasures: Psychological Responses to Design

Shyness and Embarrassment: Perspectives from Social Psychology (editor)

Understanding Shyness

Psychological Perspectives

W. Ray Crozier

palgrave

© Walter Raymond Crozier 2001

First published 2001 by
PALGRAVE
Houndmills, Basingstoke, Hampshire RG21 6XS and
175 Fifth Avenue, New York, N. Y. 10010
Companies and representatives throughout the world

PALGRAVE is the new global academic imprint of St. Martin's
Press LLC Scholarly and Reference Division and Palgrave
Publishers Ltd (formerly Macmillan Press Ltd).

ISBN 0–333–77370–5   hardcover
ISBN 0–333–77371–3   paperback

This book is printed on paper suitable for recycling and
made from fully managed and sustained forest sources.

A catalogue record for this book is available
from the British Library.

Library of Congress Cataloging-in-Publication Data
is available from the Library of Congress.

10   9   8   7   6   5   4   3   2   1
10   09   08   07   06   05   04   03   02   01

Copy-edited and typeset by Povey-Edmondson
Tavistock and Rochdale, England

Printed in China

To Sandra, John and Beth

Contents

List of Figures and Tables

Figures

Tables

Acknowledgements

I am grateful to Frances Arnold at the publishers for her encouragement and advice in the planning stage of this volume. I am also very grateful to all the following, who have helped in many different ways. The Research Committee of Cardiff University granted me a period of study leave in order to complete this project. Huw Beynon, Gareth Rees and colleagues at the School of Social Sciences have been supportive during this period. I have relied heavily on the understanding of Sandra, John and Beth Crozier, as papers and draft chapters gradually took over our home. Colleagues in the shyness research community have been enormously helpful in sending me prepublication copies of their work, in particular I would like to thank Jens Asendorpf, Bernardo Carducci, Jonathan Cheek, Mary Ann Evans, Jonathan Oakman, Nicola Yuill and Philip Zimbardo. Val Rees kindly read some of the chapters in draft form, Martin Graff helped with the figures.

I have drawn upon protocols collected during two research projects in order to illustrate points, particularly in Chapters 1 and 5. I am grateful to the anonymous participants in these studies. They have been assigned pseudonyms – English names in one study, Welsh names in the other – and minor details have been changed in order to preserve confidentiality. Alison Garbert-Jones worked with me on one of these studies. Other studies of shyness cited in the book were carried out with Maria Burnham and Delia Russell. Every research project is a team effort and I am grateful for the advice and help provided by Wynford Bellin, Dianne Bennett-Gates, Beth Crozier, John Crozier, Andrew Hill, Rob Ranyard and Val Rees.

The author and publishers are grateful to the following for permission to reprint previously published material: John Updike, Malcolm Bradbury, Bernardo Carducci, Society for Research into Child Development, Penguin Books, Alfred A. Knopf Inc. and Methuen. Excerpt from *Diagnostic and Statistical Manual, 4th edn*, reprinted with permission from the *Diagnostic and Statistical*

Manual of Mental Disorders, *4th edn*, © 1994 American Psychiatric Association; excerpt from *When Daddy Came Home* by Barry Turner and Tony Rennell (Hutchinson, 1995), reprinted with the permission of Random House Archive and Library, Barry Turner and Tony Rennell; excerpt from *You Just Don't Understand* by Deborah Tannen (Virago, 1992), reprinted with the permission of Little, Brown and Rogers Coleridge & White Limited; material in Tables 1.1 and 1.2 was published in P. G. Zimbardo, P. A. Pilkonis, and R. M. Norwood, *The Silent Prison of Shyness* (Office of Naval Research Technical Report Z-17, Stanford University, 1974) and is reprinted with the permission of Philip Zimbardo; illustration from *Developmental Science*, vol. 3, no. 2, 2000, reproduced with the permission of Dr Vasudevi Reddy and Blackwell Publishers Ltd, © Blackwell Publishers Ltd; excerpt from *Adolphe* by Benjamin Constant, translated by Leonard Tancock (Penguin, 1964), reprinted with the permission of Penguin. Figure 1.1 is based on accounts of theories presented by H. J. Eysenck (*Structure of Human Personality*, Methuen, 1970) and J. A. Gray (*The Psychology of Fear and Stress*, 2nd edn, Cambridge University Press, 1987). Box 5.1 is based on a research study described by R. S. Miller (*Embarrassment: Poise and Peril in Everyday Life*, Guilford Press, 1996, pp. 123–5). Every effort has been made to contact all the copyright-holders, but if any have been inadvertently omitted the publishers will be pleased to make the necessary arrangement at the earliest opportunity.

Introduction

'I suddenly came over all shy.' 'I am naturally shy. I never know what to say.' 'Basically, she's a very shy person.' These are typical examples, drawn from everyday conversations, of the use of the word shy. Like other short and common words it does not have a single meaning, and it is used in different ways to capture various aspects of a person's state of mind in social situations. We say that people are shy if they are quiet in company, feel ill at ease in a social gathering, are reluctant to step into the limelight or are hesitant about meeting someone for the first time. Someone is shy when he or she is self-conscious about being seen with a new hairstyle or is diffident about arriving home with a new boyfriend or girlfriend. A woman may find it hard to find the words to tell her friends that she is expecting a baby. Among children, shyness is associated with being coy, bashful and tongue-tied.

The term labels these transient feelings and behaviours but it can also be used in another way – to explain them. Being shy is the reason for having little to say or turning down an invitation. One common form of psychological explanation is couched in terms of the individual's temperament or character type, he or she is said to 'be a shy person', to have the personality trait of shyness. Someone who is this type or who has this trait finds it difficult to be bold, open, relaxed or spontaneous; he or she is wary, timid, reluctant and reticent. The trait has positive qualities too: it can describe someone who is modest or unassuming.

Applying this kind of explanation can help to make sense of an individual's style of behaviour. Someone who seems taciturn and remote, or who is arrogant or conceited, or even hostile, can appear in a new light if we realise that he or she is shy. It can make sense of our own experience of social situations, as we recognise that it has a pattern, one that is also found in the behaviour of others. The pattern has a name.

Shyness is not just a state of mind like, say, nervousness or wariness. It can have an impact on an individual's behaviour. It can take the form of reticence, an inability to contribute to a conversation or an unwillingness to make eye contact during encounters. The shy person often adopts a defensive or self-protective approach to social encounters, reluctant to express opinions or to disagree, and keeping in the background. Such behaviours have unwanted consequences. They influence the impression that others form – shy people may not appear attractive or be valued for their personal qualities. They also find it difficult to be assertive or to catch the attention of, say, superiors at work.

The difficulties experienced in social situations are of considerable interest to psychologists for both theoretical and practical reasons. Social relationships are of fundamental psychological importance. The individual's personality is shaped by his or her early relationships within the family. The child's ability to relate to other children, in play and at school, and to form friendships is significant for his or her adjustment. Effective adult life requires integration into a complex social world of family and work, business and leisure, routine social encounters and long-term commitments. One of the distinctive features of life in a modern technological society is that the regulation of social encounters has come to depend less on membership of well-defined groups or clear rules for conduct. For example, although social class still exerts a considerable influence on behaviour, it does so in a more fluid, less predictable way than in the past. The dispersal of families, technological advances in home entertainment and the replacement of routine interpersonal transactions by self-service supermarkets and 'hole in the wall' cash machines have also contributed to isolation from other people. We increasingly interact with strangers, and without clear guidelines for doing so. This may be reflected in the finding, noted in Chapter 1, that increasing numbers of people now think of themselves as shy.

The trend might also be related to evidence that there is a high prevalence of social phobia in the population. This term is used by clinicians to refer to anxiety about social interactions. Phobia is perhaps an unfortunate term, since it brings to mind quite specific fears (of spiders, snakes or enclosed spaces) whereas social anxieties are quite general. It has proved difficult to distinguish between the concepts of social phobia and shyness (Chapter 6). Clinicians have long recognised that problems with social relationships are associated with a number of psychological conditions, for example depression, but current research in psychiatry and clinical psychology has come to regard a predisposition to experience these problems as a condition in its own right. Considerable attention has been devoted to the search for suitable forms of intervention to help those with social phobia overcome their problems.

This book aims to bring together and evaluate research into shyness that has been carried out within a psychological framework. Only a few years ago this would have resulted in a very slim volume but there has recently been a surge of interest in shyness and related topics. This research has shown that understanding shyness is not simple and, in search of explanations, it has drawn upon many branches of psychology: the study of child development, behavioural genetics, the search for the basic temperaments and personality traits, the analysis of social encounters, the physiology of anxiety and blushing, and psychological and pharmacological interventions to help individuals overcome severe social anxiety.

The book has its origins in the International Conference on Shyness and Self-consciousness, which I organised in 1997 on behalf of the Welsh Branch of the British Psychological Society in conjunction with the School of Education, Cardiff University. The conference elicited an enormous public response. It received extensive coverage by the international media and this showed me and the other delegates who gave interviews how much interest there is in shyness. Whether speaking to the press or participating in radio and television programmes (as distant from Cardiff as Japan and Australia), we were asked the same questions. What is shyness? How can you tell if someone is shy? What effects does it have? Are women more shy than men are? What is the difference between shyness and embarrassment? What makes someone shy? Are some people born shy? Can people overcome their shyness? What can they do to change?

These questions have no straightforward answers. It seemed to me that it would be useful to try to address these questions at greater length, to marshal the available evidence and see what answers could be given. One of the problems with research into a topic such as shyness, which is undertaken in different branches of psychology and the findings published in a wide range of journals, is that it is difficult for the practitioner, teacher, student or interested layperson to be aware of the extent of research that is carried out and to make connections between different areas. This volume aims to do this.

Overview of the volume

The topics covered in the volume are arranged into six chapters, followed by a short epilogue. Because the book focuses on the nature of evidence supporting or challenging competing explanations of shyness it includes an extensive list of references to the research literature.

Chapter 1 begins by analysing some examples of shy behaviour and then considers definitions of shyness. The notion that shyness is a personality trait is explored in several ways. The chapter assesses the place of shyness in the major structural theories of personality and reviews evidence of it being a trait in its own right. It identifies and compares some of the common questionnaire measures of individual differences in shyness.

The organisation of the second chapter reflects a position adopted by many theorists, that shyness comprises three components: cognitive, affective and behavioural. The chapter discusses each of these components in turn and considers their roles in different explanations of shyness. Research into the cognitive component has yielded interesting findings about the nature of self-consciousness and the negative self-appraisals that are typical of many shy people. The discussion of affect concentrates on attempts to measure some of the emotional processes involved in shyness. The section on shy behaviours focuses on studies of reticence and eye contact. It includes a brief review of studies of gender differences in behaviour.

The next two chapters are devoted to the origins and development of shyness in infancy and childhood. Research in this area has been dominated by theories proposing that behavioural inhibition is a basic temperament characterised by wariness of strangers and signs of distress in unfamiliar social situations. Chapter 3 reviews evidence for inhibition as a basic temperament. It assesses whether inhibition meets four criteria for identification as a temperament, namely appearance early in life, stability over time, predictable patterns of response, and neurobiological correlates. It considers the nature of the relationship between inhibition and shyness. Chapter 4 begins with an evaluation of research into whether individual differences in shyness are innate and have a genetic basis. The study of twins has played an important part in this research. The chapter then discusses the influence upon shyness of the child's relationship with his or her parents. Two ideas are explored: that shy children construct particular 'working models' of social relationships, and that they have low expectations about their ability to function effectively in social situations. Finally, the chapter considers how shyness is related to the development of children's self-awareness and capacity for self-evaluation.

Chapter 5 asks whether shyness and embarrassment are distinct, either as emotional reactions to social dilemmas or as personality traits. The chapter identifies the kinds of situation that elicit embarrassment and compares explanations of their capacity to do so in terms of their implications for an individual's self-esteem or the embarrassed person's inability to respond appropriately to his or her predicament. It examines the psychology and physiology of blushing, which remains as much a puzzle today as it was to Charles Darwin over a century ago.

The theme of the final substantive chapter is the attempt to help individuals overcome their difficulties with social interaction. It introduces the concept of social phobia and considers whether it can be distinguished from shyness. It asks whether it is appropriate to think of social anxiety as an 'illness' that is amenable to treatment. It reviews two approaches aimed to help individuals suffering from severe social anxiety: behavioural programmes, including cognitive–behavioural approaches and social skills training, and pharmacological interventions.

Finally, a short epilogue offers a summary of the principal themes to emerge from the evaluation of the evidence. I hope that by then the book will have convinced you that shyness is a fascinating topic, worthy of further thought and empirical enquiry.

Chapter 1

The Nature of Shyness

The concept of shyness

The word *shyness* is in common use in everyday life to refer to a sense of discomfort in social situations. It does not have a precise meaning, although it has connotations of wariness, timidity and inhibition. 'Delyth' describes her shyness with a group of acquaintances:

> I felt inadequate. I believed I was too young to say anything that would have been of the slightest interest to these people. I felt awkward as if out of place even though we were all there together as we belonged to the Tennis Club. When anybody did ask me something I would be so concerned about how to reply that I could feel myself heating up and turning red. I tried to find something else to do so I could break away from the group. I don't get embarrassed or feel shy with an individual from this group but once the 'gang' is assembled I feel intimidated.

Not knowing what to say is common in descriptions of shyness. The source of Delyth's reticence seems to be preoccupation with the effect that what she says will have on others, and with the opinion of her that they may form on the basis of this. She expects that they will take a negative view – she has nothing interesting to say. This preoccupation leads to self-consciousness and an urge to escape. Delyth also implies that she is only shy in some situations. There are occasions when she is able to speak freely, for example when talking with individuals.

As we shall see, these concerns are found whenever people describe their experience of shyness. They are not restricted to contemporary life but can be found in accounts at different periods and in different cultures. For example the French novelist Benjamin Constant provided this moving description of inhibition in his novel *Adolphe*, published in 1816.

> I cannot recall ever having had one hour's serious talk with him [his father] in the first eighteen years of my life. His letters were affectionate and full of sensible and sympathetic advice, but no sooner were we in each other's presence than there came over him a sort of reserve which I could not account for and which had a chilling effect on me. At that time I did not know what shyness was – that inner suffering which dogs us even into old age, which takes our deepest feelings and rams them back into our hearts, which freezes the words on our lips, distorts everything we try to say, and only lets us express ourselves in general terms and more or less bitter sarcasm, as though we meant to take revenge on our very emotions for the pain we feel through not being able to communicate them. I did not realize that my father was shy even in front of his own son, and that many a time, after a long wait for some sign of affection from me which his own apparent coolness seemed to discourage, he left me with tears in his eyes and complained to others that I did not love him (Constant, 1816/1964, pp. 37–8).

In the course of providing a vivid account of the experience of a shy person who is unable to articulate his feelings, Constant makes several acute observations and raises a number of issues that continue to be discussed by researchers. First, this experience is not restricted to interactions with strangers or speaking in public, but can be experienced within close family relationships. This is not a peculiarity of Constant's family life or of social manners in early nineteenth-century France. There are very similar descriptions of shyness in the relationship between a father and his child in Edmund Gosse's memoir, *Father and Son*, and in the novel *The Rector's Daughter* by F. M. Mayor. It is also evident in this excerpt from an interview:

> This took place when I was about fifteen, as far as I can remember. My Uncle Bob and I worked all morning on the boat; we scrubbed down all the woodwork and polished the brass. When we had finished he said to me, 'Well, we make a good team', but I didn't say anything back to him. Not a word or a smile or anything. I don't know why but I couldn't think of anything to say to him. The moment passed, and afterwards I regretted it. Years later, I still regret it, because we were never that close again, and he's dead now. I still don't why I was so overcome with shyness. I often wonder what he must have thought of me.

This aspect of shyness has unfortunately attracted little research. That it can be experienced in close relationships has implications for understanding its causes. It qualifies the assertion made by Darwin that 'persons who are exceedingly shy are rarely shy in the presence of those with whom they are quite familiar, and of whose good opinion and sympathy they are perfectly assured' (Darwin, 1872, p. 350). Delyth's shyness seems to be largely a concern with how others in general will evaluate her, and as we shall see this concern has figured in several psychological theories of shyness. However this does not seem a very plausible explanation of Adolphe's father's shyness.

Second, shyness seems to be a characteristic of the individual, it is some quality that Adolphe's father brings to the situation, and does not seem to be simply his reaction to his son's behaviour. We are not told whether shyness was present in his other social relationships or whether it was restricted to interactions with his son. Our intuition is that it would be more widespread. Everyday language describes these widespread tendencies as *traits*: 'She is a shy person'; 'Behind that extroverted facade he's really shy'. Psychological theories have also drawn upon the trait concept. While this approach has proved useful in a number of respects, it has also led to controversy about how general traits are, and whether they can be used to explain as well as describe someone's behaviour. The notion that shyness is a personality trait is evaluated later in this chapter.

Another implication of Constant's account is that shyness is only experienced in social situations; Adolphe's father can express his warmth and sympathy and can communicate with his son by means of letters, but he cannot do this in his son's presence. Shyness is inherently a social experience. This was recognised by Darwin, who provided an example of a shy man who may be 'as bold as a hero in battle, and yet have no self-confidence about trifles in the presence of strangers' (Darwin, 1872/1965, p. 350).

Finally, shyness is expressed in behaviours that have consequences for the social encounter. Adolphe's father behaves in an apparently cold and sarcastic manner and this inhibits the kind of reaction from his son that he would have hoped for – his reserve has a 'chilling effect'. He is motivated to form a close and affectionate tie with his son and is certainly not indifferent to him, as his letters show, but his reserve creates the impression of coldness. This unfortunate consequence is exacerbated by Adolphe's lack of awareness that this behaviour is caused by shyness. In the absence of this explanation, the reticence and sarcasm would indeed be chilling. Furthermore, one can imagine that any affection displayed by Adolphe would seem to be rebuffed by his father, whose inhibition would render him incapable of making an appropriate response. Constant's description is characterised by the *temperature* of the relationship, the shy person's words are 'frozen', his behaviour is 'cool' and its effects are 'chilling'. Temperature is, I think, an effective metaphor for some of the core elements of shyness – reticence and awkwardness leave the individual in an exposed position, 'frozen' and unable to act. The shy person's reserve gives the impression that he or she is cold or remote or lacks interest in other people.

Shyness is worthy of study for both scientific and practical reasons. Its study provides insight into the processes involved in social interaction. When social encounters go smoothly the processes involved in making this happen are invisible and, indeed, seem scarcely worthy of scientific attention. However when something disrupts the encounter, and discomfort or embarrassment ensues, this provides a glimpse of what it takes for encounters to work effectively. What appears spontaneous and 'natural' is in fact the product of skilful behaviour on the part of the participants, even if this skill is normally largely unconscious. Shyness is a matter of an individual's belief that he or she is unable to make an effective contribution. The study of these beliefs can yield insight into the attributes and capacities that are necessary for someone to feel confident and at ease in a social situation.

A second reason for studying shyness is that it causes problems for large numbers of people. For many it is a 'blight' on their life, or has 'ruined' it, and is a constant source of misery. Many regard it as a handicap or illness, but one that is not recognised by others. Given these perceptions, one would imagine that shyness has been the focus of much psychological research, but until recently this was not the case and the term rarely featured in the scientific or clinical literature. In part this is because these concerns *were* recognised by psychologists but were labelled in other ways. Indeed psychologists have coined a plethora of technical terms: audience sensitivity, communication apprehensiveness, embarrassability, nonassertiveness, reticence, self-consciousness, social anxiety, social neurosis, social phobia, social skill deficit, and stage fright. In effect this plethora of terms has served to make shyness 'invisible'.

Psychologists argue that it is essential to develop such technical terms because they can be provided with unambiguous definitions and this leads to precision in making observations, taking measurements and testing hypotheses. It also helps to avoid confusion in the interpretation of research findings. For example some studies seem to show that a tendency towards withdrawn behaviour is associated with a greater risk of individuals becoming delinquent, whereas other studies indicate that it is associated with a smaller risk. These apparent differences in findings may simply reflect differences in the ways in which withdrawal has been defined in these studies (Kerr *et al.*, 1997).

Operational definitions can be tied to particular empirical referents. Everyday language, on the other hand, is more elusive: words such as shyness carry connotations that cannot be pinned down. Their meanings can vary from one group to another and can change over time. Thus shyness can have positive connotations; for example it is associated with modesty, which many would think a desirable trait, not one necessarily associated with social difficulties. Shyness has been regarded in the past as a positive trait among women, for example the middle-class women characters in Jane Austen's fiction. Researchers, it is argued, simply create confusion by basing their investigations on such a shifting foundation.

Leary (1983) has argued this point with regard to shyness, suggesting that the proliferation of terms that have rarely been explicitly defined has led to fragmentation of research and failure to make connections among parallel lines of enquiry. He prefers to use the term *social anxiety*, defined as 'anxiety resulting from the prospect or presence of interpersonal evaluation in real or imagined social settings' (Schlenker and Leary, 1982, p. 642), and to restrict the term shyness to a combination of social anxiety and inhibited behaviour.

One way forward might be for researchers to take the term 'shyness' and provide their own technical definition of it. For example one of the earliest studies of shyness defined it as:

> A state of hyper-inhibition, usually accompanied by physical symptoms like blushing, stammering, perspiring, trembling, going pale, accessory movements and increased urinary and faecal urges. The mental state is described by the individual as a feeling of inferiority, of not being wanted, of intruding; it is coupled with an inability to say the right thing at the right moment – while a hundred good answers and quick retorts can be thought of afterwards. The individual feels overconscious of himself, of his mental attitudes, his emotions, and especially of his appearance (Lewinsky, 1941, pp. 105–6).

This certainly captures many of the qualities of shyness, but it is vague – how frequently is 'usually'? Whereas it identifies a number of mental, physiological and behavioural elements in shyness, it does not say whether *all* of these elements are necessary for shyness.

Is an individual shy who has this mental state but who can manage to say the right thing at the right time? Does shyness necessarily have specific behavioural consequences? Would it be better to define it in terms of its characteristic behaviours, such as reticence? Is blushing essential for shyness? All these questions remain unresolved by the definition.

Harris (1984) has criticised this approach, arguing that psychologists should not attempt to define a term that is already current in everyday language. They should make a clear distinction between using shyness as a term with a restricted technical meaning and using it as a word with broader social meanings. Psychologists should respect the common usage of the word and be alert to its various meanings.

The implication of Harris's argument is that research in shyness must begin with a careful analysis of how the word is actually used in everyday life. He argues that psychologists can only investigate the processes involved in shyness when this step has been taken. This has seldom been the approach adopted in psychological research. One exception is a study by Cheek and Watson (1989), who contacted a sample of shy people who had written to request help with their shyness following the publication of a magazine article. The correspondents were asked, 'How do you know or how did you decide that you are shy? In other words, briefly describe the events or circumstances that led you to the conclusion that you are shy.'

The correspondents' answers to this question were coded into nine categories:

- Thoughts and worries, including self-consciousness and fear of being rejected.
- 'Somatic-emotional shyness', referring to physiological symptoms such as blushing and perspiring.
- 'Affective-emotional symptoms', such as feeling upset.
- A perceived lack of verbal skills.
- Non-verbal overt behaviour, such as averting one's gaze in conversation.
- Withdrawing from social contacts.
- Avoiding social interactions.
- Labelling, or being told by others that one is shy.
- The consequences of shyness, such as loneliness.

The most frequently mentioned reasons for the participants' belief that they were shy were thoughts and worries, affective-emotional symptoms, lack of verbal skills and a tendency to avoid interactions, that is to say, cognitive, physiological and behavioural components of shyness were all identified as factors in reaching this conclusion. Most respondents mentioned reasons from more than one category, but only 12 per cent gave reasons from all three components. Cheek and Watson (1989, p. 12) define shyness as 'the tendency to feel tense, worried, or awkward during social interactions' – this definition does not require that all three feelings are experienced. They suggest that this definition is closer to the ordinary language conception of shyness. It avoids the problems that would be caused if psychologists were to tell people that they are wrong to identify themselves as shy because their experience does not match the psychologist's definition, or that they are misguided when, say, they believe that they blush when they are shy.

A further advantage of this approach is that it does not make strong assumptions about the nature of shyness. For example, defining shyness as a form of social anxiety is essentially an assertion that shyness *is* a form of anxiety. Thus Asendorpf (1989, p. 481) asserts that, 'state shyness occurs only in social situations and always involves an elevated level of anxiety that refers to certain aspects of current or future interactions'. However alternative approaches conceptualise the experience of shyness in terms of the emotion of *shame* rather than anxiety, as we shall discuss in Chapters 2 and 5. It is surely an empirical issue rather than a matter of definition whether or not shyness is a form of anxiety.

Although people's experience can be a starting point of research, it cannot be the end point or even the criterion for evaluating research findings. The psychologist's task is to understand shyness not just in the sense of knowing what people have in mind when they describe themselves as shy or report experiences that can be categorised as shyness. The psychologist wants to be in a position to understand shyness in the stronger sense of being able to explain it.

Explanation may well be in terms of hypothetical constructs remote from the experience of shyness. For example, as we shall see in Chapter 6, variations in the level of the chemical transmitter *serotonin* in the brain are associated with changes in mood and emotion, and people suffering from depression are known to have a low level of serotonin. Medical interventions designed to increase the level of serotonin have proved effective in the treatment of depression and it is possible that these may also be effective in treating social phobia (an extreme form of social anxiety). Such findings on the contribution of serotonin to social phobia do not, in themselves, constitute an explanation, but they do point to a form that an explanation might take. It might be possible to frame an explanation of shyness in terms of a deficiency in the circulating level of serotonin and this could lead to effective treatment for people who have a problem with shyness. Furthermore these individuals might report positive changes in their experience of shyness and their perception of themselves following the treatment. The explanation would seem to be a successful one, but it would not be couched in terms of people's experience, or indeed in ordinary language. This is of course a hypothetical argument, but it does point to the need to be prepared to entertain explanations that are not suggested by common sense.

A second argument against relying upon common sense is that the assumption that shyness occurs only in social situations might reflect the *salience* of the experience in those situations rather than an emotion that is specific to them. For example, let us assume that there exists an innate fear of novel situations that is triggered by novelty wherever it is encountered – new people, new roles, new objects and new places. This fear is evoked in young infants in the presence of unfamiliar adults, and through the processes of socialisation and acquiring the vocabulary for describing feelings and behaviour it comes to be labelled shyness. As objects and places become increasingly familiar they are less likely to elicit this fear, but when they do so, this is not labelled as shyness. As the child enters a complex social world, her reactions to unfamiliar people become increasingly differentiated. The child reflects on her experience, particularly on her responsibility for it. Other people describe this experience as shyness, and perhaps label her – 'she is very shy'. The child develops ways of coping with her fear, for example by avoiding novel social situations, and these coping strategies in turn shape her experience and behaviour and influence the reactions of other people. One can end up with a complex emotional experience that *seems* to one's common sense to be specific to social situations, and yet it is not only a social one. People may not make connections between what they feel when they are introduced to someone at a party and what they feel when they drive a new car, yet the same psychological process might be involved in both.

Another method of enquiry that is close to the spirit of Harris's (1984) thesis begins by asking people whether or not they regard themselves as shy and continues by exploring what they perceive to be the implications of their shyness. This particular method does not provide respondents with a definition of shyness, only with the question, 'Do you consider yourself to be a shy person?' In the seminal, large-scale study that first adopted this approach, the further ramifications of shyness were explored by means of categories provided by the researchers and the participants were not free to describe their shyness in their own words. Nevertheless this study, carried out by Philip Zimbardo and his associates at Stanford University (hence the title of the questionnaire, the Stanford Shyness Survey), has yielded considerable insight into shyness and provided an enormous impetus for research (Zimbardo *et al.*, 1974).

The most dramatic finding of the survey was the high incidence of self-ascribed shyness. More than 40 per cent of students aged between 18 and 21 years were prepared to say that were currently shy and over 80 per cent stated that they were either shy now or had been shy at some time in their life. The survey has subsequently been replicated in many different countries, and although there is some variation from one country to another the incidence remains high, ranging from 24 per cent among a sample of Jewish Americans to 60 per cent among Hawaiian and Japanese respondents. There is less cross-cultural variation in the proportion of respondents stating that they have been shy at some point (now or in the past). This ranges from 66–92 per cent, with a median value of 84 per cent – most young adults throughout the developed world have experienced shyness at one time or another. More recent surveys suggest that there has been a trend over several years for the incidence of self-ascribed shyness to increase. The figure has apparently risen in the United States from 40 per cent to over 50 per cent (Carducci and Zimbardo, 1995).

Situations that elicit shyness

Respondents to the survey were asked about the social situations that elicit shyness. The most frequently mentioned situations, together with statistics on the proportion of respondents who endorsed each situation, are listed in Table 1.1. Table 1.2 lists the people who are most likely to elicit shyness, in terms of the percentage

Table 1.1 Situations eliciting shyness and the proportion of respondents in the Stanford survey who said they were shy in particular situations

Situation	% of shy respondents
Being the focus of attention before a large group (e.g. when giving a speech)	73
Large groups	68
Being of lower status than others present	56
Social situations in general	55
New interpersonal situations in general	55
Where assertiveness is required (e.g. when complaining about faulty service in a restaurant or the poor quality of a product)	54
Being evaluated or compared with others (e.g. when being interviewed, when being criticised)	53
Being the focus of attention of a small group (e.g. when being introduced, when being asked directly for an opinion)	52

Source: P. G. Zimbardo, P. A. Pilkonis, and R. M. Norwood, *The silent prison of shyness* (Office of Naval Research Technical Report Z-17, Stanford University, 1974). Reprinted with the permission of Philip Zimbardo.

of students who endorsed those items in the original Stanford survey and in a replication carried out twenty years later by Carducci and Clark (1999). The latter study presents results for individuals who considered themselves to be shy (as in the original survey) and also those who were chronically shy, in the sense that they indicated that they were currently shy and had been shy all their life.

The trends in these lists of situations and people are compatible with evidence from other accounts of shyness. The novelist Arnold Bennett provides the following description in his story *Buried Alive* (1912, pp. 15–16):

> He happened to be shy. He was quite different from you or me. We never feel secret qualms at the prospect of meeting strangers, or of taking quarters at a grand hotel, or of entering a large house for the first time, or of walking across a room full of seated people, or of dismissing a servant, or of arguing with a haughty female aristocrat behind a post-office counter, or of passing a shop where we owe money. As for blushing or hanging back, or even looking awkward, when faced with any such simple, everyday acts, the idea of conduct so childish would not occur to us.

Of course, as Bennett implies, it does occur to most of us.

Table 1.2 Encounters with other people that are most likely to elicit shyness: responses in the Stanford survey and a replication conducted 20 years later

| | Percentage of shy students | | |
| | | Carducci and Clark (1999) | |
Situation	Stanford survey	Overall shy	Chronically shy
Strangers	70	64	85
An opposite sex group	63	38	56
Authorities, by virtue of their knowledge (intellectual superiors, experts)	55	45	56
Authorities, by virtue of their role (police, teacher, superior at work)	40	37	48
Individual of opposite sex	49	35	48

Sources: B. J. Carducci, and D. L. Clark. `The personal and situational pervasiveness of shyness: A replication and extension of the Stanford Survey on shyness 20 years later', unpublished paper (Indiana University Southeast Shyness Institute, 1999); P. G. Zimbardo, P. A. Pilkonis, and R. M. Norwood, (1974). *The silent prison of shyness* (Office of Naval Research Technical Report Z-17, Stanford University, 1974). Reprinted with the permission of Bernardo Carducci and Philip Zimbardo.

Evidence of a different kind about the situations that elicit shyness is provided by a series of interviews that a colleague and I conducted with a sample of 21 students – 18 women and three men, all of whom had entered university as mature students (Crozier and Garbert-Jones, 1996). Their ages ranged from 24 to 59 years, with a median age of 40. Several situations recur in these students' descriptions of their experience of shyness – participating in seminars, attending an interview, being in groups of people, meeting new people and speaking to lecturers or superiors at work. Seminars (classes based on group discussions and individual presentations) seemed to hold particular anxieties. They evoked feelings that ranged from mild nervousness to extreme tension and discomfort: 'Some of the most horrific social situations you'll ever come across' ('Lawrence', aged 28).

Seminars were regarded as an ordeal, particularly during the first few months of college. For some students, simply anticipating them was sufficient to induce unpleasant emotions:

> I dreaded the word seminar before I'd actually been to them ('Jacqueline', 40).

> I think perhaps that's one of the reasons why university seemed a daunting thing, the fact that you might have to get up and speak in front of a group of people ('Debbie', 46).

Why are seminars regarded in this way? They do meet the criteria of many of the situations included in the Stanford survey, such as being the focus of attention in a large group: 'It's a case of having thirty-odd pairs of eyes staring at you' ('Lawrence'). They represent situations where one is being evaluated – 'afraid that someone might think, well, who does she think she is' ('Meryl', 52). Meryl worries about saying the right thing, apprehensive that she might say something foolish or will create a negative impression.

Respondents also mentioned speaking to lecturers. Lecturers are, in terms of the categories of the Stanford survey, authorities by virtue of both their knowledge and their role (as examiners and as people likely to put you on the spot). These roles are reflected in the following excerpts:

> The lecturers at college can make you feel difficult because you know they know what they are talking about – they know you don't know what you're talking about ('Belinda', 32).

> I feel they've got more knowledge than me – so I wouldn't – I'd feel shy about questioning them on something unless I was really sure they'd made a mistake or something – I wouldn't dream of – I'd argue a point but I wouldn't dream of saying they were wrong in any way because they – I'd say they were superior to me ('Lucy', 24)

Some students felt out of place simply because of the age difference between themselves and the majority of students: 'I kept on feeling inadequate and because I was feeling inadequate I would be reserved and that was purely and simply to do with me being out of the age group' ('Marie', 59).

The Stanford survey found that shyness varies according to the situation: shy people are not shy everywhere. Pilkonis and Zimbardo (1979) reported that a sample of shy students rated their shyness as 'varying to a large degree' (a mean of five on a seven-point scale), and only 5 per cent of shy respondents claimed to be shy in all situations. There also seems to be a considerable degree of consensus about the types of situation that elicit shyness. Russell *et al.* (1986) developed a 30-item questionnaire on shyness-eliciting situations. The items were selected from a set of situations nominated by a sample of college students. Items that elicited most shyness included the following: being asked personal questions in public; first day at a new job; at a party with strangers; emotional confrontations; and talking to a professor (all of these items had a mean rating of greater than three on a seven-point scale, showing that all elicited shyness). Nevertheless there was variation among situations, that is, some were more likely than others to elicit shyness, and this was reliable, for example the correlation between the mean shyness ratings of situations provided by two independent samples of students was 0.93.

However it is important to go beyond providing a list of situations that are likely to elicit shyness, and try to identify categories of situations that do so. This would be more satisfying from a scientific point of view, but more significantly it might yield clues about the reasons why these situations elicit shyness, and this in turn could provide insight into the causes of shyness. This is a topic to which we shall return throughout this volume.

Asendorpf (1989) argues that two kinds of concern produce inhibited behaviour – fear of the unfamiliar and fear of being negatively evaluated by others – and these concerns are triggered by two kinds of situation. The first kind involves interacting with strangers and adjusting to unfamiliar settings and novel situations. For example, in *When Daddy Came Home* Turner and Rennell (1995) present case studies of servicemen returning home at the end of the Second World War to be reunited with their families, often having been overseas for several years. These reunions could be fraught with problems as both husbands and wives were often very much changed, albeit in different ways, by their wartime experiences. It could also be difficult for children, as some were seeing their father for the first time in their memory and only knew him through letters or photographs. When reunited the children were often excessively shy. A typical example is provided by one woman's recollection of being seven years of age and seeing her father for the first time for four years (ibid., pp. 84–5).

> Although Mum had constantly talked about Dad to me, and I kissed his photograph every night so that I would not forget him, when he finally came home I felt rather shy of him. So much so that I didn't want him to be anywhere in the house when I was having my

night-time bath! I don't remember saying it, but Mum and Dad have told me since, I would say to Mum – 'I don't want him here while I am washing. Send him out!' ... I think this went on for about six months or so until I got used to having him around. It must have been very difficult for him because he had to adjust too.

The second class of events includes situations that have the potential for negative evaluation. It includes those where evaluation is salient, such as speaking up in front of others, giving a speech or attending interviews, but also routine or less public encounters such as interacting with authority figures or experts. Self-presentation concerns are exemplified by 'Bronwen's' shyness at a surprise birthday party:

> I felt shy as, because it was my 'big day' I felt as though I was expected to be 'the life and soul of the party' but I felt uncomfortable and unable to be myself among a group of strangers. ... I seemed to be answering either yes or no to several questions. I felt as though they were looking at me wondering why I was not chatty and full of lots of intellectual 'university' conversation. It felt as though I was being examined under a microscope. It felt like I was blushing every time they looked in my direction even though they were friendly, easygoing people. I kept making excuses to leave the room to escape the discomfort of the situation.

One question addressed by Asendorpf (1989) is whether both these triggers are necessary, or whether they can operate as independent causes of shyness. In many situations the two coexist, and novel situations often imply the potential for some form of evaluation. Bronwen refers to her shyness being influenced by the presence of strangers. Turner and Rennell (1995, p. 129) present an example of a woman who was apprehensive about what her returning husband would think of her. She was ashamed of being seen in her threadbare clothes (material was scarce and there was rationing of clothing; everyone was urged to 'make do and mend'). Although her reunion with her husband was, in a sense, like meeting a stranger, she was preoccupied with how she would be evaluated, an aspect missing in the examples of children.

Asendorpf (1989) provides empirical support for his claim that shyness is triggered by two separate kinds of situation. Because this is a key study in shyness research, it deserves to be described in some detail. People took part in the experiment in pairs. Each pair conversed for five minutes in a room where their behaviour was observed and recorded on videotape. Those taking part were either pairs of friends, pairs of acquaintances or pairs of strangers. Thus the extent to which the participants were familiar with one another varied. In one part of the experiment, half of the participants were instructed to interact with their partner in order to evaluate each other's personality; the other half did not receive this instruction. Hence the instruction attempted to manipulate the extent to which evaluation by the partner was salient to the individual. A number of measures were taken:

- Self and partner ratings of the participants' shyness in the situation.
- Observer ratings of the participants' shyness and their body posture during the conversation.
- The researcher went through the videotape of the conversation with each participant and asked about thoughts and feelings at the time.

Analysis of the measures confirmed that the instruction about the prospect of evaluation did have the predicted impact. Participants assigned to the 'evaluation' condition rated themselves more highly on an item referring to fear of being evaluated and they made more spontaneous mention of this fear during the videotape reconstruction. The principal finding was that both the unfamiliarity of the partner and the evaluation instruction produced an increase in shyness, whether this was self-rated, partner-rated, or observer-rated. The two effects – unfamiliarity and the prospect of evaluation – were 'additive', that is, each factor was varied independently of the other and each had a separate, significant effect on shyness. To take one finding as an example, there were differences in body posture associated with the degree of familiarity of the partner. A closed body posture was observed more often during conversations between pairs of strangers and pairs of acquaintances than between pairs of friends. However there were no differences in body posture between those who anticipated being evaluated and those who did not.

In summary, Asendorpf provides evidence that shyness is elicited by two kinds of social situations: encounters with unfamiliar people, and those where one fears being evaluated by others. This distinction has been important in shyness research. It raises questions about the unitary nature of shyness, whether these two kinds of situation elicit different experiences, say, shyness on the one hand and anxiety or embarrassment on the other, or whether both elicit shyness. It also raises questions about the origins and development of shyness in infancy and childhood. Whereas fear of the unfamiliar can be observed in very young children, it is commonly thought that fear of being evaluated entails a level of sophistication and self-awareness that only comes later in development. We shall return to this issue in Chapter 4.

Schlenker and Leary (1982) provide an alternative analysis of the reasons why certain situations elicit shyness. They propose that anxiety is elicited whenever an individual is motivated to create a desired impression on other people but doubts that he or she is able to do so. This differs from Asendorpf's account in two ways. First, novelty is not regarded as a category in its own right and only elicits shyness to the extent that it creates impression management concerns. However, as we shall see, a recurrent theme in shyness research is that novelty is a prime cause in its own right. For example it is an important cause of anxiety in Gray's (1987) theory of personality (see pp. 22–3), and reactions to the unfamiliar play a key role in Kagan's (1994) theory of temperament (this volume, Chapter 3). Second, Schlenker and Leary (1982) do not regard fear of being negatively evaluated as the issue. Rather the individual is concerned about creating a desired impression, thus wanting to be liked or even feared might be the individual's goal and finding that people are indifferent, rather than critical, would be regarded as failure. In one of my own studies (Crozier, 1981) I found that shyness was closer to fear of lacking social competence than to fear of negative evaluation. Of course in many shyness-eliciting situations it can be difficult to disentangle these types of fear.

Individual differences in shyness

The trait concept

A distinction between state shyness and trait shyness is important in shyness research. So far we have discussed the trait element of shyness only in terms of people's perception of themselves. However the dominant position within psychology is to take a stronger view of traits, conceptualising them as stable internal attributes that influence behaviour across a range of situations. The status of the concept of personality traits has proved controversial in psychological research. First, there is disagreement about whether traits explain behaviour, or simply describe it. Am I reticent in unfamiliar situations because of my underlying shyness, or are reticence and shyness merely alternative ways of describing the same observed pattern of behaviour? Another issue is whether observed regularities in behaviour are the product of underlying psychological entities or simply matters of perception, that is to say, conspicuous tendencies in behaviour are labelled and their origins attributed to the individual. Alternatively, recurrent tendencies might be patterns of response that are elicited by certain kinds of situation and are specific to those situations. Perhaps shyness is only a disposition in the weak sense of a learned habitual response to a particular class of stimuli rather than a product of some internal characteristics of the person. Is attributing an explanation to trait characteristics merely a sign of ignorance about the 'real' causes of behaviour, namely the properties of social situations?

These controversies dominated research into personality for decades following Walter Mischel's (1968) accusation that psychologists had failed to demonstrate consistency in behaviour across different situations, which was assumed in their definitions of traits (see Caspi, 1998, for a recent account of this issue). Mischel cast doubts on the value of traits such as shyness when it could be shown that someone who was shy in one situation was not shy in another. Indeed he argued that scores obtained from questionnaire measures of traits such as shyness had only very low correlations with measures based on actual behaviour. The inconsistency alleged by Mischel takes different forms: low correlations between questionnaire scores and measures of behaviour; variability in the observed behaviour of individuals across different situations; and disagreement between different informants in respect of the ratings they make of the same individual. Of course no one doubts that all these forms of inconsistency can be observed. The issue is whether they call into question the value of the concept of personality trait or whether they simply show that certain behaviour in any particular situation is caused by a multiplicity of factors.

One line of defence of the trait position was that Mischel was attacking a soft target, challenging a simplistic position that had never been adopted by personality theorists. They had always recognised that certain behaviour in a given situation could be caused by a variety of factors and no one had claimed that it could be predicted solely by questionnaire measures of personality traits.

Individuals do behave differently in different situations for reasons that are readily understood and which are not incompatible with the notion of trait. Different observers reach different conclusions because overt behaviour is only a partial guide to the existence of a trait and because people adjust their behaviour in the light of the opportunities and constraints provided by situations.

Consider the consistencies in the findings of Asendorpf's (1989) study. The scores obtained on the questionnaire measure of trait shyness were systematically associated with both self-ratings and ratings made by other people during the short conversation. The study also found that shy people tend to adopt a different sitting posture from their less shy peers. To be sure, these differences are statistical ones and the trait measure does not predict an individual's behaviour in a straightforward causal fashion, but it is surely not necessary for the trait position that it does so. Rather the critic of the trait position has to show why there are systematic differences in, say, posture, particularly as this is not obviously part of the common-sense notion of shyness and it is unlikely that shy people are aware of this tendency in themselves.

It is also conceivable that dispositionally shy people might not experience or exhibit shyness in the specific conversational setting arranged for the purposes of a study. As Asendorpf has shown, many shy people are apprehensive about being negatively evaluated by others. However, whether or not this fear will be evoked is a subjective matter and not an objective property of social situations. The individual might fail to pick up cues that he or she faces the prospect of being evaluated and hence will not feel shy. However noticing the cues will tend to elicit shyness.

I have observed this in myself in social situations. I might be at ease in a social gathering until some subtle change is introduced into the situation, for example the topic of conversation might switch to some matter that I believe has implications for my esteem in the eyes of others. Alternatively someone else might join the group, my employer perhaps, or an attractive person whom I would like to impress. Following this change I can suddenly become uncomfortable and experience shyness. Hypothetically, some of the other people present in this situation might have been feeling shy until that same moment, but the arrival of the newcomer puts them at ease, perhaps because this is a person they know very well and of whose opinion they are confident. In terms of an objective description of the situation this is a small change but its implications for shyness can be considerable. Although an individual's behaviour changes as a function of the situation, this might be entirely predictable from knowledge of the relevant personality trait and of his or her assessment of the situation. Failure to predict behaviour in a given situation may be because the observer does not have the necessary information.

The same point applies to the common finding that separate informants can arrive at different impressions of the same target individual since they will inevitably have different knowledge of that person. Furthermore people occupy different roles relative to the target – as employer, employee, co-worker, teacher, parent, sibling, friend or rival – and this will be reflected in the information they have about and influence their understanding of that individual. Nevertheless it should be pointed out that in many circumstances judges do agree. Thus in Asendorpf's study three independent judges provided very similar ratings of the body posture of the participants.

More generally, as for example Achenbach *et al.* (1987) have reported, informants who see the same person in the same context do tend to agree with each other. These researchers found a considerable degree of consensus in parents' ratings of their own children, the average interparent correlation being 0.59. Fergusson and Horwood (1987) have found a similar pattern. They report a significant degree of agreement between pairs of informants who see a child in similar situations, in this case different teachers of the same child, but disagreement between those who see the child in different contexts, such as a teacher and the child's mother.

Shyness as a personality trait

I shall now consider the evidence for shyness as a personality trait. First, this section will briefly review some of the most influential approaches to identifying fundamental personality traits and consider the place of shyness within the models of personality that have emerged from these enquiries. Second, it will assess evidence of the need to make a distinction between the traits of shyness and introversion which, at first sight, seem to have much in common. Third, it will discuss whether there is convincing evidence for the existence of a personality trait of shyness. Finally, it will consider whether shyness is itself a unitary trait or whether there are different types of shyness.

There have been several systematic attempts to identify the fundamental traits of personality. These attempts have drawn upon the mathematical technique of factor analysis. This is based on the analysis of the table (or matrix) of correlations that is produced if scores are collected on a set of variables and the correlations between every pair of variables are computed. The goal of the analysis is to find the smallest number of common factors that could reproduce the correlations between these variables. The technique assumes that the variation in a set of test scores reflects two kinds of factor in addition to the inevitable errors in measurement that are entailed in any test. There are factors that are specific to performance in that test, and factors involved in that test and that are shared by other tests.

This technique aims to identify a small number of common factors within a set of measures. Factors found to be common to measures of personality (typically the responses of large samples of people to self-report questionnaires or rating scales) are provisionally identified as fundamental personality types or traits. However factor analysis is not a single technique that yields a unique solution for any set of data, but a family of techniques that differ in the assumptions they make about the data and about procedures for finding solutions. In particular, two key issues have divided personality theorists. How many factors constitute the minimum necessary to reproduce the correlations among variables? On what criteria can the researcher choose between different factor solutions, all of which are compatible with the data? Consequently much of the dispute between different trait theories of personality has concerned technical interpretations of factor analysis. For many years the study of personality traits was dominated by the theories and research programmes of Raymond Cattell and Hans Eysenck, and by a long-standing dispute between them as to which of their explanations of the structure of personality was the correct one.

Cattell (1973) applied factor analysis to measures of individual differences in performance in laboratory tasks, to people's self-reports in questionnaires and to people's ratings of friends and acquaintances. Although the same factors did not emerge in all these types of data, Cattell did identify 16 factors or 'source traits', which can be identified in ratings and self-report questionnaires. One of the 16 factors identified in this manner was labelled *threctia* versus *parmia.* Those whose scores are at the threctia pole of this trait tend to endorse questionnaire items on keeping in the background on social occasions, feeling embarrassed when the focus of attention and finding it difficult to speak in front of a group. They tend not to endorse items that refer to being sociable or outgoing. The factor seems on the face of it to be a measure of shyness, and this view is held by Cattell *et al.* (1970, p. 91), who describe this trait as 'shy, timid, restrained, threat-sensitive versus adventurous, "thick-skinned", socially bold'.

Eysenck's (1970) research has its origins in an attempt to devise brief screening measures for service personnel who presented with psychiatric problems in London during the Second World War. Self-report checklists were devised to help decide whether individuals required more intensive psychiatric investigation. Factor analysis of the responses to these checklists yielded two factors. One reflected the severity of neurotic conditions and formed the basis of a personality trait that Eysenck labelled as neuroticism. The second factor reflected the type of neurotic condition, which Eysenck identified as a dimension with extraversion and introversion as its poles (he preferred to write about personality 'types', but he treated them as continuous dimensions rather than discrete categories and that is how they will be described here). These two factors provided the basis for various self-report questionnaires that measured two orthogonal personality dimensions: extraversion–introversion and neuroticism (see Figure 1.1). Eysenck subsequently proposed a third dimension, which he identified as psychoticism.

The extraversion–introversion dimension can be decomposed into two separate, albeit correlated factors: sociability and impulsivity. The typical extravert is socially outgoing, likes company, is easy-going, optimistic, takes risks and is adventurous, whereas the introvert is quiet, passive, introspective, prefers more solitary pursuits, avoids risks and is happier to make plans than to act upon impulse. Neuroticism is related to emotions that are strong and easily aroused. Those who obtain high scores in this dimension are anxious, moody, restless and excitable. Individuals who score high in the psychoticism dimension are antisocial, cold, aggressive and lack empathy. Those who score high on the neuroticism or psychoticism scales are predisposed to neurotic or psychotic conditions, respectively, but whether or not these conditions actually develop depends on other factors as well.

More generally, Eysenck proposed a hierarchical model of personality where three levels can be distinguished. The three dimensions described here are at the top, higher-order level. Below this

Figure 1.1 Personality dimensions in the theories of H. J. Eysenck and J. A. Gray

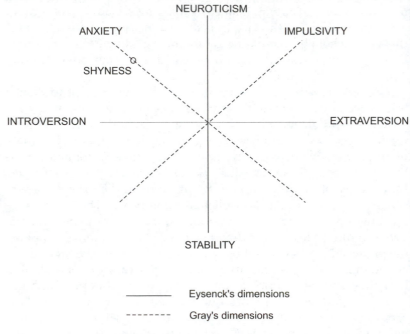

level are traits that correlate with each other to produce these dimensions. Thus, for example, the traits involved in psychoticism are aggression, coldness, antisocial behaviour, egocentricity, lack of empathy, impersonality, creativity, tough-mindedness and impulsiveness (Eysenck, 1995, p. 205). At the bottom level are primary traits that cannot be broken down into further factors.

An alternative explanation of Eysenck's dimensions of extraversion–introversion and neuroticism has been proposed by Gray (1987; see Matthews and Gilliland, 1999, for a detailed comparison of the two theories). Gray has proposed that the two-dimensional factor solution identified by Eysenck can be rotated to provide two different dimensions: impulsivity and anxiety (Figure 1.1). There are no mathematical grounds for preferring one rotation to another, but Gray argues that other kinds of research support his interpretation of the factors. He proposes that anxiety represents heightened susceptibility to signals of punishment (or the loss of a reward) whereas impulsivity is associated with susceptibility to signals of reward. Neurotic individuals (in terms of Eysenck's dimension) are most sensitive to reinforcing events, whether rewarding or punishing. Eysenck's neurotic introvert (Gray's anxious person) is most sensitive to cues for punishment whereas the neurotic extravert (impulsive person) is most susceptible to cues for reward.

Gray argues that this interpretation is grounded in psychophysiological evidence about the brain systems involved in reward and punishment, particularly evidence on the effects of drugs that reduce anxiety. He has proposed a 'behavioural inhibition system', which responds to signals of punishment or non-reward (these include novel situations such as meeting strangers) by inhibiting behaviour, increasing the level of arousal and focusing attention on the environment. Individual differences in anxiety are due to differences in the reactivity of the behavioural inhibition system. The notion that novel situations and threatening social situations are associated with individual differences in inhibition will strike a chord with researchers into shyness, if only because of the familiarity of the vocabulary. We shall see below that factor analytic studies of shyness locate it at the anxiety pole of Gray's dimension.

Shyness occupies an uncertain position in Eysenck's theory. Sometimes he seemed to consider it as a trait located in the introversion branch of the hierarchy, whereas at other times he regarded it as belonging to the neuroticism branch. The only item in the Eysenck Personality Inventory (EPI) that explicitly mentions shyness is included in the neuroticism scale. Although he was one of the most prolific writers on personality and related themes, Eysenck himself paid very little attention to shyness. However he did propose a distinction between two different forms: introverted shyness, where the individual is unsociable; and neurotic shyness, where the individual is self-conscious, lonely and tends to worry about humiliating experiences. We shall return to this duality of shyness after introducing a third approach to the identification of the fundamental personality traits.

Is personality better described by Cattell's 16 source traits or by Eysenck's three dimensions? This question has been the subject of controversy for many years. The source traits in Cattell's scheme can themselves be submitted to factor analysis. This produces eight second-order factors, including two that have been labelled *exvia* and *anxiety*. These are very similar to Eysenck's dimensions of extraversion–introversion and neuroticism.

These two factors also appear in the most recent attempt to identify the basic factors of personality. The set of fundamental traits that has been proposed in this account is familiarly known as the 'Big Five' because adherents of this position argue that factor analysis of personality data converges on five factors: openness, conscientiousness, extraversion, agreeableness and neuroticism (Costa and McCrae, 1995). According to this model the typical extravert is active, adventurous, assertive, impulsive, self-confident and sociable, whereas the introvert is reserved, submissive and timid. This obviously bears a close resemblance to Eysenck's dimension of the same name and can likewise be decomposed into two dimensions. However in the Big Five model these two dimensions are confidence and sociability rather than impulsivity and sociability (Feist, 1998). Neuroticism contrasts individuals who tend to be anxious, depressed, emotional, excitable, insecure and tense with those who tend to be well-adjusted, calm, free of guilt, happy and stable (ibid.).

Thus the three major systematic approaches to the identification of the basic factors of personality agree that there are at least two fundamental higher-order dimensions: extraversion–introversion and neuroticism (or anxiety). Shyness seems to be related to both of these. For example Cattell's *threctia* factor has significant loadings on the two second-order factors: *exvia* and *anxiety*. Crozier (1979) has reviewed several studies and concludes that shyness correlates with measures of both introversion and neuroticism. Pilkonis (1977a) has found significant correlations between self-ratings of shyness and both the extraversion and neuroticism scales of the EPI. Briggs and Smith (1986) report significant correlations between five separate measures of shyness and a measure of extraversion (mean $r = -0.38$) and a measure of neuroticism (mean $r = 0.35$). Asendorpf and Wilpers (1998) find that shyness correlates substantially with two Big Five trait scales (0.45 with neuroticism and -0.67 with extraversion).

Briggs (1988) administered the EPI, together with a set of 74 items drawn from four shyness scales, to a sample of 290 university students. The large majority of items (56 out of 74) correlated moderately and equally highly with both the EPI extraversion and the neuroticism factors. Only a few items had markedly higher correlations with one of the dimensions and many of these may have been affected by similarities of wording across items. For example shyness items that mentioned worrying, feeling relaxed and getting nervous had higher correlations with neuroticism than with introversion, but these words were also frequently represented in the neuroticism items of the EPI. Briggs concludes that 'In a hierarchical model of personality, shyness might best be represented as a primary factor situated between and contributing to both introversion and neuroticism.... To be precise, shyness should be located between the sociability component of introversion on one side and the low self-confidence aspect of neuroticism on the other side' (ibid., p. 305).

According to these analyses, shyness is not synonymous with introversion in that it also has elements of neuroticism. But can shyness be distinguished more clearly from introversion? There is some evidence that it can. Eysenck (1956; see Crozier, 1979) undertook an analysis of a number of scales from Guilford's personality inventory, including the shyness, introversion and neuroticism scales. Eysenck was able to identify within the shyness scale a set of items that correlated with introversion but not with neuroticism (these items referred to liking to mix socially with people and keeping in the background on social occasions) and another set of items that correlated with neuroticism but not with introversion (these items referred to feelings of loneliness and self-consciousness).

Cheek and Buss (1981) developed self-report measures of shyness and sociability and found further evidence of separate factors. Factor analysis of the set of items confirmed the presence of two distinct factors. The factor they labelled 'shyness' was represented by items referring to feeling tense with people one did not know well and to feeling inhibited in social situations. The 'sociability' factor included items referring to liking to be with people and welcoming the opportunity to mix with people. The correlation between the two sets of items was only moderate.

Cheek and Buss extended their research to assess how a sample of women who had obtained different score patterns in the shyness and sociability factors behaved during the course of a (surreptitiously) videotaped conversation with a stranger. They found that the shy participants talked significantly less than the non-shy participants. Shy women also rated themselves as more tense and inhibited than non-shy participants. However there were differences within the group of shy women: between those who were both shy and sociable and those who obtained high scores on the shyness scale but low scores on the sociability scale. Those who scored high on both the shyness and sociable scales made more anxious gestures (touching the face or body with the hands). They also spent less time looking at their partner; observers rated them as more tense and inhibited.

Schmidt and Fox (1994) have obtained similar results. Those participants in their study who scored high on both the shyness and sociability measures had a significantly higher but more stable heart rate when anticipating a novel social encounter than both shy participants who were less sociable and participants who were not shy.

Eisenberg *et al.* (1995) have also reported differences between shy and less sociable participants in a number of self-report measures of emotionality and regulation. They measured three aspects of emotionality: (1) emotional reactivity and intensity (for example 'my palms sweat during an important event'); (2) characteristic levels of positive or negative affect; and (3) a tendency to experience negative emotional reactions such as worrying. Shyness was associated with high levels of emotional reactivity and intensity, negative affect and negative emotional intensity. Low sociability, in contrast, was associated with less reactivity and was not related to measures of negative affect. Measures of regulation included emotional control ('I find it hard to get thoughts that upset me out of my mind') and coping style. Shyness was associated with low levels of regulation and control and less effective ways of coping. These trends were not found among those with low sociability. These findings reinforce the value of distinguishing introversion from shyness.

However Bruch *et al.* (1989) have obtained counterfindings. They report the results of a factor analysis of the Cheek–Buss shyness and sociability scales, which show that while there is evidence of two distinct factors, they are more highly correlated than suggested by previous research (a correlation between the factors of –0.56, compared with the coefficient of –0.28 reported by Cheek and Buss). Bruch *et al.* also carried out an observational study where students with different patterns of scores on the two scales took part in a conversation with an opposite-sex person (actually a confederate of the researcher). There were differences between shy and non-shy participants in a number of measures, including the frequency of positive and negative self-statements, non-verbal signs of anxiety and changes in heart rate. However there was no indication that shy-sociable participants were the most anxious group. There were a number of differences between this investigation and the original study by Cheek and Buss that make it difficult to compare them. Nevertheless the findings do illustrate the value of distinguishing between shyness and low sociability, since there were few significant effects that could be attributed to sociability.

In summary, shyness, conceived as a personality trait, is neither the same as introversion nor the opposite of sociability. It is possible to be both shy and sociable, and those who are both tend to be more anxious in a social encounter than those who are simply shy or less sociable. This pattern might be understood in terms of the goals that individuals set for themselves. Someone who is both sociable and shy wants to mix with others but lacks confidence in her or his ability to do so. Those who are shy without being sociable lack confidence but do not have the same motivation, and may find it easier to find a lifestyle that can accommodate their shyness. Those who are introverted without shyness are content with their own company and feel no need to be with others; nor do social situations pose them any kind of threat.

The measurement of shyness

I have argued elsewhere (Crozier, 1979) that a shyness factor has consistently emerged throughout the history of factor analytical studies of personality. The more recent attention that has been paid to shyness has resulted in the development of a number of questionnaire scales to measure this factor and these are now considered. Table 1.3 lists a number of these scales.

Table 1.3   Questionnaire measures of shyness

Scale	Author	Number of items
Shyness scale *	Cheek and Buss (1981)	9
Social reticence scale *	Jones and Russell (1982)	21
Morris shyness scale *	Morris (1982)	14
Trait shyness scale	Aikawa (1991)	16
Interaction anxiousness *	Leary (1983)	15
Shyness scale	McCroskey et al. (1981)	14
Personal report of communication apprehension	McCroskey (1970)	25
Social anxiety scale	Fenigstein et al. (1975)	6
Children's shyness scale	Crozier (1995)	26

*   Measures included in the Briggs and Smith (1986) comparative study (see text for details).

There are differences in the conceptualisation of shyness underlying the construction of these scales. The items in Leary's Interaction Anxiousness Scale refer only to self-reported anxiety and omit any reference to behaviour. This decision is based on Leary's analysis of shyness. Leary (1983, p. 23) argues that shyness is not equivalent to anxiety but is a combination of anxiety and inhibited behaviour. Thus it avoids confusion if anxiety and behaviour are measured separately. McCroskey (see McCroskey and Beatty, 1986) has devised two separate questionnaires. The shyness scale eschews reference to anxiety and its items refer to lack of talkativeness, quietness and shyness. The Personal Report of Communication Apprehension (PRCA) measures anxiety in four types of situation: group discussions, meetings, conversations and delivering a speech. Anxiety is assessed by reference to feeling afraid, feeling nervous, tension, inability to think clearly, not being calm or relaxed, and lack of confidence – no items mention behaviour.

The remaining scales include items that refer explicitly to shyness (only the PRCA among the scales in Table 1.3 has no item mentioning shyness), and to a mixture of cognitive, affective and behavioural aspects. Despite this mixture, the unsystematic sampling of the domain of shyness and variation in the number of items in the scales, the scales are correlated with one another to a substantial degree and seem to be measuring a common factor. Briggs and Smith (1986) undertook an analysis of five scales (marked with an asterisk in Table 1.3). They report correlations between pairs of scales ranging from 0.70 to 0.86, with a mean correlation of 0.77. The internal reliability of each of the five scales is acceptable, with values of Cronbach's alpha coefficient ranging from 0.82 to 0.92.

The demonstration that scales have effective psychometric properties is only one step towards establishing whether shyness can usefully be conceived as a personality trait. Research has also to establish whether the scales have construct validity, that is, can be grounded in a body of theory on and research into the construct of shyness. A number of studies have addressed this question, examining the implications of shyness for social behaviour. They have assessed similarities and differences between measures of shyness and related constructs, and investigated the relationship between individuals' scores in self-report questionnaire measures of shyness and the rating of these individuals by friends, acquaintances and observers (Briggs and Smith, 1986; Cheek and Briggs, 1990). They conclude that despite problems with definitions, research into shy-

ness has proved fruitful. Of course much of this book is directly concerned with the construct validity of shyness when it reviews relevant empirical research.

Different types of shyness

Briggs (1988) argues that shyness is a primary trait that cannot be
factor analysed into further traits. Others, however, argue that there
are distinct *forms* of shyness. Pilkonis and Zimbardo (1979) distinguish between *public* and *private* shyness, based on an analysis of
participants' rating of the importance to them of five aspects of shyness: feeling discomfort in social situations; fear of being negatively
evaluated by others; tendency to avoid social situations; failure to
respond appropriately (for example, being quiet or avoiding eye
contact); and responding in an awkward way. One group of participants, who emphasised internal discomfort and fear of negative
evaluation, were labelled 'privately shy' because of their concern
with their internal state. Two other groups were similar to each
other in their emphasis on failure to respond, awkward behaviour
and fear of negative evaluation. These groups were labelled 'pub-
licly shy' because they emphasised their behaviour rather than any
internal feelings.

Factor analysis has not demonstrated that shyness can be decomposed into public and private factors. Nevertheless people seem to
reach judgments about their own shyness in terms of three components – cognitive, affective and behavioural – and there are differences among individuals in the weight that they assign to these in
reaching their judgments. In a sense the study by Pilkonis and
Zimbardo is similar to that of Cheek and Watson (1989) and the
findings are comparable (see this volume, p. 6).

A smaller grouping in Zimbardo and Pilkonis's study, but not
considered further by them, comprised participants who emphasised avoidance of social situations. Cheek and Krasnoperova (1999)
distinguish between *withdrawn shyness*, which is characterised by
inhibition, reticence and social avoidance, and *dependent shyness*,
which is characterised by the conformity and attitude neutrality
that are elements of the protective, self-presentational style adopted
by many shy people. These two forms may reflect alternative strategies pursued by shy people in order to accommodate their shyness
to the demands of social interaction. A shy individual either tries to
avoid such situations or, if this is not wanted or is impossible in

practice, plays a passive and compliant role, hoping by this means to avoid being the centre of attention.

Arnold Buss (1986) distinguishes between fearful and self-conscious shyness. According to Buss, novelty and intrusion into a social situation elicit fearful shyness; self-conscious shyness is produced by formal situations and breaches of privacy, and is also a result of being scrutinised and being uniquely different. This theory also has a developmental aspect, related to the cognitive demands of self-consciousness. Fearful shyness emerges early in life and is associated with inhibition in new situations, especially contact with strangers. This type does not require self-awareness of any degree of complexity. However the later-appearing self-conscious type is associated with awareness of the self as a social object. We shall discuss the developmental aspects of this thesis in Chapter 4.

Buss's thesis has prompted some empirical research Bruch *et al.* (1986) have classified young adults into the two types according to their profile of scores on questionnaire measures of shyness, fearfulness and public self-consciousness. Following a proposal by Buss (1986), fearful shyness is defined as shyness accompanied by a score of one standard deviation above the mean fearfulness score and one standard deviation below the mean self-consciousness score. Conversely, self-conscious shyness is defined in terms of shyness accompanied by a score of one standard deviation above the mean self-consciousness score and one standard deviation below the mean fearfulness score. There were some significant differences between the two groups thus classified; specifically, there was support (at least from respondents' retrospective reports on the onset of shyness) for the hypothesis that fearful shyness develops earlier in life than self-conscious shyness. Further evidence for the distinction between early and late appearing shyness comes from retrospective accounts of the onset of shyness collected by Cheek and Krasnoperova (1999). Shyness was a more stable trait among those respondents who claimed that their shyness had begun earlier in life. More specifically, 72 per cent of those who said they had been shy before they started elementary school still considered themselves to be shy, compared with 48 per cent of those who believed that the onset of their shyness had happened later than elementary school.

Schmidt and Robinson (1992) adopted Buss's recommended approach to the classification of the two forms of shyness and found that fearful shy participants had lower self-esteem than self-conscious shy participants. They interpreted this trend in terms of fearful shy individuals' more enduring fear of negative evaluation, restricting opportunities for the development of social skills and self-efficacy. Bruch *et al.* (1986) had found that their fearful shy participants obtained significantly lower scores than non-shy participants in a test of responses to hypothetical problematic social situations (the self-conscious group was not different from the non-shy group).

Despite the differences between groups of participants demonstrated by operationalising the two types of shyness in this way, research is hampered by the absence of any reliable psychometric measures of the two types. Indeed one argument against the existence of different types of shyness is the consistent finding of substantial correlations between the shyness measures discussed earlier in this chapter. This argument is reinforced by evidence of a common factor underlying shyness items drawn from different scales and by the lack of evidence for separate factors relating to fearfulness and self-consciousness (Briggs and Smith, 1986). A problem with this specific approach to identifying the two types of shyness in the research summarised here is that findings may be influenced by the contribution of self-consciousness scores to the selection of subjects. For example self-consciousness tends to have a lower correlation with self-esteem than does shyness (Bruch *et al.*, 1995), and this has to be kept in mind when interpreting self-esteem differences between fearful and self-conscious shy participants.

Summary

Shyness is a common word in everyday language that has a range of meanings in respect of the difficulties people face in social encounters. It refers both to transient experiences and to more stable characteristics of individuals. When writers or participants in psychological research describe their shyness, there is a large degree of consensus in their accounts. Classifying the elements of shyness into three categories – cognitive, somatic and behavioural – can capture this. When people experience shyness they tend to refer to feeling self-conscious, to worrying about what other people present might think. They feel flustered and ill at ease, and perhaps blush. They remain quiet, stay in the background, avoid the limelight and possibly even avoid or escape the situation altogether. Not all of these are necessary for someone to think of him- or herself as shy. Individuals will differ from each other in the extent to which they emphasise particular elements. This is not an altogether tidy picture, but most of our everyday psychological concepts have some degree of uncertainty.

There seem to be individual differences in the propensity to experience shyness and this too is captured in ordinary language. In an attempt to understand the extent of individual variation, whether in cognition or in personality, and to explain these differences, lay people and psychologists alike have traditionally drawn upon the concept of the trait. Traits are used to describe consistencies in behaviour. They are also used to explain regularities and peculiarities in thoughts, feelings and behaviour, and many psychologists adopt a realist conception of traits, regarding them as stable, internal characteristics of people.

What is the status of shyness as a trait? There exists in psychology a 'technology of traits', which draws upon factor analysis and empirical research methods in an attempt to establish the reality of particular traits. If these methods are applied to shyness then there does seem evidence for the existence of a trait (which might be labelled by different theorists as 'shyness', 'social anxiety' or even the neutral 'S') that bears resemblance to the ordinary language conception of shyness. This position can be criticised on several grounds. Some psychologists dispute the value of the notion of traits, reject a realist conception of traits or believe that the case for shyness as a trait has not been made. Others worry that the use of an everyday word as a technical term only results in confusion. A particularly telling criticism is that the population of people to whom the concept of shyness is applied is too heterogeneous for the classification to be useful – the term is used to describe a wide range of individuals who do not necessarily share the same concerns. It brings together into a single group disparate individuals who may have little in common; it misleads researchers who think they may be talking about the same thing but really have different things in mind.

These criticisms caution us against casual use of the term shyness, and warn us that when we interpret studies we should carefully examine what definition of shyness is involved. Bearing this in mind, the next chapter will examine in more detail the cognitive, affective and behavioural aspects of shyness and consider the impact of shyness upon the lives of shy individuals.

Chapter 2
Analysing Shyness

Shyness and emotion

It was proposed in Chapter 1 that shyness consists of cognitive, affective and behavioural components. In this chapter we take each of these components and provide a brief overview of research. We first consider how the components fit together to produce the experience of shyness. We take as our starting point a model of the processes that take place between noticing a stimulus and making an appropriate response. The model is outlined in Figure 2.1.

This figure provides a simplified picture of a highly complex process. Two core elements are omitted. First, the sequence of events forms a system that is regulated by one or more executive processes. It is difficult to think of these processes without falling into the trap of inventing a homunculus, a miniature 'person' within the brain who directs activities in the manner of the conductor of an orchestra. Yet even the first stage in the sequence – noticing a stimulus – must involve procedures for regulating the activities of several systems. These include allocating attention, holding information in the short-term memory, retrieving information from the long-term memory in order to recognise the stimulus

Figure 2.1 Emotion as a process

Stimulus ⇨ Appraisal ⇨ Mobilise resources ⇨ Select action ⇨ Implement action

Stream of thoughts

by matching the information with stored data, and so on. Executive processes play an important part in theories of emotion, but they are little understood. Leary and Downs (1995) have identified an executive process they call the *sociometer*. This monitors the degree to which an individual is accepted and valued by other people. It is sensitive to cues that the person is at risk of rejection or devaluation and facilitates behaviour to head off the threat. When it detects a potential threat it evokes an emotional response. Although people often consciously think about the impression they are making, the sociometer is regarded as an executive process that can operate outside conscious awareness.

Further omissions are the feedback loops that must exist between the stages. For example awareness of somatic changes, such as an increase in heart rate, can feed back to the appraisal stage. The fact that symptoms of anxiety are being experienced in itself provides evidence that there is something to be anxious about. Self-monitoring must also involve feedback loops since the effectiveness of any remedial action that is taken must be assessed and the outcome of this assessment evaluated by the sociometer.

In addition to the sequence of stages the model postulates a continuing stream of consciousness that, it is assumed, accompanies all waking life. This may take the form of thoughts or visual images, and we shall see later in the chapter that attempts have been made to study the contents of thoughts in the context of anxiety and shyness. These thoughts affect the emotional process in a number of ways. First, they can provide the starting point for the process, so that remembering a past event or anticipating a future one can produce an emotional reaction. Thus the stimulus need not be an external one.

Second, the perception of threat can so capture a person's attention that the thinking process becomes dominated by it. In the study of anxiety this process is known as *worry*. It can be persistent, pervasive, intrusive and uncontrollable, making it difficult for the worried person to concentrate on anything else. In shyness, the contents of worrisome thinking can be the individual's own social performance, the impression that is being made on other people and the costs of making a poor impression.

Third, thinking can influence the somatic and behavioural components. It can interfere with attention that ought to be paid to task-relevant activity. Eysenck (1992) offers an explanation of this interference in terms of the implications of worry for the efficient

processing of information during performance of a task. The explanation draws upon a model of working memory that comprises a
central executive together with two 'slave' systems that function to
keep material available for processing. As the word 'working'
implies, the theory is an attempt to understand the role that memory plays in processing information. In many activities, such as following a conversation or thinking of something to say, information
has to be held in the cognitive system long enough for it to be
related to information that has just been received or is stored elsewhere in the system, and so on. Worry can pre-empt some of
the capacity of the working memory so that it is unavailable for
task-relevant processing. Alternatively, worry obliges the central
executive to allocate extra resources to the task, so that it can be
completed, but much less efficiently.

A further influence of thinking on behaviour is demonstrated by
self-consciousness. When one is conscious of being observed by
others, even well-practised activities such as walking or swimming
can become stiff, awkward or unnatural. An early account of self-
consciousness was provided by Baldwin in 1902 (quoted in Harris,
1990, pp. 67–8):

> This 'sense of other persons' may break up all the mental processes.
> The present writer cannot think the same thoughts, nor follow the
> same plan of action, nor control the muscles with the same sufficiency,
> nor concentrate the attention with the same directness, nor, in fact, do
> any blessed thing as well, when this sense of the presence of others is
> upon him.

When I am conversing with someone I divide my attention among
many tasks. I listen to what is being said and pick up non-verbal signals. I construct some sense of what is going on, of the underlying
meaning and purpose of the conversation. I plan my own contribution, seek an opportunity to utter it, modify it as the conversation
changes course, utter it, gauge its effect and so on. My sense of self
does not normally intrude but if I am shy some of my attention
becomes focused on myself. This presumably reduces the amount of
attention I can pay to other aspects of the situation and thereby produces the incapacity and lack of concentration noted by Baldwin.
This may be a matter of attention having a limited capacity; alternatively it might be that the new focus is absorbing, generating
fresh trains of thought and hence capturing attention.

There is an intimate relationship between thinking and affect. Nevertheless it would be misleading to equate the cognitive component of shyness with conscious thought. Much cognitive activity is unconscious, as demonstrated by the classic experiments carried out by Zajonc (1980). He argues that emotional reactions are rapid and usually precede any elaborate cognitive processing. It is only afterwards that people explain or rationalise their reactions. Zajonc supports his argument with experimental evidence. In typical studies, stimuli are presented for very brief exposure times – fractions of a second – and on a variable number of occasions. Participants judge these stimuli in terms of whether or not they like them and whether or not they recognise them. They tend to like best the stimuli they have most often encountered, irrespective of whether or not they recognise them, that is to say, liking appears to be independent of subjective recognition. Many emotional reactions are in place before the individual becomes aware, say, that there is a threat, which implies that there has been *pre-attentive* processing of threat-related information.

We consider each of the stages in turn and suggest that there are differences among people at each stage of the process:

- There are individual differences in the kinds of situation that elicit anxiety, for some it is spiders, for others it is high places. Where social fears are concerned, these seem to be quite general and encompass a range of situations. Furthermore shy individuals and less shy people agree on the types of situation that elicit shyness, which implies that individual differences are larger at subsequent stages of the process.
- There is considerable evidence of individual differences in the appraisal of situations. Socially anxious people are more sensitive to threat, and they perceive themselves as lacking the skills necessary to get what they want out of social encounters. People develop *schemas*, or mental models of the nature of recurring situations, and these influence subsequent stages in the process.
- There may be individual differences in the tendency to react emotionally to situations, for example some may have a more reactive arousal system. This chapter reviews evidence of differences in two indices of emotional reaction: heart rate and activation of the brain hemispheres.
- Research shows that socially anxious individuals develop characteristic ways of coping with social situations, and these may

be thought of as *strategies* to avoid threat or to escape from it. These strategies seem to be successful in the short term, but eventually they are counterproductive, denying individuals the rewards that can be obtained from social encounters and the opportunity to practise more effective ways of behaving. They also sustain the shy person's negative view of him- or herself.

- There are behavioural differences between the shy and the less shy, and reticence has been regarded as a defining characteristic. Nevertheless there are reasons for being quiet that are not due to personality factors; furthermore shy people are not always reticent and shyness can manifest itself in talking too much, or 'gabbling'. This chapter examines evidence of quietness and other non-verbal behaviours.

We shall consider each of the stages in turn, paying particular attention to the nature of the evidence they contribute to our understanding of the three components of shyness.

Stages of the emotion process

The stimulus

When anxiety is elicited by an external event, the individual should be able to report on this. Such reports help researchers to identify the kinds of situation that elicit social anxiety and can also provide psychologists with a starting point for the development of a programme to help people overcome their anxiety. However, as we have noted, the trigger for an emotional reaction need not be an external event but can come from memory or the imagination. Perhaps the nature of the reaction differs depending on whether it is externally or internally generated. For example it could be argued that the distinction between fear and anxiety is that fear is a response to an actual stimulus whereas anxiety is a response to the anticipation or imagination of an event. Anxiety may also be more diffuse in that the individual cannot always identify its source; someone may be nervous before going to a social function but cannot quite say what it is he or she is nervous about. Much worrying seems to involve the mental rehearsal of eventualities, specifically the potential negative outcomes of events. 'Worst case' scenarios figure largely. The contents of worries are often self-deprecatory and self-blaming. Although these processes are not externally generated they are, of course, felt to be real and are a source of anguish. In shyness the feared outcomes are looking foolish, losing face and being embarrassed or humiliated, yet these are presumably rare events. Shy people try to ensure that they do not happen by adopting self-protective strategies or *safety behaviours* (discussed pp. 43–4). Although social situations can provide cues for threat, the feared outcomes are seldom encountered.

Appraisal

An accurate appraisal of threat is of obvious survival value for any species and it is to be expected that they will evolve systems for monitoring the environment and detecting signs of danger. An appraisal process is subject to bias, in particular it can be adjusted to reduce the value of the threshold at which it is decided that a threat is imminent. This will result in an increase in the number of 'false alarms', the detection of a threat where none exists. However it might be better to be anxious without good cause than to fail to identify a danger, and this is likely to be the case when the cost of failure is very high, for example life-threatening.

There is empirical evidence of bias in highly anxious people. They tend to interpret ambiguous information as threatening. If they are requested to write down words that are read aloud to them they are more likely to write the more threatening of a pair of homophones, 'die' rather than 'dye', or 'pain' rather than 'pane' (Eysenck, 1992).

One programme of research uses the Stroop paradigm. Subjects are presented with either a threatening or a non-threatening word printed in a particular colour and their task is to name the *colour* as quickly as they can while ignoring the semantic content. For example subjects who have a phobia about eating in public might be presented with a set of words printed in different colours where one of the stimulus words is 'menu'. Anxious subjects take longer to name the colour when the word is threatening (menu) than when it is non-threatening (mail). People take longer to name the colours when the stimulus word is relevant to their particular worries. For example people with social phobia are slower to name the colour of words when they relate to social threat, but this delay does not occur for words referring to physical threats (McLeod, 1996).

Another form of bias is that the appraisal is not commensurate with the danger. The likelihood of the feared outcome or its magnitude can be exaggerated. Studies of the belief systems of individuals high in test anxiety have demonstrated their preoccupation with the negative consequences of their failure, anticipating the worst outcome and thinking of it in catastrophic terms.

Mobilising for action

It is important to regard somatic reactions as preparations for action, since emotions serve adaptive functions. Because shyness and anxiety are unpleasant states, it is tempting to think of emotions as disruptive or unwanted experiences. This can be misleading, and these problems may be due to an inappropriate response to threat rather than to anxiety processes in themselves. The somatic component of shyness has mostly been discussed in terms of anxiety, and the physiological processes involved in anxiety have been intensively studied in recent years. The role of the autonomic nervous system (ANS) in fear and anxiety has been recognised ever since the pioneering investigations carried out by the American physiologist Walter Cannon and published in 1919 in his book *Bodily Changes in Pain, Hunger, Fear and Rage*.

The automatic nervous system has two divisions, the sympathetic and the parasympathetic, and these work together to maintain the body's internal environment. They tend to have opposing actions, thus stimulation of the sympathetic division increases the heart rate, whereas stimulation of the parasympathetic division decreases it. In general, activation of the sympathetic system prepares the body for action, particularly when emergency action is needed. The heart rate increases, producing an increased flow of blood to the skeletal muscles. The body temperature rises, and increased sweating regulates this. Blood is diverted from the surface of the skin (producing skin pallor) and from internal organs such as the stomach and intestine, giving rise to the sensation of 'butterflies' or churning in the stomach.

These changes are detectable and can be reported upon by the shy person. Sweating, skin pallor, muscular changes such as trembling, shaking or nervous hand movements, stammering or a higher frequency of the voice can be reported upon by observers. Thus self-reports by shy people and ratings of shyness by observers constitute one source of evidence of anxiety. Respondents in the Stanford survey reported that shyness was accompanied by increased pulse rate, pounding heart, blushing, perspiration and butterflies in the stomach. There is also empirical evidence. Following a conversation with a stranger, shy participants reported more tension, worries and inhibition than did those who were not shy (Cheek and Buss, 1981). Observers of their behaviour reported that they seemed more tense, inhibited and unfriendly during the conversation.

Relationships between shyness and anxiety are also apparent in ratings of children made by parents and teachers. Mothers of shy children judged them as having more fears and worries than did mothers of less shy children (Kagan *et al.*, 1984; Stevenson-Hinde and Glover, 1996). Playgroup leaders judged shy children as having withdrawal problems, including reluctance to speak, being easily upset, tearful and very fearful (Stevenson-Hinde and Glover, 1996).

Of course an individual might experience anxiety without being conscious of any of these symptoms, or might have some or all of these symptoms without interpreting them as anxiety. Similarly an observer might not notice these signs in another person or might label them incorrectly. Peripheral physiological measures of heart rate, blood pressure, respiration, hand temperature and sweating (galvanic skin response measures the electrical conductance of skin) are also available and provide another source of evidence. Research into the relationship between shyness and heart rate is summarised below.

Recent research has aimed to identify the neuro-anatomical structures involved in emotion. Structures in the limbic area of the midbrain have been targeted, including the thalamus, amygdala, hypothalamus and hippocampus, and their projections to the cortex and the brain stem. The amygdala (a complex nucleus that lies in the medial wall of the temporal lobe) has been a focus of research into fear and anxiety. One important source of evidence draws upon clinical samples, studying the effects of lesions or electrical stimulation. For example stimulation of the amygdala gives rise to the experience of fear, but there is no fear response if the amygdala has been damaged (LeDoux, 1998, pp. 172–3). Recognition of facial expressions of fear, but not of other emotions, is impaired by damage to the amygdala (Davidson and Irwin, 1999).

Research has found that the appraisal of threat can lead directly to somatic changes without the necessity for cognitive processing. The thalamus plays a central part in this process. It receives information about an emotional stimulus prior to its receipt by the sensory cortex and sends messages about the stimulus directly to the amygdala, which can orchestrate an emotional reaction. Because this information bypasses the cortex only a rough representation of the stimulus is provided, but the process is quick and can provoke a rapid response before the person is fully aware of the danger.

The study of cortical activity has also contributed to the understanding of emotion. Measurements of electrical activity by means of electroencephalography (EEG), where electrodes are attached to the scalp, provide a significant source of evidence. Research using this technique indicates that there are differences between the two cortical hemispheres in the regulation of emotion, and anxious people show greater EEG activity in the right hemisphere of the prefrontal cortex (Davidson *et al.*, 1990).

More recent developments in brain imaging techniques, such as positron emission tomography (PET) and functional magnetic resonance imaging (fMRI), are enhancing knowledge of the structures and circuits underlying the experience of emotion among human participants with intact brain structures. The measurement of glucose metabolism or cerebral blood flow indicates which parts of the brain are active while a specific task is being performed, for example while the participant is looking at unpleasant pictures or imagining frightening events. These measures provide additional evidence of the contributions of the prefrontal cortex and the amygdala in emotion. For example Birmbaumer *et al.* (1998, cited in Davidson and Irwin, 1999) used fMRI and found evidence of activation in the amygdala of social phobics as they looked at pictures of facial expressions.

In summary, emotion, specifically fear, is the outcome of a complex system of interactions. The complexity of the system and the interactions between its components means that the measurement of emotion is not straightforward. A number of approaches have been adopted, and all offer insights into the subjective feelings, bodily changes and behaviours that are associated with fear and anxiety. Nevertheless the various measures are not always intercorrelated and different anxiety conditions or different individuals may show diverse patterns of physiological reactions (Kagan, 1994, p. 152). More generally, the question of the reliability of physiological measures has to be considered when interpreting findings.

Selection of action

The classic responses to fear are flight and fight. The organism escapes the threat or defends itself against attack. Fears and anxieties about social situations can require a more complex response.

Avoidance of situations and escape from them are sometimes options but there are pressures of many kinds to participate in social situations. Some of these originate in the demands of work and family, and the need to interact with neighbours, shop assistants, co-workers and officials. Others originate in the self and shy people often experience a conflict between their motivation to socialise and their lack of confidence. They find it difficult to select an action. Not knowing what to say and being at a loss for words is a common complaint of the shy. Being embarrassed is literally to encounter a barrier in social interaction, and the individual finds it hard to know what to do to get the process going again.

Implementation of action

The Stanford survey found that shy people are silent, avoid making eye contact and keep in the background on social occasions. They are reluctant to express an opinion or interject a remark into a conversation, and when they speak they do so in a quiet voice. These characteristic behaviours may have a variety of causes or serve a number of different functions. Shy people may be relatively unskilled in behaviour. Interfering thoughts or self-consciousness might make it difficult to plan and produce utterances. They might set unrealistic standards for their contribution, rehearsing and rejecting remarks before they are uttered. They may be apprehensive that their contribution will lead to embarrassment, ridicule or rejection. They may fear that their contribution will lead to further interaction that they will be unable to sustain.

Hill (1989) has examined three explanations of the behaviour of shy people: they lack knowledge of appropriate behaviour, they are reluctant to enact appropriate behaviours, or they lack confidence in their ability to enact the behaviours. These were explored by means of self-report questionnaires. Shy and non-shy participants (assessed by a modified version of the Stanford survey) differed on measures related to all three hypotheses, implying that all contribute in some way to their behaviour. Nevertheless, support for the hypothesis that shy people lack confidence in their social ability was stronger than that for the other two explanations.

Shy people adopt various strategies to cope with their social difficulties. Staying in the background, being reticent, offering answers to questions that are short or framed to discourage further conversation, and avoiding self-assertion or the expression of attitudes that are controversial or will demand a further contribution, are all behavioural tendencies mentioned by shy people. Bruce (1997) provides an interesting discussion of 'niceness', defined as a 'courteous, deferential, non-assertive, non-confrontational manner'. Although this can lead to smooth, conflict-free social interactions, these are achieved at a cost. Being nice involves a narrow range of behaviours and hence stunts the development of the social skills that are necessary for effective social functioning. It is a form of 'hiding', which can lead to being ignored by others or even distrusted by them ('What's he really like?'). It is difficult to be nice at the same time as being frank. For example a teacher does students no favours by failing to tell them that an assignment is unsatisfactory. An employer who does not confront employees with their shortcomings puts up with shoddy work and makes it more difficult to deal with any future confrontation. To be nice means having to forego being a leader, standing up for your rights or those of people close to you, being funny or being intimate.

Self-protective strategies have been discussed in the context of social phobia. Wells *et al.* (1995) have explored the concept of *safety behaviours*. These are adopted in order to reduce the risk of being negatively evaluated by others. Examples of these behaviours are avoiding social situations, minimising eye contact, mentally rehearsing sentences, avoiding eating or drinking in public, and concentrating on gripping utensils or cups in order to reduce the risk of appearing clumsy or having accidents when eating or drinking in public. These behaviours are maintained and become habitual, but although they create a sense of safety they have considerable costs. Avoiding social situations reduces the chance of boosting self-confidence by having successful experiences, and it minimises opportunities to learn and practise less defensive strategies.

Paulhus and Morgan (1997) found that shy participants in a discussion group were rated by other group members as less intelligent (although this effect diminished over time). The main reasons for these ratings, as stated by the group members themselves, were quietness (36 per cent of the reasons given) and the poor quality of the shy participants' contribution to the discussion (35 per cent). When amount of talk was controlled statistically, the correlation between shyness and judgment of intelligence was no longer significant. It is perhaps necessary to point out that there was no correlation between shyness and an objective measure of intelligence (scores in an IQ test). Irrespective of whether quietness is a freezing response to perceived threat, an outcome of a process of cognitive interference or the result of a coping strategy it inevitably creates an impression in other people that can influence subsequent encounters.

Safety behaviours create a public image or 'personality' that may be unsuccessful or unwanted and may serve to constrain other activities. Thus if one avoids speaking up in class, one creates for oneself a more impoverished learning environment. Someone who fails to take the initiative in forming friendships or blocks approaches by others will end up with fewer friends. Application of safety behaviours to job interviews or promotion panels, or simply failing to catch the attention of superiors will have adverse consequences for the development of one's career. Wells *et al.* (1995) argue that safety behaviours also serve to maintain social phobia, and they provide evidence that dropping these behaviours can reduce patients' anxiety.

Self-consciousness

Cheek and Watson (1989) define the cognitive component of shyness in terms of the individual's thoughts and worries, including self-consciousness and fear of being evaluated. There is a high degree of consensus that self-consciousness is at the heart of shyness. The Stanford survey identified self-consciousness and apprehension about being evaluated by others as the most frequently endorsed characteristics of shyness (self-consciousness was reported by 85 per cent of participants). Woody *et al.* (1997, p. 118) claim that 'negative self-judging cognitions are endemic to social phobia'.

One meaning of self-consciousness is the capacity for self-awareness and self-reflection (developments in the ability to think about the self are relevant to shyness and are discussed in Chapter 4). However this is not what shy people have in mind when they say that they are self-conscious. They are drawing a distinction between what they feel when they are shy and what they feel when they are not shy; self-consciousness is somehow an abnormal state. Harris (1990) proposes that it is also an inherently unpleasant state and argues that its negative quality is due to a person's awareness of a discrepancy between the self-image that is sought and the image that is projected to others. Clark and Wells (1995) suggest that self-focused attention results in enhanced awareness of unwanted somatic responses and this contributes to socially anxious people's negative view of themselves through a process of reasoning from consequences. Insight into the nature of this process can be obtained from two social psychological approaches to the self, which study the effects of self-awareness and cognitive interference. We shall consider each in turn.

Self-awareness theory

This theory proposes that attention can either be directed outwards towards the environment or inwards towards the self. The flurry of interest in this proposition in the 1970s and 1980s (see Carver and Scheier, 1987, for a review) was influenced by evidence that straightforward experimental manipulations in the laboratory could alter the direction of attention in a reliable way. There was greater self-focused attention when participants acted in front of a mirror or a camera or while their tape-recorded voice was played to them.

An illustration of this research is a study by Hass (1984), where a participant was asked to draw a letter E on his or her forehead. There are two ways of drawing this, either oriented towards an external observer, or oriented towards the self, in which case it would appear in reverse to the observer. If a state of self-awareness was elicited, say by pointing a camera at the participant, the external orientation was adopted on 55 per cent of occasions compared with 18 per cent when the camera was pointed elsewhere. A similar effect was obtained when the participant was made aware of the presence of a tape-recorder.

There is substantial evidence that inducing self-focused attention by these means can lead to increased negative affect, less self-confidence in conversations and lower self-ratings of social skill (see Woody *et al.*, 1997, for a review of these studies). Woody *et al.* (1997) also found that post-therapeutic gains in self-confidence and reductions in anxiety among a sample of social phobic patients were associated with decreased self-focus, as assessed by the self-report questionnaires on focus of attention that patients completed immediately after a social episode. Bögels *et al.* (1997) report that a treatment approach aimed at reducing self-focused attention reduced the tendency to blush and the fear of blushing among a sample of individuals with a chronic blushing problem.

Self-consciousness was defined within this framework as a trait-like predisposition to self-focused attention. A questionnaire measure of this trait was developed (Fenigstein *et al.*, 1975) and factor analysis of the items identified three factors. *Public self-consciousness* is the tendency to focus on the self as a public object. *Private self-consciousness* is the tendency to focus attention on one's thoughts and feelings. The test items in *social anxiety* refer to shyness and embarrassment. Individual differences assessed by these means parallel experimental manipulations. For example scores on the public self-consciousness scale are correlated with a tendency to adopt an external perspective in the E-drawing paradigm (Hass, 1984).

The predictions of this theory have received substantial empirical support, particularly where the public self-consciousness scale is concerned. Scores on this scale have been shown to be significantly correlated with shyness (Pilkonis, 1977a) and with a measure of predisposition to embarrassment (Miller, 1995). Public self-consciousness also helps to distinguish between different types of shyness. Cheek and Krasnoperova (1999) report that a 'secure-shy' group of participants, that is, those who were less dependent and withdrawn than other shy people, obtained lower scores for public self-consciousness than either dependent shy or withdrawn shy participants.

There is also relevant evidence from studies of social interactions. Hope and Heimberg (1988) report that, among a sample of men and women who had been diagnosed as having social phobia, public self-consciousness was associated with less social skill, greater anxiety and a higher frequency of negative thoughts during social interaction. Froming *et al.* (1990) found that students with high public self-consciousness were quicker to escape from the situation where they had to sing a song in front of another student, and this was the case irrespective of how well they knew the other student. On the other hand, those with low public self-consciousness were less embarrassed overall, and their degree of embarrassment was smaller when the one-person audience was either a friend or a complete stranger rather than someone whom they expected to meet afterwards to discuss their performance.

Bruch *et al.* (1995) compared the ratings provided by two groups of men about their conversations with an attractive woman stranger. One group varied in shyness (on the Cheek–Buss scale) and the other varied in public self-consciousness. Both groups were asked to rate the extent of any symptoms of shyness they had experienced (nervousness, awkwardness and inhibition) and to judge the likelihood that the woman had formed a negative impression of them. They estimated the proportion of time spent focusing on themselves, and listed the thoughts that had gone through their minds during the conversation (these thoughts were subsequently coded as positive, negative or neutral). Both shyness and public self-consciousness were associated with more symptoms of shyness; however shyness (but not public self-consciousness) was correlated with greater concern about the woman's evaluation, more self-focused attention and recollection of more negative than positive thoughts. There was no tendency for shyness and public self-consciousness to interact with each other to produce more intense shyness or discomfort during the conversation.

In summary, this study suggests that feeling awkward and inhibited in a conversation can be produced by both shyness and public self-consciousness; however in the case of shyness these feelings coincide with self-doubt and low expectations of a successful encounter. This correlation is not found where public self-consciousness is involved, nor is the tendency of shy people to report a belief of low self-efficacy in respect of social interaction augmented by public self-consciousness.

The theory of self-awareness generated a substantial amount of research within a short period of time and the self-consciousness measure has continued to be valuable in the study of personality. Nevertheless the theory has not altogether fulfilled its promise in the area of shyness research. It influenced Harris's (1990) model of self-consciousness discussed above, but the latter has not attracted further investigation. The theory does offer an interpretation of disruption of behaviour if it is assumed that self-focused attention is at the expense of task-focused attention. It also offers an interpretation of negative affect, in that the theory proposes that self-consciousness arises from a discrepancy between the individual's standards and his or her behaviour.

Cognitive interference

When taking examinations or tests, anxious people are self-absorbed rather than task-absorbed. For example Blankstein et al. (1989) invited those who had participated in an anagram solution task to list the thoughts they could remember having during the task. These thoughts were categorised as negative, neutral or positive, and as self-referential, task-referential or unrelated to self or task. The more negative, self-referential thoughts that were recalled, the worse the task performance.

Melchior and Cheek (1990) investigated the relationship between self-focused attention and anxious thoughts and symptoms among a sample of women students. Following a conversation with a stranger, the women provided numerical estimates of the proportion of time they had spent focusing attention on themselves ('I spent X% of the time thinking about what I was going to say next or about what kind of impression I was making'). They also estimated the proportion of time spent focusing on what the other person had been saying and doing, and rated themselves on a set of 21 items relating to social anxiety symptoms. Shy participants reported significantly more self-focus than did non-shy participants, and the extent of self-focus was correlated with scores on the social anxiety items. These results were interpreted as evidence of anxious self-preoccupation among the shy women.

The study by Bruch *et al.* (1995) summarised above also included the Melchior–Cheek self-focus item, together with a 'thought listing' measure where the participants listed all the thoughts they could recall having during their conversation with a stranger. The thoughts were coded as positive (facilitating the conversation), neutral or negative (not facilitating the conversation, for example not knowing what to say). Shy participants (defined in terms of scores on the Cheek–Buss scale) reported more self-focus and also recalled more negative thoughts. The frequency of negative thoughts was correlated with the number of shyness symptoms, concerns about negative evaluation and concerns about protective self-presentation. These findings confirmed earlier research showing that shy people use more negative adjectives to describe themselves (Cacioppo *et al.*, 1979) and recall more negative self-referent information (Breck and Smith, 1983).

A more structured approach to tapping negative thoughts during social interaction uses rating scales where participants rate the frequency of a set of items reflecting positive and negative thoughts. Bruch *et al.* (1989) administered one of the scales, the social interaction self-statement test (SISST; developed by Glass *et al.*, 1982, see Bruch *et al.*, 1989), which comprises 15 positive items and 15 negative items, each rated on a five-point scale. Ratings were provided after a conversation between each participant and a stranger. Shy participants gave significantly higher ratings of negative thoughts than non-shy participants (a mean score of 36.8 versus 25.8) and significantly lower ratings on the positive items (mean of 44.4 compared with 48.8). It can be seen from these mean scores that shy people report positive thoughts as well as negative ones, but negative thinking is much less salient for the non-shy.

It would be useful to show not only that shyness is associated with intrusive thoughts but also that these have an effect on some other aspects of the shy person's functioning. Karafa and Cozzarelli (1997) considered whether cognitive interference could carry over from one situation to another. They examined the influence of shyness (Cheek–Buss scale scores) and cognitive interference, assessed by means of an index of mind wandering and lack of concentration, on the self-reported sexual arousal of men while they were watching a sexually explicit videotape. The researchers attempted to influence participants' anxiety about being socially evaluated by an observer, and before watching the videotape the men were either interviewed and (allegedly) filmed or else completed questionnaires privately. Two results are of particular interest here. First, taking part in the interview had a powerful effect on the shy men. The combination of shyness and social interaction reduced sexual arousal the most. Indeed, among those who had not taken part in an interview there were only slight differences between shy and non-shy men in levels of arousal. Second, the effects on sexual arousal were mediated by cognitive interference. Arousal was lowest among those shy individuals who participated in the interview and scored highest on the index of intrusive thoughts. The results suggest that interference induced by social interaction carried over to another situation.

Shy individuals tend to perceive themselves as inadequate. A number of studies have shown that they underestimate their social competence (Bieling and Alden, 1997; Jackson et al.,1997; Kowalski and Leary, 1990; Stopa and Clark, 1993). In the study by Bruch et al. (1989) summarised above, shy participants believed that they exhibited more signs of nervousness than were perceived by their partner in the conversation, and this tendency was more pronounced when a higher frequency of negative thoughts were reported. Research has also found that shy people have a greater expectation of being negatively evaluated and rejected by others (Jackson et al., 1997).

The evidence on perfectionism is less decisive. Clark and Wells (1995, p. 75) argue that social phobics hold excessively high standards in respect of their social performance. Bieling and Alden

(1997) report greater perfectionism among a sample of social phobics. Specifically, the sample gave higher scores on a scale assessing
the extent to which they perceived that other people required high
standards from them. Furthermore the more perfectionist they
were, the higher the standards they believed were expected. On the
other hand they did not differ from a control group when perfectionism was defined in terms of the standards people set for themselves, implying that socially anxious individuals feel that the exacting standards they find difficult to meet are set by other people
rather than by themselves. However Jackson *et al.* (1997) found no
differences in either measure of perfectionism between shy and less
shy people when using the Cheek–Buss scale to assess shyness.
Whether the difference between a clinical sample and a random
sample of undergraduate students is relevant to explaining the differences in the findings awaits further research.

Self-consciousness in shyness

Each of these approaches has been usefully applied to shyness, but
it is questionable whether they can explain an aspect of perspective-
taking that has been emphasised in philosophical accounts of shyness, shame and embarrassment. This stresses the role of spectators
in the actor's behaviour. More specifically it argues that:

- The person views his or her behaviour from the perspective of
  an audience.
- The view that is held is negative.
- The actor is aware that he or she ought not to be seen in that
  light.

This audience need not be physically present, and an audience that
is present need not hold this view of the actor – it is sufficient that
the actor recognises that his or her conduct *could* be seen in that
light. Taylor (1985, p. 26) describes the audience as a 'possible
detached observer-description' of the actor's conduct in order to
capture the notion that the view of the actor need not be held by any
actual individual. This account has implications for the person's
sense of responsibility for her or his predicament, and we shall discuss this in Chapter 5. Here we concentrate on the shift in perspective that is proposed. It is the audience that distinguishes self-
consciousness from egocentrism. More precisely, it is the audience

as conceived in the mind of the self-conscious person. This audience can be imagined or actual; it can be generalised ('What would people say!') or specific ('What would your mother say!'). What is salient is what one's position looks like, or would look like, to the audience. In its eyes one is humiliated or exposed, and whether or not one deserves to be seen in this way is not germane.

This emphasis on the individual's sense of how he or she *might* be seen rather than on the individual's negative view of him- or herself is a potentially important one for several reasons. First, according to this account, low self-esteem is not a prerequisite for self-consciousness. This can be contrasted with the widely held view among researchers that low self-esteem and shyness are similar constructs (Cheek and Melchior, 1990) and that shyness can be related specifically to personal insecurity about social interactions (Cheek and Briggs, 1990). There is substantial empirical evidence of a correlation between measures of shyness and self-esteem among both children and adults (Cheek *et al.*, 1986; Crozier, 1981, 1995). Whether this is an indication of a difference between shyness on the one hand, and shame and embarrassment on the other, or whether there are different dimensions of shyness, some related to low self-esteem and others not, is a matter for further enquiry.

Second, the notion that someone adopts a 'possible detached observer' perspective on the self might help explain why people feel *shy* when they believe that they are not in a position to contribute effectively to a social encounter rather than, say, feel depressed or angry or disgusted with themselves. Perhaps their state of mind is characterised by uncertainty and apprehension about whether a possible view of the self might be realised in practice.

Third, accounts of self-consciousness in both shame and embarrassment assume that there is something specific for individuals to feel ashamed or embarrassed about. They have performed some action, have failed to perform some action or are associated with someone else's action, there is something untoward about their appearance, or they are found in an inappropriate place. Any of these can give rise to a judgment with which they will feel uncomfortable, whether or not it is deserved. You knock over a pile of vegetables in a crowded supermarket. You find yourself at a loss to recall someone's name at the moment when you are obliged to introduce him. Your child spills drink over your host's carpet. You discover that you have a pimple on your nose. You realise when your host answers the door in his bathrobe that you have arrived for the dinner party on the wrong evening. All these can give rise to self-consciousness and the source is palpable in each case. But what is the source of self-consciousness in shyness? Perhaps shyness is anticipatory, in the sense that the shy person is afraid of committing one of these actions rather than finding that one has been committed. More likely, I suspect, is that the shy person believes that the predicament will reveal some aspects of a social self that will be found to be wanting.

Cognitive interference theory does not specifically address this shift in perspective. Presumably any self-absorbed thoughts can affect performance, whatever perspective is adopted. The focal thoughts in shyness concern not knowing what to say, the rehearsal of possible utterances, speculation on what others are thinking and so on. Is shyness simply a matter of the contents of thoughts or is there a further dimension, relating to a shift in attention or the perspective from which the self is viewed?

Self-awareness theory deals more specifically with shifts in attention but its position on the distinction between egocentrism and self-consciousness is not clear. From a phenomenological stance, different experiences can ensue when I focus attention on myself. If I catch a glimpse of myself reflected in a shop window I might be critical of how I look, judging myself to be overweight or shabbily dressed. Here I am egocentric and the perspective I adopt is my own. I am the spectator and judge of my image, even though it is my public image that I am judging. Alternatively I may become aware that I am being photographed or filmed and may again be critical of how I look. This awareness of my appearance seems intuitively to have a different quality and this might be because I am now seeing myself as if through the eyes of another. Moreover this difference does not map onto the distinction between private and public self-consciousness. When looking at myself in the window I am not more aware of my somatic state; on both occasions I am conscious of my public image, the only difference, if there is one, is the source of the observing eye.

Alternatively self-consciousness might represent bias in the operation of a cognitive system dedicated to detecting whether one is being looked at (Figure 2.2). The threshold criterion for detection scrutiny might be lowered, leading to a greater number of 'false alarm' decisions and an overestimation of the frequency with which one is the object of others' attention. Where the criterion is set is a function of the benefits and costs associated with making correct

Figure 2.2 A cognitive system for detecting scrutiny by others

	Someone is looking	No one is looking
Believe self is being looked at	Correct recognition	False alarm
Believe self is not being looked at	Miss	Correct

and incorrect decisions. This bias might be operative in self-consciousness because of the importance the individual attaches to creating a desired impression or because of her or his low level of subjective probability of doing so. This notion should be amenable to empirical investigation, perhaps using videotaped sequences of someone looking in the direction of the subject, who has to decide whether he or she is being looked at.

Shyness and affect

Heart rate

The balance between the two divisions of the ANS can be seen in their influence on heart rate. The vagus is the primary nerve of the parasympathetic system. It originates in the brain stem and projects to many organs, including the heart. Vagal tone is defined as the rate of parasympathetic efferent activity and is assessed by heart rate variability. An index of this is respiratory sinus arrhythmia (RSA), which is a naturally occurring correspondence between the phases of breathing and a rhythmic increase and decrease in heart rate (Porges *et al.*, 1994). When you breathe out (expiration) your heart rate decreases, that is, there is a longer interval between heart-beats. When you breathe in (inspiration) there is a relatively short interval between beats. RSA can be measured by taking the average difference between the shortest interval between heartbeats during inspiration and the longest interval during expiration, the so-called 'peak-valley' method (Jennings and McKnight, 1994). Alternatively, power spectral analysis of heart rate can be used. The variation in heart rate is divided into different frequency components, isolating those frequency components that correspond to respiratory rate and are associated with parasympathetic system activity.

When there is increased heart rate activity, for example when an individual is exposed to a stressful event, the predominance of sympathetic over parasympathetic activity produces more inhibition of vagal tone, and a smaller reduction in heart rate during expiration, and hence less variability in heart rate. As sympathetic activity increases the heart rate increases and also becomes more stable.

Considerable information on the relationship between heart rate measures and shyness is provided by longitudinal studies undertaken by Kagan and his associates at Harvard University. We shall discuss this research in Chapter 3, where we examine children's temperament as a factor in the development of shyness. Here we shall concentrate on physiological measures and their findings. A summary of the main findings of the investigations discussed in this section is provided in Table 2.1.

The Harvard study began by gathering a sample of 28 extremely inhibited and 30 extremely uninhibited children at the age of 21 months. The measurement of inhibition was based on systematic observations of the children while they were engaged in a number of novel activities, including a brief separation from their mothers. Inhibition was defined in terms of a long latency to interact with a stranger and distress at separation. Although inhibition is regarded by Kagan as a reaction to novel and unfamiliar events of all kinds, shy and timid behaviours have been explicitly linked to inhibition (for example Kagan *et al.*, 1987, p. 1461).

Heart rate and heart rate variability were measured when these children were 21 months, 4 years, $5^{1/2}$ years and $7^{1/2}$ years. Recordings were made during a baseline condition and when the children were undertaking a sequence of tasks, some of them quiet, such as listening to a story, and others more active, such as constructing objects or telling a story. The longitudinal study provides evidence of temporal stability in heart period and heart period vari-

Table 2.1 Selected studies of heart rate in infancy and childhood

Authors	Average age	Sample size[1]	Heart period baseline	Heart period activity	Heart variability baseline	Heart variability activity
Harvard studies						
Garcia-Coll *et al.*						
(1984)	1:9	55 [58]	No	Yes	No	Yes
Kagan *et al.*						
(1984)	4:0	43	No	Yes	No	Yes
Reznick *et al.*						
(1986)	5:6	58 [64]	Yes	Yes	Yes	Yes
Kagan *et al.*						
(1988)	7:6	41	No	No	No	No
Madingley study						
Marshall and						
Stevenson						
-Hinde (1998)	4:6	57 [126]	No[2]	No	No	No

Notes:
'No' refers to no relationship between heart rate and inhibition, 'Yes' to a statistically significant relationship.
1. Sample size refers to the number of children for whom heart rate data were available; the numbers in parentheses refer to the original sample size.
2. Heart measurements were taken during four episodes, the first of which involved the mother and child sitting quietly.

ability (Table 2. 2). Heart period is a measure of the interval between beats; therefore a short period means a fast heart rate. The standard deviation of heart rate provides a measure of variability, and a large value represents high variability.

The correlation coefficients are statistically significant, albeit modestly so. When considered as evidence of test-retest reliability they might be thought to be disappointing. However the coefficients are not very much smaller than those found in comparisons of the inhibition scores over the equivalent period of time (Table 2.2). These are aggregates of a number of measures of inhibition and hence might be expected to be relatively stable over time. We should bear in mind that these data were collected from samples of very young children. There are methodological problems with taking physiological measures at these ages. Furthermore it is difficult to be certain that the activities provided for the children were equivalent at different ages. At each time of testing the tasks were chosen

Table 2.2 Temporal stability of heart rate measures. Correlation of measurement made at $7^{1}/_{2}$ years with measurements made at 21 months, 4 years and $5^{1}/_{2}$ years

	21 months	4 years	$5^{1}/_2$ years
Measure at $7^{1}/_{2}$			
Inhibition	0.67	0.54	0.57
Mean heart period	0.62	0.56	0.58
Heart variability	0.54	0.48	0.46

Source: J. Kagan, J. S. Reznick, N. Snidman, J. Gibbons, and M. O. Johnson, 'Childhood derivatives of inhibition and lack of inhibition to the unfamiliar', *Child Development*, **59** (1988), p. 1589. Reprinted with permission of the Society for Research in Child Development, Inc.

to be cognitively demanding, and social episodes were structured in an attempt to expose the children to unfamiliar people and events. However it is difficult to know whether the tasks were equivalent in respect of level of difficulty or familiarity at different ages, particularly as the children themselves were changing rapidly during this period of their life. Perhaps, too, inhibited and uninhibited children were developing in different ways or at different paces, given the pressures they faced as they moved away from dependence on the family towards a social world with large numbers of other children and unfamiliar adults such as playgroup leaders and teachers.

The studies are also informative about cross-situational consistency in heart rate measurement. It will be remembered that the children participated in a sequence of episodes, some of which were more cognitively demanding than others, and some of which required more active participation than others. The heart rate measurements can be compared across different episodes. The cross-episode correlations are substantial and indicate a considerable degree of consistency between episodes.

When assessed at the first three ages there were negative correlations between inhibition and both the mean and standard deviation of heart period. Inhibited children had a faster and a more stable heart rate, implying greater sympathetic nervous system activity. At any given age the coefficients were moderate, showing that between 11 per cent and 21 per cent of the variation in heart rate scores can been explained by individual differences in inhibition, with the remainder due to other factors, measurement errors and so on.

There is also evidence that the relationship with inhibition was stronger when the child was faced with a challenging situation than in the baseline condition.

However the relationship between inhibition and heart rate was not found at $7^1/_2$ years. The correlations were, in general, not significant. Furthermore, although heart period and heart period variability at $5^1/_2$ years could be predicted by the children's inhibition when this had been assessed at 21 months, heart rate at $7^1/_2$ years could not be predicted by the inhibition scores obtained at any of the three earlier ages.

Despite findings suggestive of a heightened level of sympathetic nervous system activity among shy children, there remains the question of why early inhibition only aided prediction of the heart rate variables up to the sixth year. Kagan *et al.* (1988) also reported that the differences between the cortisol levels in the saliva of inhibited and uninhibited children at the age of $5^1/_2$ years could not be replicated when the children were $7^1/_2$. Does some change in the nature of inhibition take place after five years that weakens its link with physiological measures?

The picture is complicated by the fact that other studies of the relationship between inhibition and the two heart rate measures have failed to find significant relationships even at the younger ages. A longitudinal study in Maryland, USA (Calkins and Fox, 1992) assessed children when they were only two days old, with subsequent assessments at five months, 14 months and 24 months. Inhibition (assessed at 24 months) was not correlated with heart period or heart rate variability (RSA) at any age. Marshall and Stevenson-Hinde (1998) also report non-significant findings from a study in Cambridge, England on a sample of children at the age of $4^1/_2$ and 7 years.

These findings are inconclusive about the significance of the weaker relationship between heart rate measures and inhibition that is found among children when they reach school age. They suggest that increasing maturity weakens this link, either because of development of the limbic and autonomic systems, which facilitate greater self-regulation of emotional reactions to events, or because cognitive developments lead to more familiarity with and understanding of recurring social situations and more strategies to cope with them. Neither unfamiliarity nor difficulty is an objective property of situations, and perceptions of these will change with experience.

EEG measures and right frontal asymmetry

A substantial body of research has been undertaken by Fox and his associates, who have examined the relationship between right hemisphere frontal activation and emotional reactions to novel situations, including social interactions with strangers. In these studies electrodes were attached to the scalp at sites corresponding to the frontal and parietal areas of the brain. EEG recordings were taken over a period of several minutes while the participant was attending, say, to computer-generated stimuli. The electrical signals were sent to separate amplifiers and recorded for subsequent analysis by computer. Power density was computed within a range of frequency bands, typically between 1 Hz and 20 Hz. It was assumed that decreases in power would correspond to increases in activation (Fox and Davidson, 1987). The research focused on asymmetry in activation between the right and left hemispheres, and this was usually indexed by a formula comparing power in recordings made in the right (R) and the left (L) hemisphere:

$$\text{Frontal asymmetry} = (R-L)/(R+L)$$

A positive score on this index represents relatively more power in the right hemisphere, and hence less activation in that hemisphere.

The research shows that left frontal asymmetry is associated with the experience of positive emotions whereas right frontal asymmetry is associated with more negative ones (Fox *et al.*, 1995). This pattern is also evident in emotions elicited in social situations. Fox and Davidson (1987) studied the responses of a sample of girls aged 10 months to a strange situation. The sequence of episodes involved approach by a stranger while the mother was present, approach by the mother in the absence of the stranger, separation from the mother, approach by a stranger while the mother was absent, and finally the return of the mother. The children's facial expressions and preselected behaviours were observed during these episodes. EEG recordings were made by means of electrodes attached to a cap worn by the children, which enabled reliable measurements to be taken of power density during the episode where the mother approached and reached towards her daughter, and during maternal separation.

Left frontal asymmetry was greater when the mother entered and reached for the child and this action was also associated with more vocalisation by the child and more joyful facial expressions. Those children who cried during separation from the mother showed a larger relative increase in right frontal activation than those who did not cry. All the differences found involved the frontal sites; there were no equivalent differences at the parietal sites.

Schmidt and Fox (1996) found parallel results with a sample of young children. EEG recordings were made when the children were only four months old, and their behaviour was observed at 14 months. Children with left hemisphere asymmetry exhibited more positive responses to the stranger and their mothers rated them as more sociable in temperament.

Fox *et al.* (1995) related EEG measurements to an index of inhibition in a sample of four-year-olds. The children were systematically observed while taking part in play sessions. The inhibition index was an aggregate of several measures based on these observations, including time taken (latency) to first spontaneous utterance, amount of time spent talking, amount of looking on rather than joining in, and signs of anxiety (for example, thumb sucking, crying). EEG measurements were not taken during the play sessions, but on a separate occasion, two weeks later, while each child was attending to a computer display in a quiet room. Frontal asymmetry, computed by means of the formula used in previous research, did not correlate significantly with the inhibition score (r = –0.16). However, when scores from the EEG recordings at different sites were computed in order to divide the power score into components that reflected the unique contribution of each hemisphere to the score, and a fresh asymmetry score was computed based on these values, a statistically significant correlation was obtained (r = –0.35). Using this index, right frontal asymmetry was (just) significantly correlated with the mothers' ratings of their children's shyness. A measure of sociability and social competence based on observations of play behaviour correlated with both traditional and new asymmetry measures. Sociable children had greater relative left frontal asymmetry.

In a study of much younger children, Calkins *et al.* (1996) took EEG measurements at nine months and assessed inhibition at 14 months. Their sample was selected at the age of four months on the basis of extreme scores on levels of motor activity, positive affect (indicated by vocalisation and smiling) and negative affect (fretting and crying). Inhibition was assessed at 14 months based on latency to vocalise and approach novel toys, proximity to mother and negative affect. Observed measures were recorded while the children were in an unfamiliar room, with a stranger and when faced with a novel object. Analysis of the EEG recordings revealed that those children who demonstrated high levels of motor activity and negative affect at four months showed more EEG right frontal activation at nine months than both the high motor/high positive affect group and the low reactivity group. However, although inhibition at 14 months was predicted by high motor/high negative affect status, it was not related to the EEG measurements. Nevertheless these results confirmed the finding of previous research that temperamental measurements taken at a very early age are associated with right frontal region activity, a pattern that is involved in negative affect in later childhood and adulthood. This implies that there is a biological basis for individual differences in predisposition to experiencing negative emotions, including anxiety.

Studies of the relationship between shyness and frontal asymmetry have also been carried out with adults, with a similar pattern of findings when shyness is measured on the Cheek–Buss self-report scale. Shy adults show greater right frontal asymmetry than the less shy. There are also differences in left hemisphere power (Schmidt and Fox, 1994). Those who score high on both shyness and sociability have less power (that is, greater activation) in the left frontal measure than either the shy-low sociable or the non-shy. This pattern is compatible with the notion, discussed in Chapter 1, that shy and sociable individuals experience an approach–avoidance conflict in respect of social situations, in that encounters with others are seen as potentially rewarding as well as threatening.

The differences in frontal hemispheres identified by EEG methods are also apparent in research using neuroimaging techniques. When individuals are exposed to pictures that have been rated 'unpleasant', positron emission tomography (PET) shows heightened metabolic activity in the right hemisphere, whereas pleasant stimuli elicit more activity in the left hemisphere. Anxious individuals who are exposed to pictures of fear-inducing objects or situations show greater activation in the right hemisphere, for example arachnophobes produce such a response when shown pictures of spiders (Davidson and Irwin, 1999).

Acting shy

In the previous two sections we have seen support for the notion that shy people differ from the less shy in their perceptions of social situations and in their somatic reactions to them. We now consider the behavioural component of shyness. Do shy people behave in different ways from those who are less shy? There is less consensus among theorists on this issue; for some shyness is a matter of reticence, for others it is the cognitive and somatic components that define shyness. In one of the first empirical investigations into this subject, Pilkonis (1977a) concluded that there are differences among shy people in the balance of somatic and behavioural components. For some, shyness is largely a matter of being anxious in social situations whereas for others it is their inadequate or inappropriate behaviour that defines their shyness. This implies that differences in overt behaviour might not always distinguish the shy individual from his or her socially confident peers, since the behaviour of at least some shy people will be unproblematic and it is possible that any signs of anxiety will not be noticed. There do seem to be people who give the impression of being poised or even extroverted or outgoing but who claim that, behind this confident facade, they are shy.

In this section we consider evidence that shy people do behave differently from others and we begin by considering what kinds of difference one might expect to find. We know from subjective reports and from the Stanford survey that shy people are wary of novel situations or situations where they suspect others will evaluate them. They prefer to keep in the background on social occasions, they are hesitant about speaking out, especially in front of a group of people, and they often do not know what to say. These self-reports do not tell us whether observations of behaviour will actually reveal such differences. As we have seen, shy people may believe that they act differently from other people (this is, at least in part, what leads them to call themselves shy), but we need to know whether this belief has any basis in reality. Perhaps, in practice, shy people behave in a rather similar fashion to everybody else. We have noted that shy people tend to underestimate their social skills relative to the ratings by observers of their behaviour, and also regard themselves as more nervous than do those who observe them (Bruch *et al.*, 1989).

A large number of studies have systematically observed how shy and less shy people behave in social situations. Usually the researchers arrange for a participant to join a group of individuals who do not know each other, or to have a conversation with a stranger. Alternatively participants are observed unobtrusively in natural settings, such as a playgroup or a classroom. They will have been separately assessed as shy or less shy, for example on the basis of their responses to an appropriate questionnaire, but the observers are not informed about the shyness status of any participant. Arrangements are also made to prevent the participants from becoming aware that these meetings, or their behaviour in them, are actually the focus of the investigation or the target of observation. The participant's behaviour during the social episode is either coded at the time (from behind a one-way viewing screen) or video-taped for later analysis. The observers are given prearranged categories of behaviour to look out for, and they count the frequency of behaviours falling into each category within a specified interval of time. Comparisons are then made between the frequency of these coded behaviours for shy and less shy participants.

The most common categories include measures that relate to the timing and frequency of speech acts, such as the time elapsing before the target person makes his or her first spoken contribution to the conversation or play activity (latency of first utterance) or the first spontaneous contribution. Other categories related to speech include the proportion of time or the amount of time spent talking, and the average length of utterances, measured in numbers of words or morphemes. The prediction is that shy people are more reticent than less shy people.

Non-verbal behaviours are also counted, including direction of gaze or the amount of time spent looking at the face of the other person. The prediction is that shy people spend less time looking at the other person. The timing of looking plays a significant role in the regulation of social encounters for a number of reasons. A conversation involves the participants taking turns to speak and to listen, and looking provides one cue for an individual that the other person is about to finish their turn and that they may begin their own. Looking at the listener also gives the speaker an idea of the effect that his or her contribution is having and this helps the speaker to plan what to say next, or how to say it. The listener can make eye contact, stare, glare, nod, shake the head, smile, frown, blush, raise the eyebrows, put a hand over the mouth, look away, close the eyes, yawn and so on. These are all visual cues that can influence the speaker, and are often the mode in which messages are sent intentionally by the listener to help sustain, develop or change the direction of the conversation.

Related to these functions, the amount of looking by an individual can be informative about his or her attitude to the encounter. If you tend not to look at the other person you might be thought to be uninterested in the topic or that person, or unfriendly. Looking can provide information about someone's personality. Holding the gaze is regarded as reflecting self-confidence and trustworthiness whereas gaze avoidance or looking down at one's feet is an aspect of shyness or shiftiness. The amount of time spent looking also provides information about the relationship between the people involved, for example about intimacy or power relationships. Less looking by the shy person therefore has implications for the smooth running of conversations and the development of relationships.

Notwithstanding these functions of looking, interpretation of this aspect of behaviour is not necessarily straightforward. Asendorpf (1990a, p. 104) draws attention to an important distinction between looking at someone as part of social interaction and looking without social interaction. In the latter case a child might be an *onlooker*, watching what is going on from a safe distance. This pattern of looking on, labelled 'wait and hover', has been reported in a number of studies of shy infants and children. More generally, the different functions of looking can be hard to disentangle, making it difficult for a clear picture of differences between shy and less shy people to emerge. A shy child might look more often to the adult researcher for guidance in an uncertain situation, but might make less eye contact with another child during a joint activity. If the frequencies of these categories are simply added together, the average frequencies of looking seem to be comparable for shy and non-shy children.

Other aspects of behaviour are also potentially relevant to shyness. A shy person might keep a greater distance from another person, a trend reported by Pilkonis (1977b) and Carducci and Webber (1979). The individual's posture can also be measured. It is predicted that shy individuals are more likely to adopt a stiff, awkward posture, a closed rather than an open posture (arms folded, fists clenched, legs close together), or turn his or her body away from the other person; again there is support for these predictions (Asendorpf, 1990a). Finally, nervous movements such as fidgeting, touching the face, hiding the face or biting the lip or fingernails can be observed and their frequency counted.

Perhaps the dress style adopted by shy people is also a factor, although to my knowledge it has not been examined, and one might query whether it should in fact be regarded as an aspect of behaviour. Nevertheless clothing does reflect an active choice, whether or not it is made consciously, that people make about their appearance, and it is potentially relevant to shyness for a number of reasons. Styles of dress are related to conspicuousness, since brightly coloured clothing, unconventional, highly fashionable or indeed extremely unfashionable attire or styles that expose more of the body or accentuate its form all draw attention to the self. They might also serve as a trigger for initiating social interaction. These styles are not conducive to keeping in the background or minimising social contact. The way one dresses is also relevant to the coping strategy of attitude neutrality, since it can make a positive statement about the self, about one's tastes or affiliations, or else it can be neutral and uninformative.

Furthermore appearance is a potent source of self-consciousness and can give rise to embarrassment or even shame. For example schoolchildren can be extremely nervous about the demeanour of their parents when they visit the school for, say, sports day, and feel apprehensive about the impression their parents will make on their fellow pupils. I have noticed, too, that many shy people wear a coat and keep it buttoned, even on a warm day, and often dress rather formally, whereas many less shy people seem to be more at ease in shirt sleeves or with bare shoulders. This pattern of shy behaviour seems to be related to inhibition, and is perhaps correlated with a tendency to adopt a closed posture.

Empirical studies

Evidence is available about the behaviour of both children and adults. As mentioned above, Asendorpf (1990a) has provided a valuable review of the research findings up to 1990. Here we concentrate on two aspects of behaviour: observed differences in verbal behaviour (because reticence is often regarded as an essential part of shyness) and measures of gaze, including looking away from the other person and avoiding eye contact. Table 2.3 summarises the principal findings on these aspects of behaviour in a selection of studies on shyness and social inhibition. These studies were carried

Table 2.3 Selected observational studies of speech and looking behaviour

Author	Age	Sample size	Situation	Shyness measure	Shyness related to
Cheek and Buss (1981)	Adult	40	Pairs in conversation	Cheek–Buss scale	Less time spent talking (in minutes); less time looking at partner's face
Evans (1987)	Kindergarten	14	'Sharing time' session in class	Observed reticence	Fewer topics per turn; fewer words per topic; smaller mean length of utterance; smaller percentage of self-initiated words; fewer utterances volunteered per topic
Eisenberg et al. (1998)	(1) 7½	82	(1) Free play	Parent and teacher checklist	(1) More onlooker behaviour, solitary activity, less conversation*
	(2) 9 years	77	(2) Meet stranger		(2) Longer latency to first spontaneous comment; fewer spontaneous comments *
Kagan et al. (1987)	5½	60	Interaction with examiner	Index of inhibition at 2½ years	Longer latency of first or second comment; fewer comments in total
Reznick et al. (1986)	5½	46	Observation of play in school	Index of inhibition at 21 months	Lower on aggregate of social interaction; less talking talking with another person; less onlooker behaviour
Kagan et al. (1988)	7½	41	Interaction with examiner	Index of inhibition at 21 months	Longer latency to sixth spontaneous comment; fewer spontaneous comments; less time spent talking
Asendorpf (1990b)	4–8 years	99	(1) Interaction with stranger	Parent rating of inhibition at age 4	(1) Longer latency to first unsolicited utterance to stranger
			(2) Free play with unfamiliar child		(2) Longer latency of first request to child
Asendorpf (1991)	4–8 years	87	(3) Free play period in school Play session with another child	Parent rating of inhibition at ages 4, 6 and 8	(3) Higher rate of wait and hover Longer latency of first request to playmate at ages 4, 6 and 8
Asendorpf (1987)	4 years	(1) 87 (2) 79	(1) Interaction with stranger (2) Free play in class	Parent rating of shyness with stranger	(1) Longer time spent silent and longer periods of silence (2) More wait and hover sequences
Asendorpf and Meier (1993)	German school grade 2	41	Monitored in natural settings: (1) school; (2) out of school	Parent rating of shyness	(1) Less speech at school entry, break, leaving school, during lessons (2) Speak less in less familiar settings
Bruch et al. (1989)	Adult	84	Conversation with opposite-sex partner	Cheek–Buss scale	Fewer utterances; higher in index of anxiety, including gaze aversion

* These differences were only reliable for parental ratings of girls; there were fewer differences in the ratings for boys and teacher ratings.

out with children of various ages and with adults, almost invariably university students. They all involve systematic observation of behaviour.

The most common situation where children are observed is a play session, with one or more other children, either in the laboratory or in a natural setting. They are also observed in the 'strange situation', where social interactions are set up between the child and an adult stranger (typically a confederate of the researcher, often following a pre-established 'script'). It should be noted that much of this research forms part of research programmes into inhibition as a dimension of children's temperament. Children are identified as either inhibited or uninhibited on the basis of an assessment of their behaviour, frequently in the strange situation, and measures of verbal and non-verbal behaviour are typically part of this assessment. For example the index of inhibition used to identify children at 21 months of age in the Harvard studies is an aggregate of a number of observed behaviours. These include a long latency to interact with the unfamiliar adult and cessation of vocalisation in the presence of the adult (Garcia-Coll *et al.*, 1984). In similar fashion the index of inhibition in the longitudinal study by Calkins *et al.* (1996) includes latency of vocalisation. In a sense these measures are built into the researcher's definition of shyness. Nevertheless it remains to be seen whether an index of inhibition that is developed at one age can be predictive of a child's behaviour in different settings. For example, does a child's behaviour in the presence of an unfamiliar adult provide an accurate prediction of how he or she will behave in the company of an unfamiliar child or a familiar child? Asendorpf (1993, p. 1071) summarises the relevant findings of two studies. In one, shyness with strangers was not associated with shyness with familiar peers; in the other, shyness was correlated with low rates of vocalisation during conversations with strangers but not with people with whom the child was more familiar.

Furthermore, Asendorpf and Meier (1993) draw attention to an important distinction between a child's reaction to a specific situation (particularly one that has been so arranged as to be challenging) and his or her spontaneous behaviour in more naturally occurring settings. In reality a child's personality characteristics will influence the situations that he or she will try to encounter or avoid. A shy child may also try to manipulate the situation to make it as comfortable as possible, for example by establishing proximity to a play leader, seeking out familiar playmates or declining to volunteer for activities that would make him or her the centre of attention. There is some evidence from a study that compared children's behaviour in a more constrained situation – that is in school – with their behaviour in a setting where they had a greater opportunity to choose their own activities. Asendorpf and Meier recorded the verbal behaviour of children during certain periods over several days. The time periods in question were when the children were at school in the morning and when they were free to choose their own activities in the afternoon. Throughout these periods the children wore a small portable microcomputer that picked up and recorded their vocalisations. It was found that shy children spoke significantly less than non-shy children in the school setting, in lessons as well as break time, and this difference was most pronounced in the 10-minute period before the start of the first lesson. In the afternoon they spoke less when they were in unfamiliar situations, but they did not differ from their non-shy peers when they were in familiar situations.

The findings summarised in Table 2.3 suggest that where speech acts are concerned shy children do behave differently from their less shy peers when they encounter a novel social situation. They tend to wait on the sidelines when their peers are playing. They are slower to speak to other children, for example to ask for something. Overall they speak rather less than other children, and their interactions include longer periods of silence. When they speak up in front of a group of other children, for example to talk to their classmates about recent events in a 'sharing time' session, they speak less, talk about fewer topics and make shorter utterances. When they do contribute they tend to provide straightforward descriptions of objects they have brought with them rather than develop narratives or more extensive or complex forms of discourse (Evans, 1987).

A similar picture of hesitation and quietness emerges from observations of children's interactions with unfamiliar adults. Studies of inhibited children have consistently found that a longer period of time elapses before they make their first unsolicited utterance, and their spontaneous contributions are much rarer throughout the social encounter. For example inhibited children aged seven-and-a-half took an average of 27 minutes to reach a set number of spontaneous comments during a test session in the company of a woman examiner compared with an average of 11 minutes for their uninhibited peers (Kagan *et al.*, 1988, p. 1586). Observers' ratings of a child's shyness are strongly influenced by the child's patterns of speech. Asendorpf (1987) found that the shyness ratings of four-year-old children were positively correlated with the overall length of time the child spent silent and the average length of the silences, and were negatively correlated with the average length of utterances.

Measures of looking behaviour during social interaction, other than assessments of looking on or 'wait and hover', have not been common in studies of children's behaviour, and have not tended to figure in observations of play or reactions to the 'strange situation'. Where measures of looking to the examiner in test situations are concerned, the interpretation of differences between shy and less shy children is ambiguous – is the shy child looking for additional guidance on what to do, or is he or she avoiding the examiner's gaze? Certainly, neither Reznick *et al.* (1986) nor Asendorpf (1987) found any significant correlations between measures of inhibition or shyness and the frequency of gazing at the adult.

In comparison with studies of children, few systematic observations have been made on the social behaviour of adults. Pilkonis (1977b) observed shy and non-shy students in conversation with a member of the opposite sex. Shy adults were slower to make their first contribution, they spoke for a smaller proportion of the time, there were more silences (defined as pauses longer than ten seconds) in their conversations and they were less likely to break silences. But when they did speak their utterances were no shorter than those of their less shy peers. There were no overall differences between shy and less shy students in measures of looking, but these measures were influenced by gender. Shy men looked at their partner the least of all the participants, and non-shy men the most, while the women, whether or not they were shy, were intermediate between the two groups of men. Overall women made more eye contact than men.

Cheek and Buss (1981) observed speech and looking behaviours in a sample of university students. In this case all the participants were women, although their conversation partner could be of either gender. Shy women talked for significantly less time than non-shy women and spent marginally less time looking at the partner's face. The differences in looking behaviour were more pronounced for a subgroup of participants who were both shy and sociable.

Bruch *et al.* (1989) also found that shy individuals (the sample included both men and women) talked less than those who were not shy during a conversation with someone of the opposite sex. Their procedure did not incorporate a direct measure of looking, but gaze avoidance was one item within an aggregate of thirteen observed indices of anxiety that were coded from videotapes of the conversation. Shy participants scored significantly higher on this aggregate measure than non-shy participants, although there was a significant interaction effect involving shyness and gender. It is not possible to separate out gaze aversion from the other anxiety items.

These studies support the finding of observations of children that shy people are more hesitant about talking when they are conversing with an unfamiliar person. There are mixed findings where the total amount of talk is concerned. The relationship between shyness and gaze avoidance seems to be more consistent in the three studies of adults, although this may be less a matter of the age of the participants than of the setting in which they were observed. As mentioned above, looking plays an important role in conversations. However conversations between pairs of children have been studied little in comparison with observations of activities involving children and unfamiliar adults.

Gender differences

Studies suggest that gender is a factor in differences between shy and less shy people in these situations. Pilkonis (1977b) found that, where both speech behaviour and looking were concerned, the differences between shy men and non-shy men were larger than the differences between the two samples of women. Shy men were slowest to speak and contributed least to the conversation whereas non-shy men were least hesitant and spoke the most. Similarly shy men looked the least, and made least eye contact with their partner, whereas non-shy men engaged in most looking and eye contact. Bruch *et al.* (1989) found that the non-shy women had the lowest score among the participants on the aggregate anxiety measure, while the other three groups – shy women, and shy and non-shy men – did not differ in observed anxiety. Shy men also reported having had more negative self-related thoughts during the encounter. However, unlike in Pilkonis' study, gender did not modify the finding that shy participants spoke less than the non-shy; both shy men and shy women spoke less.

It seems that shy men experience more difficulties in their conversations with women than do shy women with men. Pilkonis (1977b) suggests that shyness among women is expressed in a more reactive mode (involving more nodding and smiling) because the cultural convention is for women to take less of a lead and be less assertive in such situations. Men are expected to take the initiative, and shyness affects their ability to do so. Clearly there are social expectations about the roles that women and men should play in such encounters, although these expectations may not be the same for different groups in society. For example the participants in all these studies were at an age when their preoccupation with dating and finding partners, and their concern about their attractiveness to the opposite sex, were at their most salient. It remains to be seen whether similar findings would be obtained among older participants or in conversations between people who know each other rather better than the partners in these experiments.

Nevertheless it is the case that there are gender differences in patterns of talking. In general males talk more in public settings: in classrooms, in meetings and at conferences. Tannen (1992, p. 77) argues that talk serves different functions for men and women:

> For most women, the language of conversation is primarily a language of rapport: a way of establishing connections and negotiating relationships. Emphasis is placed on displaying similarities or matching experiences.... For most men, talk is primarily a means to preserve independence and negotiate and maintain status in a hierarchical social order. This is done by exhibiting knowledge and skill, and by holding center stage through verbal performance such as story telling, joking, or imparting information.

If talk does serve these various functions for men and women, in general it would not be surprising if shyness affected men and women in different ways. Since shy people doubt their ability to perform skilfully in social situations, the greater the demand for skilled performance the greater the impact of shyness on their behaviour.

Conversely a woman's language style can lead to shyness, particularly in public settings. Tannen (ibid., p. 87) provides an example where a woman (Rebecca), who is generally more talkative than her husband (Stuart) at home, becomes tongue-tied when she goes to a meeting, say, at a school parents' evening, whereas he is prepared to stand up and ask questions:

> In that situation it is Rebecca who is silent, her tongue tied by an acute awareness of all the negative reactions people could have to what she might say, all the mistakes she might make in trying to express her ideas. If she musters her courage and prepares to say something, she

needs time to formulate it and then waits to be recognized by the chair. She cannot jump up and start talking the way Stuart and some other men can.

Gender has an impact on shyness in other ways. If someone has developed a reticent, non-assertive style to cope with shyness, this style will be challenged by situations requiring assertiveness. If cultural conventions oblige a man to be more assertive than a woman in a particular situation then shyness should affect a man more than a woman in this situation. Courtship, or at least as it has been practised in past years, provides an example of this. There is evidence from longitudinal studies following the life paths of shy children that shy men tend to get married at a somewhat later age than less shy men (a difference of some three years) whereas there is no comparable trend among women (Caspi *et al.*, 1988). This is compatible with the notion that finding a partner and establishing a lasting relationship make different demands on men and women.

The thesis that gender differences are ubiquitous implies that their influence on shyness should also be noticeable in children, since sex roles develop from childhood. There is some evidence of this. Asendorpf (1987) reports the findings of a study where four-year-olds interacted with an adult stranger. Those boys who were more hesitant about initiating contact looked much less at the stranger, whereas there was no significant correlation between latency to interact and looking behaviour among the girls. After the process of interaction had begun, there were no gender differences in the pattern of looking, suggesting that the differences between boys and girls related specifically to different ways of responding to the initial uncertainty about the encounter. In the context of Tannen's analysis, one is tempted to speculate that girls are more ready to look to the adult for cues, reflecting their concern for affiliation, whereas boys are more overawed by the problem of fitting into dominance relationships.

Stevenson-Hinde and Glover (1996) looked at shyness in four-year-old boys and girls and found a complex pattern of gender differences. Children were classified as either *extremely shy* (rated as shy at home and extremely shy in the laboratory), *low in shyness* (not shy at home and receiving a low rating in the laboratory) or *medium shy* (a medium rating in the laboratory, irrespective of the rating at home). In the case of mothers being observed while interacting with their child at home, analysis of the ratings of their behaviour revealed that mothers of extremely shy boys were most positive and had the most gentle, sensitive and relaxed style with their children, whereas mothers of extremely shy girls were the least positive of all. On the other hand, when mothers and children were observed while carrying out a joint activity, the mothers of medium-shy girls were more positive towards their children than were the mothers of extremely shy girls or medium-shy boys. Finally, there was a subgroup of six shy boys who behaved in a very shy way at home but were much less shy in the laboratory. These children attracted much less positive attitudes from their mothers than the other groups of boys.

Only a small number of children participated in this study, particularly in the case of the subgroups of shy children, and this makes it difficult to interpret the pattern of findings. Yet even at this early age the shy boys elicited a different response from their mothers than did the shy girls from theirs, and this presumably reflects more general assumptions that adults share about the social desirability of shyness in boys and girls. Is shyness more acceptable in girls? Does a shy son worry his parents in ways that a shy daughter does not? If so, does this reflect a cultural stereotype of girls as modest, unassuming and indeed 'nice', and of boys as powerful and having to stand up for themselves, in short, 'being men'? Of course we must take care not to frame these questions in such a way as to assume that children are simply either shy or not shy. Some kinds of shy behaviour might be difficult for parents of boys to accept whereas other kinds might be seen as tolerable or regarded as a positive trait.

Tannen raises some fundamental issues about research into the influence of shyness on how the individual uses language. She is sceptical of analysing conversations in terms of simple frequency counts of verbal behaviours. For example the interpretation of silences, breaks in silences or interruptions requires some knowledge of the relationship between partners, their conversational style and the topic of conversation. At another level one has to analyse the conversation very closely to see what contribution the silence or the break in silence is making. An interruption can serve various purposes. It might represent someone's attempt to take over the topic of conversation, it could be intended to add meaning to another's contribution, or it could be to steer the conversation away from a topic that would embarrass or hurt one of the people present. Conversations are complex social activities. Very little research has examined the speech of shy people in this qualitative fashion.

Summary

Shyness can be regarded as comprising cognitive, affective and behavioural components. Research into the behaviours characteristic of shyness has concentrated on measures of speech (particularly delay in making spontaneous utterances) and eye contact. While differences in looking or gazing have been found, they can be difficult to interpret. Reticence seems to be central to shyness, particularly when the individual is interacting with unfamiliar people. Quietness can have long-term consequences for the individual. He or she may regard it as evidence of their social inadequacy. Others can interpret it as unwillingness to put any effort into the conversation, self-absorption or a lack of interest in other people. Shy people feel more anxious in social situations and they also create that impression in others, although when their self-perceptions are compared with assessments by observers they seem to have exaggerated their difficulties. Some studies have attempted to gauge levels of anxiety, for example by taking peripheral measures of activity of the sympathetic nervous system. A substantial body of research has shown that there are differences in a number of measures, including mean heart rate, heart rate variability and circulating levels of cortisol. The differences in reactivity that can be detected in younger children are not always obtained with older children or adults. However such measurement is notoriously difficult to take and is confounded by many extraneous factors. This is an issue that needs further research. There are also differences between the shy and the less shy on EEG recordings of right frontal hemisphere activity, and this is a promising area for future investigation.

There is evidence that shy and socially anxious individuals think differently about themselves than their less anxious peers; they are preoccupied with their inadequacies and the impression they are making on others. The empirical findings are similar to those obtained in research into test anxiety. Many writers on shyness and embarrassment have assigned a key role to feelings of self-consciousness. Research into anxiety has emphasised the role of worry, or pervasive self-deprecatory thinking, and perhaps what is called self-consciousness is an example of this. However an alternative position, which has been developed in studies of shame and embarrassment, is that self-consciousness is a distinctive state that involves taking a different perspective on the self. The self-awareness paradigm seemed to offer a promising approach to capture this aspect of shyness but it has yet to deliver on that promise. We shall return to this issue in Chapter 4.

The chapter began with an outline model of shyness as an emotional process. There is evidence of individual variation at different stages of the process. Shy people are biased in the situations they encounter, in their appraisal of them, the mobilisation of resources for action and the selection and implementation of actions. The following two chapters consider the origins of these individual differences in childhood.

Chapter 3

Shyness and Temperament

Introduction

The preceding chapters have presented evidence for the existence of individual differences in shyness and argued that self-report questionnaire measures of shyness have construct and predictive validity. Shy people differ from their less shy peers along cognitive, somatic and behavioural lines. They are predisposed towards self-consciousness and reduced confidence in their ability to perform to their satisfaction in social situations. They consider themselves to be anxious in these situations and are rated as such by observers of their behaviour. Measures of heart rate and heart rate variability distinguish the shy from the less shy, although these differences are not apparent in every age group studied. Finally, shy people are, in general, more hesitant about contributing to social encounters, talk less and avoid making eye contact, tendencies that are most apparent when they meet strangers or deal with novel situations, or when they fear that they will be negatively evaluated. In more familiar settings shy people can be just as talkative as others and make as much eye contact.

Many of these individual differences can be observed in early childhood, implying that these differences might emerge early in life. This chapter addresses the question of the origins of shyness. Historically, the question of the origins of personality was initially posed in terms of a dichotomy: nature versus nurture. According to this approach, personality characteristics are either inherited or acquired during the individual's lifetime through processes of acculturation and socialisation. As statistical methods became more sophisticated in the early years of the twentieth century and the first empirical investigations were carried out into the extent of family resemblance in psychological characteristics, particularly in studies of twins, the question changed. Rather than attempting to explain differences in terms of a simple dichotomy between heredity and environment, researchers now asked what proportion of the variability in a psychological trait was due to inheritance and what proportion was due to environmental factors. In more recent years psychologists have recognised that there are complex interactions between genetic and environmental factors, making it more problematic to allocate the proportions of variability to different factors. An individual's genetic endowment will influence the environment in which he or she is brought up, and the environment will affect the ways in which genetic factors shape behaviour.

For example societies may differ from each other in their attitude towards shyness or the expression of shyness in men and women. Shyness might be regarded as an attractive quality in a woman, as a sign that she is gentle, modest or perhaps flirtatious, whereas it might be seen in a man as a sign of weakness or a lack of appropriate assertiveness. Stevenson-Hinde and Shouldice (1993) have found that parents have a more positive attitude towards their daughters' shyness but that this is less acceptable in sons, particularly as they grow older.

Assuming for the moment that shyness is inherited, a boy who is born shy might be subject to pressure from his parents to behave in a less shy way, whereas a shy girl might not be discouraged from being shy. The shy boy might be a disappointment to his parents and they might communicate this to him in one way or another, with consequent effects on his sense of self-worth. However as he grows older he has increasing opportunities to create for himself an environment that he finds more congenial, perhaps reading, playing computer games or listening to music in his bedroom. In school he may have recourse to daydreaming, to keeping in the background, to avoiding challenges. He avoids catching the teacher's eye and does the minimal amount of school-work to make this possible, he never volunteers to join in any activities and he responds to questions by the teacher in ways intended to discourage any further conversation.

Meanwhile less shy peers are seeking out the contact of other children and developing more extensive networks of relationships outside the home. A peer could, of course, be the shy boy's brother; research has demonstrated that large differences in personality can be found within the same family, a finding which indicates the significant role of genetic factors in personality. The non-shy child is, in his own way, also creating an environment that he finds more congenial. However in this case his behaviour is likely to elicit a positive response from those with whom he is interacting. These reactions will help him to develop positive self-esteem and increase his social competence as he faces new challenges, extends his repertoire of social skills and meets a range of people who have diverse personalities, experiences and attitudes.

To complicate matters, shy children may have parents or carers who are shy themselves. A shy parent might have sufficient influence over the family's activities to produce a social life where relationships outside the family are kept to a minimum. Confident behaviour by the adult may not be available as a model for the child's own behaviour. These circumstances might be particularly injurious for the shy child, since his bolder brother might have sufficient motivation and resources to establish relationships beyond the influence of the family. He might look to a less shy parent as a model for his own behaviour or take advantage of access to the social situations made available by that parent.

Of course I am presenting two caricatures here, but the point is to pose the following questions. If one was to study either of these boys could one say that their shyness was either inherited or acquired? How would they have developed if they had been raised in families or even societies that had a different attitude towards shyness? This chapter surveys an approach to the origins of shyness based on the notion of temperament. Chapter 4 will look at evidence for genetic and environmental influences upon shyness.

The concept of temperament

Psychologists have drawn upon the concept of temperament in order to explain the variation in responses that can be observed early in life. There exist several definitions of this concept. Common themes are that temperament refers to individual differences that appear early in life, are stable over time, lead to predictable patterns of behaviour and have a biological basis. The fact that temperamental characteristics appear so early in life distinguishes them from other personality traits. There is also an emphasis in many approaches to temperament upon the infant's reactions to stimulation rather than on his or her seeking out and shaping experience. Obviously an infant has limited mobility and is heavily dependent

on other people. Nevertheless the construct of temperament emphasises what the infant *brings* to any situation rather than simply
regarding him or her as reactive. Furthermore, what the infant
brings will tend to shape the reactions of others. Babies who have
irregular patterns of sleep, cry a lot or resist being soothed or cud-
dled will elicit different responses from their carers than regular
sleepers, settled babies or those who respond appreciatively to
being picked up. The interaction between an infant and his or her
caregiver is a continuous and dynamic process of negotiation,
where each accommodates the other's preferences while simultaneously trying to satisfy her or his own needs. Thus from the outset
the infant's temperament has an important role in structuring his or
her environment.

Temperament should not be regarded as an adult personality
characteristic that is also seen in infancy, nor should it be thought of
as simply maturing into this characteristic. Rather, personality traits
are produced by an interaction among temperament, properties of
the child's environment and the course of his or her life.

Search for the basic temperaments

Much research has been concerned with the identification of a set of
fundamental temperaments that might underlie the range of apparent differences among infants. Clearly one of the goals of research is
that of classification, of bringing order to observations. In addition
to the intrinsic merits of this endeavour, identification of a small set
of temperaments provides an impetus to research since it facilitates
comparisons between different investigations, helps in the development of measurement techniques and is a source of fresh hypotheses. On the other hand a proliferation of terms hinders research, lim-
its communication among researchers and is wasteful of effort. The
success of the Big Five theory of personality dimensions is a case in
point. It has invigorated research into individual differences,
brought an end to the increasingly sterile debate on the nature of
'true' personality factors and helped to forge links between different
areas of psychology, for example between the fields of personality
and child development. Taxonomies of dimensions of individual
differences have heuristic value. They should not be regarded as
providing the only picture of personality, and should be open to
revision in the light of fresh evidence.

The seminal investigation was the New York Longitudinal Study, organised by Thomas, Chess, Birch and their colleagues. The study was initiated in 1956 and followed a sample of 133 individuals from 84 families, from three months of age into adulthood (see for example Chess and Thomas, 1986). The research began with detailed interviews with the parents of 22 infants aged between three and six months. Nine temperaments were identified on the basis of analysis of the contents of these interviews. The nine temperaments were classified into three types: the *easy child*, the *difficult child* and the *slow to warm up child*. The easy child has a positive mood quality, follows a regular sleep and feeding rhythm, readily approaches new situations and is adaptable. The difficult child has more intense reactions to stimulation, has a negative mood quality, does not establish regular patterns, withdraws from novel situations and tends not to adapt to change. The slow to warm-up child has a low activity level, less positive moods, withdraws from novel situations and shows a low-intensity reaction to stimulation. Several of these temperaments are relevant to the development of shyness, for example the tendency to withdraw from novel situations, which is a characteristic of both the difficult and the slow to warm up child.

Subsequent research into the Thomas–Chess model made use of parental rating scales to supplement the judgments made by researchers. Parents provided numerical ratings in response to questionnaire items, ratings that were assumed to reflect the extent to which they believed items such as 'tends to be shy' or 'is very energetic' were characteristic of their child. Factor analysis of the ratings data provided the basis for further attempts to identify core temperaments. According to Rothbart and Bates (1998), studies of infants (typically younger than twelve months) have indicated six dimensions of temperament: (1) positive affect, with a tendency towards smiling and laughter; (2) fearful distress or withdrawal; (3) irritability and fussiness; (4) activity level; (5) attention span and persistence; and (6) rhythmicity and regularity of sleep and feeding patterns. Studies of older children have also produced a list of dimensions that show considerable overlap with those identified in infancy (Caspi, 1998; Rothbart and Bates, 1998) and also with the set obtained in the New York study. These dimensions are (1) positive affect; (2) inhibition and harm avoidance; (3) irritability and fussiness; (4) activity level; and (5) attention control and persistence.

A factor of positive affect tends to emerge in all studies, one that includes positive mood quality and a willingness to approach new situations. This factor is similar to the personality dimension of extraversion, which is consistently found in studies of adult personality (see Chapter 1). Negative affect tends to be represented by two factors, one related to inhibition and anxiety and the other to irritability. Inhibition and anxiety bear considerable resemblance to the adult personality dimension of neuroticism, and of course this factor is similar to shyness. We shall now consider evidence for shyness as a temperament.

Shyness as a temperament

Buss and Plomin's EAS model

Factor analysis of parental ratings data provides the foundation for Buss and Plomin's (1984) theory of temperament. They reviewed studies of rating scales based on the New York longitudinal study and concluded that the statistical evidence did not support the existence of the nine temperaments. Instead they argued that the data identified four temperaments: emotionality, activity, sociability and impulsivity. Questionnaires were designed to measure the four temperaments, but subsequently the impulsivity scale was omitted. Several versions of the EAS ratings scale were constructed, as well as a self-report questionnaire for adults, in order to measure the three remaining temperaments. Emotionality and activity were similar to the temperaments proposed in the Thomas–Chess model. However the sociability scale changed in nature during the revisions of the test. Items in the original version of the EAS referred to sociability, as it is usually conceived (preference for the company of other people). Subsequently, two measures were developed: the Colorado Childhood Temperament Inventory (CCTI) and a revised EAS. The sociability scale of the CCTI turned into a measure of shyness. The revised EAS included both sociability and shyness scales as well as emotionality and activity scales, with five items measuring each of the four scales. The items refer to behaviours that can be observed in children from twelve months of age. Shyness items refer to being shy, slow to 'warm up' to strangers, not sociable, not making friends easily, and not being friendly with strangers. Boer and Westenberg (1994) carried out factor analyses of the EAS, which was administered to a sample of 230 mothers and 172 fathers of children aged between four and 12 years. A factor consistently emerged with the shyness items represented. This was the case whether factor analysis was applied to ratings of boys or girls, to ratings of younger or older children, or to ratings provided by fathers or mothers. Sociability emerged less consistently as a factor, but where it did so, it was distinct from shyness.

It would seem that the three basic temperaments, which are reliably found in these parental ratings data, are emotionality, activity and shyness. There is some overlap between this scheme and the list of temperaments put forward by Chess and Thomas (1986) and Rothbart and Bates (1998). This trio of temperaments can be identified from the ratings made by parents of children of different ages, ranging from five months (Rowe and Plomin, 1977, cited in Boer and Westenberg, 1994) to 12 years. However this consistency does not in itself prove that children who are rated as shy at one age will also be rated as shy at a later age. For this, longitudinal studies are needed. Furthermore rating scale data are not sufficient in themselves to provide evidence of the origins of these individual differences. We now examine a highly influential theory of behavioural inhibition that has explicitly addressed these issues and has led to a surge of research into shyness in infancy and childhood.

Kagan's theory of behavioural inhibition

We have already introduced this theory in the course of our review of studies of physiological correlates of shyness. Kagan and his colleagues at Harvard University have been studying inhibition as a temperament that is evident in children's behaviour such as crying, withdrawal, timidity, and inhibition of vocalisation and motor behaviour when confronted with novelty, be this new places, events or people (Garcia-Coll et al., 1984). In their initial study the parents of a sample of 305 21-month-old children were contacted by telephone and asked a series of questions about their children's behaviour in unfamiliar situations. On the basis of these interviews, 56 children were classified as inhibited and 104 as uninhibited. In the next stage of the investigation 117 of these children were observed in unfamiliar situations such as meeting a strange adult or being exposed to novel toys and objects (see Table 3.1 for an outline description of the procedure). The children's behaviour was observed during six episodes. Inhibition was interpreted in terms of fretting, crying, making distress calls, withdrawal and the absence of spontaneous interaction with the researcher across all six

Table 3.1 Typical procedures in laboratory studies of inhibition

Typical situations

- Unfamiliar adult enters and tries to engage the child in play.
- Mother and child are left in room with novel objects.
- An unfamiliar adult demonstrates an activity to the child.
- An unusual toy, for example a large robot, is revealed and the child is encouraged to play with it.
- Mother leaves child alone with the researcher.

Typical measures of inhibition

- Ratings of overt signs of distress (fussing, fretting, crying).
- Frequency of overt signs of distress.
- Number of spontaneous approaches to unfamiliar adult.
- Latency to approach adult.
- Latency of vocalisation to adult.
- Time spent in proximity to the mother.
- Latency to approach novel object or to play with it.

episodes, and also in terms of reactions to specific episodes. Physiological measurements such as heart period and heart period variability were also taken, as described in Chapter 2. Each parent completed a temperament questionnaire about their child and this was scored according to the nine basic temperaments in the New York study. Finally, each mother was interviewed about her child's responses to unfamiliar situations in everyday life. Children were assigned to the categories of inhibited or uninhibited on the basis of the set of observational measures carried out in the laboratory, and this allowed the researchers to examine the consistency of classification across different contexts of measurement – home versus laboratory; parents' judgments versus researchers' classifications.

It is important to draw attention to a fundamental distinction between the approaches of Buss and Plomin (1984) and Kagan. The former consider temperament as a dimension, and the location of individuals on the dimension can be measured by their pattern of responses to questionnaires. Thus individuals vary along a continuum of shyness, ranging from extremely shy to moderately shy to scarcely shy at all. Every child can be located at some point on the continuum. On the other hand Kagan conceptualises inhibition as a category to which a given individual does or does not belong.

Similarly, lack of inhibition is a separate category. Thus many children will not belong to either category. According to Buss and Plomin, differences between individuals in shyness are quantitative; in Kagan's theory the differences are qualitative.

This difference between the theories has significant implications for the design of investigations. Buss and Plomin's theory lends itself to correlational designs, whereas these are not appropriate for Kagan's theory; his strategy has been to examine differences between samples of individuals belonging to the categories. The inappropriateness of correlational designs becomes apparent if it is considered that the absence of a significant correlation between two measures taken in an unselected sample of people might lead to the erroneous conclusion that there are no relationships between the measures. Variables may well be uncorrelated in the sample as a whole or in the population from which the sample has been selected but can be correlated within a subsample, and this finding might be of considerable theoretical interest. The following example is provided by Kagan et al. (1993, p. 26):

> Only a small proportion of infants – about 10% – show a combination of high motor activity and frequent crying at four months, high fear in the second year, and large cardiac accelerations to psychological stress. These variables are not positively correlated in a large unselected sample, only in a small group of individuals who inherit a particular temperamental profile.

From an historical perspective, the emphasis on different types of person is a very old one. According to Galen (a writer and scientist who acted as physician to several Roman emperors and produced his theory of temperament during the second century) there were four types: choleric, melancholic, phlegmatic and sanguine. Which type an individual was depended on the relative amount he or she had of one of the four 'bodily humours', yellow bile, black bile, phlegm and blood. This early theory proposed a biological basis for temperament; obviously one based on the knowledge of the time. Eysenck has regularly pointed out that the quadrants constructed by the intersection of the two orthogonal dimensions of extraversion–introversion and neuroticism–stability map on to Galen's types: stable extravert (sanguine), unstable extravert (choleric), stable introvert (phlegmatic) and unstable introvert (melancholic) (see Figure 1.1). He claims that his theory is one of personality types, but in practice the measurement of these dimensions is routinely based on quantitative differences in people's responses to questionnaires. Factor analysis has played a key role in establishing the validity of the theory (see Chapter 1) and the correlational design has dominated research inspired by it. Although a decision can be taken to the effect that extremely high scores on the extraversion–introversion dimension indicate that an individual with such and such a score belongs to the extravert type, the choice of cut-off score for assignment to the category is an arbitrary one and cannot be derived from the theory itself. Furthermore this approach fails to capture the interrelationships among dimensions, which is one of the central features of a typology. Kagan has referred to this feature in justifying his categorical approach to personality, as illustrated in the quotation above. Traits combine and interact with one another to produce emergent qualities that cannot be reduced to the component traits.

Ultimately the test of whether it is better to conceptualise temperament in terms of discrete categories or continuous dimensions is whether it provides greater understanding of the phenomena associated with temperament. It is also important to point out that whereas the Buss–Plomin theory emphasises shyness as a distinct dimension of temperament, Kagan regards inhibition to the unfamiliar as a much broader category than shyness and argues that shyness should not be equated with inhibition. Only some shy children have an inhibited temperament and some inhibited children may not be shy.

Research findings

We now offer a brief overview of research into the construct of inhibition, organised on the basis of common criteria for the identification of temperament: appearance early in life, stability over time, predictable patterns of reactions and evidence of a biological basis.

Appearance early in life

The Harvard study was initiated not with very young infants, but with a sample of young children aged 21 months. This age was selected because there was evidence that all children go through a phase of inhibition to unfamiliar people and objects during the latter part of the first year (Rothbart and Bates, 1998, p. 135). They show heightened fear of strangers and of being left by the mother between 8 and 16 months and timidity about interacting with new children between 18 and 21 months (Kagan, 1994, p. 125). Hence there were advantages in studying individual differences after this period, when the magnitude of these differences would not be obscured by the overall age trend.

Nevertheless subsequent research has looked at infants younger than 21 months. Kagan (1994, 1998) reports his findings on a sample of 16-week-old infants, which he divided into two groups, labelled *high reactive* (comprising 20 per cent of the sample) and *low reactive* (40 per cent of the sample). The division was based on signs of distress (facial expression of fear, crying, fretting) and increased motor activity (movement of the limbs and arching of the back) when faced with novel sights, sounds and smells. These included mobile toys, tape recordings of voices and cotton swabs dipped in dilute butyl alcohol and held to the nostrils. Infants who were highly reactive to these stimuli at 16 weeks tended to cry in distress when they were assessed at both 14 and 21 months in a range of novel situations, including exposure to novel toys, flashing lights and unfamiliar adults. Only 3 per cent of the high reactive group showed minimal signs of fear whereas 35 per cent were fearful in four or more situations. The reverse pattern was obtained for the low reactive group. Girls were somewhat more fearful than boys. Eighty-six per cent of the infants who displayed most fear at both 14 and 21 months were girls (Kagan, 1994, p. 195). The gender difference was most marked when the infants were confronted with an adult dressed in a clown's costume.

There is also evidence of physiological differences between high reactive and low reactive infants, at least in measurements taken early in life. Kagan (ibid.) reports differences in a number of measures. Here we shall focus on heart rate. Kagan found that more high reactive than low reactive infants had higher foetal heart rates when these were measured approximately two weeks prior to the child's birth. They were also more likely to have higher heart rates when this was measured at two weeks of age while asleep and being held upright by the mother (this posture stimulates sympathetic nervous system activity, relative to lying down, ibid., p. 210). However measurements of resting heart rate taken at four months did not differ between the two groups.

Nevertheless large increases in heart rate contingent upon stimulation, for example when a drop of lemon juice was placed on the tongue, were found more frequently among the high reactive group than among the low reactive group when this was administered at nine and 14 months. Again there was a gender difference, specifically an interaction effect between gender and reactivity. More high reactive girls than low reactive girls showed large increases in heart rate. However there was no corresponding difference in heart rate increase among boys. On the other hand, more low reactive boys than high reactive boys had very low heart rates in this situation.

Calkins *et al.* (1996) have also examined differences between groups of infants selected on the basis of their distress and motor activity in response to stressful events. At four months of age infants were tested in their own homes, where they were exposed to a range of situations similar to those employed in the Harvard studies – novel visual and auditory stimuli and a dilution of butyl alcohol applied to the nostrils. Three groups were formed on the basis of measures of motor activity, positive affect and negative affect. The negative group (14 per cent of the sample) was similar to the Harvard high reactive group: high in both motor activity and signs of distress. The positive group (9 per cent) was high in motor activity and positive affect (smiling, making vocalisations). The low group (15 per cent) was below the average in motor activity, with few signs of either positive or negative affect.

As discussed in Chapter 2, Calkins *et al.* (1996) report evidence of physiological differences at nine months of age among the three groups. The negative group (the equivalent of the high reactive group) demonstrated significantly greater right frontal asymmetry derived from EEG measurements of brain activity than either of the other groups. These group differences were also obtained when EEG was recorded at 24 months (Schmidt and Fox, 1999). The negative group also exhibited the most inhibited behaviour when this was assessed at the age of 14 months. Inhibition was assessed by the child's reaction to the arrival of a stranger in the playroom and this adult's attempt to initiate interaction with the child. The positive group (high motor activity/positive affect) demonstrated least inhibition. Further evidence of group differences in behaviour came from a follow-up study conducted by Schmidt *et al.* (1997). There was greater shyness among the children who had been in the negative group at four months than among the children who had been in the other two groups. Children who had been inhibited at 14 months were observed to be more wary during the free play session when they were four years of age.

These studies show that individual differences in inhibited behaviour can be predicted by young infants' reactions to stressful situations that involve some degree of novelty. These findings suggest that inhibition does meet this criterion for consideration as a basic temperament.

Stability over time

The issue of temporal stability of psychological characteristics is a complex one, particularly if one considers the enormous changes that take place during the childhood years, both within the growing child and in his or her social environment. Even if temperament is stable over time the behaviours that serve as good indicators of temperament at one age might not do so at another age. The frequency of behaviours such as crying or fretting changes with time and so do the psychological meanings of these behaviours. The brain and nervous system develop as the child matures and this has implications for interpreting data on peripheral physiological reactions collected at different ages. There are systematic changes in children's ability to control and direct their attention (Rothbart and Bates, 1998, p. 118). Children learn to regulate their emotions, so they are able to control their crying in many of the mildly stressful situations that would previously have elicited distress.

There are also important cognitive developments, particularly during the second year of life. Children form mental representations of objects and events, their language develops rapidly and they engage in symbolic forms of play. Two-year-olds become self-conscious in the sense of being able to think about themselves and their own qualities.

The child's environment also undergoes dramatic changes, from the newborn's daily cycle of feeding, winding, eliminating, sleeping and dependence on the mother or other caregivers to the relative autonomy of older children. They increasingly regulate their own behaviour, take responsibility for it, exercise choices about their school studies and form their own tastes and preferences. They establish friendships with their peers and interact with a variety of adults and other children outside the family. They learn about themselves and the world through the media and electronic channels such as the Internet.

These changes affect researchers' attempts to establish the consistency of temperament. However it should not be overlooked that a further source of apparent instability is that temperaments themselves may change over time (Rothbart and Bates, 1998). Different kinds of evidence can be adduced to decide about the temporal dimension of temperament:

● When individuals are regarded as belonging to a temperament category, as in Kagan's theory of inhibition, one can investigate whether individuals who are assigned to one category are in the same category when they are assessed at a later time.
● When a temperament is regarded as a continuum, one can test whether there is a sizeable correlation between temperament scores taken at different ages.
● One can use measures of temperament made at one age to predict later behaviours when there is some theoretical rationale for expecting the behaviour to be relevant to the temperament.
● If a number of measures contribute to an index of temperament one can test whether the pattern of intercorrelations between measures is similar from one age group to another.
● If a physiological basis is claimed for a temperament one can assess the degree to which peripheral measures of activity of the physiological system are associated with the temperament at different ages.

The Harvard study assessed inhibition at the ages of 21 months, four years, five years and seven years. The correlations between measures of inhibition taken at different times provide one estimate of the stability of the inhibited temperament. It should be kept in mind that these correlation coefficients are based on samples selected for being inhibited or uninhibited, and hence can be expected to be higher than correlations obtained from a random sample of children, in general. Inhibition assessed at 21 months correlated with assessments at four years ($r = 0.46$), five years (0.52) and seven years (0.78). All the correlations are statistically significant, and all are sizeable.

A separate indication of the stability of this temperament is obtained if we consider whether children who are in one category at one age still belong to the same category at a later age. Relevant data are available from the Harvard cohort of high reactive and low reactive children (Kagan, 1994, p. 191). Of the 20 infants who were high reactive at four months, eight were inhibited at $3^1/2$ years. Of the 28 who were low reactive, 14 were uninhibited at the later age. Thus 40 per cent of the high reactive group and 50 per cent of the low reactive group were in the predicted category three years later. Although this seems to be only modest evidence for stability, it is difficult to make successful predictions between these ages, given the enormous changes that take place during these years. Similar modest correlations are obtained for measures of intelligence, which do not become stable until middle childhood. Kagan *et al.* (1988) found a more convincing trend in their own longitudinal studies of inhibition: 75 per cent of children who were inhibited at 21 months were shy six years later.

There is also evidence that inhibition assessed at one age allows prediction of relevant characteristics or behaviours on subsequent occasions. In the study reported by Schmidt *et al.* (1997) the correlation between inhibition at four months and mothers' ratings of shyness at four years was 0.52. In the Harvard cohort the inhibition index at 21 months was correlated with mother's ratings of the child's shyness at $5^1/2$ years (0.55) and $7^1/2$ years (0.66).

The measures contributing to the index of the inhibited temperament are not always the same from one time to another, for example reactions to strange toys and other objects are less appropriate for older children. There is less attention to interactions with the mother whereas interactions with peers become more salient. There is increasing emphasis on the frequency of spontaneous speech in the presence of an unfamiliar adult or in a test situation. Nevertheless the measures are theoretically coherent, and they intercorrelate sufficiently to enable a meaningful aggregate index to be drawn up at each age, an index that is relatively consistent from one age to another.

At 21 months the measures include latency to approach an unfamiliar object or adult, clinging to the mother, crying or fretting, facial signs of distress and cessation of play. At four years measures are taken, during free play, of latency to approach another child, time spent close to the mother, frequency of glances at mother and another child, and frequency of approach to the other child. At $7^1/2$ years, systematic observations of children in free play situations assess the distance kept from other children, frequency of speaking to other children and to adults, and frequency of shouting, smiling and laughing. In a more formal test session, children are assessed on latency to spontaneous comments to the adult examiner, and frequency of hand and body movements, frequency of smiling and laughter, and ratings of softness of voice.

We have seen that the effectiveness of peripheral physiological measures varies from one age to another. Among younger children the measurement of heart rate and salivary cortisol is successful in distinguishing between inhibited and uninhibited children but it is less successful with four-year-olds (Schmidt *et al.*, 1997) and $7^{1/2}$ year-olds (Kagan *et al.*, 1988). The inconsistencies in these findings may not be due to the age of testing as such, but to age-related changes in the kinds of unfamiliar situation where variation among children can be detected. Thus in a study of seven-year-olds the introduction of an embarrassing task – having to give a speech, which the child believed would be videotaped and shown to other children – led to significant correlations between changes in cortisol levels and self-perceived social competence (Schmidt *et al.*, 1999). Nevertheless, given the general difficulties of interpreting physiological measures, the theoretical framework that has been proposed for the construct of inhibition has received substantial empirical support, particularly when aggregate physiological measures are used.

In summary, there exists evidence of various kinds to suggest that the temperamental category of inhibition remains relatively stable throughout the childhood years. This implies that the origins of shyness can be traced, for some children at least, to infancy. Nevertheless there are indications that children can change category from one time of testing to another. It remains to be seen to what extent this reflects something about the nature of temperament, the influence of the social environment upon temperament or the limitations of current approaches to measurement.

Some researchers have examined stability over more extended periods of time. Kerr *et al.* (1994) report the findings of a longitudinal study of children born in Sweden between 1955 and 1958. Children were rated for shyness by mothers and psychologists on four occasions in the first year of life and regularly afterwards until the age of six years (in the case of psychologists' ratings) and 16 years (mothers' ratings). In order to compare the estimates of temporal stability with estimates obtained in the studies undertaken by the Harvard group, ratings were made at 21 months. Consistent with the American findings, there was a moderate degree of stability from 21 months to six years ($r = 0.51$ among girls and 0.54 among boys) in samples of children scoring at the extremes of the inhibition dimension. When the children were monitored to 16 years, there was greater stability of inhibition among girls who had been rated as extremely inhibited in early childhood. Ratings of girls in the extreme uninhibited group tended to regress towards the mean rating for the sample. There was also less stability over time among boys. These trends were more conspicuous for the extreme groups, in support of Kagan's claim that the differences between inhibited and uninhibited children are qualitative rather than quantitative.

There is also evidence from longitudinal studies carried out in the United States and Sweden that the influence of shyness persists well into adulthood (Caspi *et al.*, 1988; Kerr *et al.*, 1996). Shy men marry significantly later than non-shy men (three years later, on average) and start their family later (about three years' difference). There are no equivalent differences among women. There is evidence from the United States (but not Sweden) that shy men are slower to enter a settled career and have lower incomes than non-shy men, and evidence from Sweden that shy women tend to have lower educational attainments than non-shy women. The two societies differ in numerous ways – in work and marriage patterns, in the role of women in society and in attitudes towards shyness (shyness seems to be regarded more negatively in the United States than in Sweden) – making the differences in findings difficult to interpret. Nevertheless the results show the impact of shyness upon men's dating and their establishment of close relationships.

Research also shows that inhibition and shyness have implications for other areas of children's development. Eisenberg *et al.* (1998) report that shyness in childhood is correlated with a measure of internalising negative emotion, including measures for anxiety, nervousness and distress. Hirschfeld *et al.* (1992) have found that consistently inhibited children – those who are inhibited in assessments made at different times – are more likely to suffer from anxiety disorders than children who are inhibited at the first assessment (at the age of 21 months) but not on subsequent occasions. Van Ameringen *et al.* (1998) report the findings of a study where a sample of adult patients attending a clinic for anxiety disorders provided retrospective accounts of inhibition in childhood. Scores on the social fears subscale of the inhibition questionnaire were correlated with scores on anxiety scales. Patients with a primary diagnosis of social phobia obtained higher social fears scores than patients with an alternative primary diagnosis.

Inhibition can also serve to 'inoculate' against problems of adjustment. Kerr *et al.* (1997) have found that boys who are identified as inhibited at 10–12 years of age are less likely to report a history of criminal activities at 13–15 years, even if they also show signs of disruptive behaviour at the earlier age.

Shyness also has an impact on adults' longer-term social relationships. Asendorpf and Wilpers (1998) studied the relationships of a sample of students for a period of 18 months, beginning with their entry to university. The shyer the student the slower the growth of his or her network of peers during the first year, their networks being half the size of those non-shy students at the end of that period. However their networks continued to expand over the next six months, during which time the network increase among the non-shy tapered off. Shy students were also slower to form a romantic attachment (the probability of doing so by the end of 18 months was 37 per cent compared with 73 per cent in the case of the non-shy).

Predictable modes of response

We have already discussed some evidence suggesting that inhibition is associated with predictable modes of response. These are related to distress and wariness when confronted with novel or unfamiliar people or events. By the age of seven, children are at school and are becoming used to interacting with large numbers of adults and children outside the immediate family. Temperamental differences are now becoming closely linked with reticence, and speech measures consistently discriminate between the shy and the less shy. Mary Ann Evans has produced an important body of research findings on the impact of shyness and reticence upon the development of children's language, conducted at the University of Guelph in Canada, and we shall briefly examine her work here.

Evans (1987) observed individual differences in the language of kindergarten children during 'sharing time' sessions in their classrooms. In these sessions individual pupils took turns to tell the teacher and their classmates about things they had recently done or seen. Reticent children introduced fewer topics, spoke fewer words about each topic and produced shorter utterances on average. Their contributions were simpler and tied to objects they had brought with them, and they were less likely to develop a narrative about the object. They volunteered less information. They were more likely to offer either no response or only a very minimal answer to teachers' questions and this tended to result in stilted conversation.

According to Evans and Bienert (1992), teachers found the silences and minimal responses of shy children uncomfortable and coped with their own discomfort by producing yet further questions; however this tended to encourage an even more minimal response as the teacher began to control the conversation rather than create the conditions for a dialogue to take place. In general, children were less fluent when the teacher asked direct questions (those which could be answered yes or no, and those which were prefaced with 'how' or with 'wh-' type words – who, why, where, when, what). Children were more fluent when the teacher adopted a more conversational style, elaborating on the children's contributions and introducing their own personal contributions. It is interesting that differences are apparent in settings such as 'show and tell' and 'sharing time' since these are well-structured, in the sense that each child has his or her turn to speak, it is clear what is expected and they are relatively familiar experiences, taking place perhaps every day with the same adult and the same group of children.

There is evidence that such differences between shy and less shy children extend to their performance in standardised language assessments, including tests of both expressive and receptive vocabulary. Evans (1993) provides a review of the literature relating to children in the age range of three to 11 years. She classifies three groups of studies: standardised assessments of language performance, linguistic measures in recorded social interactions, and 'hypothetical-reflective performance', where children state how they think they would behave in particular scenarios. Poor performance by shy children relative to their peers has been interpreted in all of these kinds of study in terms of a process whereby the social withdrawal of shy children results in fewer opportunities for social interaction, and this in turn has an impact on the development of language competence.

When interpreting these findings it is essential to distinguish between performance and competence. Evans' interpretation is that shy children lack competence; she assumes that these tests provide an accurate assessment of these children's abilities. An alternative explanation is that shyness affects the assessment process. Most of the studies assess linguistic performance through face-to-face testing. It is clear from the research into inhibition reviewed above that interactions with unfamiliar adults and test situations produce the largest differences in performance between inhibited and uninhibited children.

There are several potential mechanisms by which shyness can influence performance. This might be through attention processes (see Chapter 2). Shyness produces cognitive interference that could, for example, inhibit the generation of responses in vocabulary tests. Alternatively shy children might set themselves a more rigorous criterion for response selection in an effort to minimise the chance of producing a wrong answer and causing themselves embarrassment. If this strategy is adopted it will result in longer latencies of response or even a reluctance to respond at all. These alternative hypotheses imply that such tests underestimate children's abilities. However Evans (1993, p. 203) explicitly rejects this interpretation of the findings. She argues that the relatively poor performance of shy children is also evident in vocabulary tests that require either no verbal response or only very minimal response, whereas these performance deficits are not apparent in assessments of non-verbal tasks. This issue clearly warrants further empirical examination.

Tests of language present a consistent picture, particularly when the frequency or latency of spontaneous contributions to conversations in unfamiliar social situations is measured. Reticence is the *sine qua non* of shyness among older children and, as we saw in Chapter 2, among adults as well. The implication of the temperament model is that there is continuity between these behaviours and the wariness and distress shown by inhibited infants when confronted with novel or stressful situations of any kind. Kagan's (1994) interpretation of reticence draws upon similarities in fear reactions between human and non-human species. Silence is a kind of freezing. Kagan supports this argument with a substantial body of evidence suggesting that the reactions of inhibited children are mediated by those cortical and limbic structures and neurotransmitters that regulate fear, and he assigns a central role to the amygdala and its projections to the lower brain stem. The following section summarises evidence on neurobiological bases of temperament. It also presents some quite surprising findings about the differences between inhibited and uninhibited children, for example in eye colour and facial shape, evidence that is not yet completely understood but provides further indication of the physiological basis of temperament.

Biological bases

The system responsible for the experience of fear and the bodily changes that prepare the individual to take aggressive or avoidant action is complex, but research is beginning to tease out the contribution of various components of the system. The roles played by the frontal cortex and parts of the limbic system, including the amygdala (particularly the central nucleus), the hippocampus and the hypothalamic–pituitary–adrenal system, are being identified using both animal and human studies. Research into the temperament of inhibition has focused on a number of peripheral measures of this system, including heart rate, heart rate stability, right frontal EEG asymmetry and levels of salivary cortisol. Heart rate and heart rate variability are indicators of increased sympathetic nervous system activity in response to threat, and this involves projections from the central nucleus of the amygdala to the hypothalamus, with consequent changes in heart rate, and to the medulla, which releases epinephrine, which also affects heart rate. The frontal cortex is involved in the tendency to experience emotion, and right frontal asymmetry seems to be associated with negative emotions such as depression and, more specifically, inhibition, individual differences in infants' anxiety about strangers and distress at separation from the mother (see, for example, Fox and Davidson, 1987). Cortisol is a hormone that is released into the bloodstream to trigger the release of protein to provide extra energy for fight or flight responses.

Kagan (1994) has argued that individual differences in the response to unfamiliarity and stress are associated with greater sympathetic nervous system reactivity, and this is due to innate differences in the threshold of excitability of the amygdala and its projections to the hypothalamus, cingulate, central grey matter, medulla and ventral striatum. Tests of this theory compare inhibited and uninhibited children on measures of sympathetic nervous system activity.

In addition to findings of individual differences in autonomic indices, for example measures related to heart rate (see Chapter 2), there is also evidence that shy/inhibited children show evidence of heightened activity mediated by the adrenocortical system. They secrete more morning salivary cortisol, have a higher concentration of norepinephrine in samples of urine and greater right frontal EEG activation. Bell et al. (1997) report a significant relationship between shyness and opioid peptide activity among a sample of elderly people, finding higher morning plasma beta-endorphin levels among those who are shy. This peptide is involved in the regulation of blood pressure and arousal. Although the findings are not always convincing, it is not so much the series of separate findings that is significant but the *pattern* of differences, because the pattern can be related to what is known about the physiology of the system.

Furthermore the findings can be compared with the results of studies of non-human species. For example LeDoux (1998) and his colleagues have used conditioning procedures to study emotional responses. Conditioning is a process of learning where links are established between different stimuli. In Pavlov's classic demonstrations the presentation of food was systematically accompanied by the ringing of a bell, and eventually hungry dogs salivated at the ringing of the bell in the absence of food. The food is an example of an *unconditioned stimulus*; the bell and other previously neutral stimuli are examples of the *conditioned stimulus*. In the fear-conditioning paradigm, a previously neutral stimulus is paired with an emotionally charged stimulus; for example a sound is associated with the administration of a brief electric shock – when the sound stops the shock is applied. The sound becomes a conditioned stimulus and elicits the same pattern of responses that were evoked by the shock.

If a conditioned stimulus is presented while an animal is carrying out an activity such as pressing a lever in order to obtain food, the animal will immediately cease that activity and 'freeze'. This inhibition of the animal's response has been regarded as similar to the cessation of play and inhibition of exploratory behaviour demonstrated by a shy/inhibited child when he or she encounters a strange room, is separated from the mother or is approached by an unfamiliar adult. Animal studies can also be used to examine the physiological correlates of this pattern of responding, and these can be compared with the correlates identified in studies of individual variation in inhibition among humans. This research has provided evidence of changes in the reactivity of the autonomic nervous system and increased release of cortisol and catecholamines. It has established the role of the amygdala and the hippocampus and their projections to the autonomic system and the hypothalamic-pituitary–adrenal system in the regulation of these responses (LeDoux, 1998). Thus the findings from human and non-human studies converge on a theory where inhibition is related to systems regulating fear and/or anxiety responses. There remain theoretical differences concerning the precise relationships between fear and anxiety and between inhibition and these emotional states, for example between Gray's theory of anxiety and accounts that emphasise the regulatory function of the amygdala (Kagan, 1998). Future research will undoubtedly examine more closely the psychophysiology of these reactions.

Differences between inhibited and uninhibited individuals are not restricted to these laboratory measures of reactions to stressful or unfamiliar events. A body of evidence is currently being collected on other differences that cannot be predicted by common-sense notions of shyness or by theories that regard it as a purely learned pattern of behaviour. Presented below are brief summaries of some illustrative research into differences in the distribution of eye colour, in the characteristic shape of body and face, and in susceptibility to allergies and particular forms of illness.

Eye colour

More children with blue eyes are found in samples of inhibited children than might be expected on the basis of the distribution of blue eyes in the population. Studies carried out by Rosenberg and Kagan (cited in Kagan, 1994, pp. 161–2) found that 60 per cent of the five- to six-year-old inhibited children in their sample were blue-eyed (in the general population some 40–45 per cent have blue eyes). This tendency was stronger among the boys in the sample. Inhibited children are also more likely to have relatives with blue eyes. These investigations compared samples of children selected for inhibited or uninhibited temperament, but Coplan *et al.* (1998) studied the distribution of eye colour in an unselected sample of 152 preschool children. Ratings of the participants' temperaments and characteristic behaviour were also collected in the study. One measure was the Colorado Child Temperament Inventory, which includes parent ratings of shyness and (low) sociability; scores on these subscales were combined to yield an index of inhibition. Other measures were teacher ratings of reticent behaviour and teacher assessments of internalising problems (fears and worries). Eye colour was identified on the basis of parental reports.

Children with blue eyes were rated as more reticent than children with brown eyes, although no statistically significant differences in either temperament or internalising problems were found. However gender had a strong influence on the pattern of results. Blue-eyed boys were more reticent, had more internalising problems and a more inhibited temperament than brown-eyed boys. Among the girls there were no differences associated with eye colour in the two teacher-provided ratings, although blue-eyed girls were rated as *less* inhibited by parents than were girls with brown eyes.

Other evidence suggests that these differences based on eye colour are also moderated by age. They are not apparent in children below the age of twelve months (when iris pigmentation has not yet been established) and they have not been found in studies of older children (for example among nine-year-olds; Coplan *et al.*, 1998, p. 41).

Physique and shape of face

The notion that people with different personalities have different body shapes is an ancient one and prompted empirical research during the twentieth century, including the attempt to identify typologies of body shape by Kretschmer (1925) and Sheldon (1940). Sheldon's classification is based on analysis of large sets of photographs of people and comprises three types. The *ectomorph* is tall and thin, the *endomorph* fat and rounded and the *mesomorph* broad and muscular. Sherlock Holmes, Falstaff and Superman perhaps serve as familiar fictional prototypes of each of these physiques. The frequency with which individuals with contrasting physiques provide a source of humour suggests that we may be predisposed to expect an interaction between different personalities: Don Quixote and Sancho Panza, Laurel and Hardy, Morecambe and Wise. To many, these approaches are absurd simplifications and attempts to relate personality to physical characteristics have also been regarded as objectionable. Kagan (1994, p. 8) suggests that this approach is too similar to the dogma of the eugenics movement in Germany and America, which became influential during the period in which Sheldon's approach was developed, and this stigma has persisted. In more recent years there has been controversy about the breach of privacy involved in the taking and storing of the photographs of university students that contributed to the database for Sheldon's research. When the existence of this archive of photographs became known, many of the subjects – who were, of course, now mature adults – expressed their resentment of having been included in the research without being asked for their informed consent.

Nor has this approach found favour among psychologists, and any empirical findings of correlations between body shape and personality characteristics have often been dismissed as evidence of the influence of social stereotypes upon personality. Over the years Eysenck (1970) claimed that the dimensions of personality in his theory were associated with individual variation in body shape, proposing that the introvert tends to be an ectomorph and the extravert an endomorph, again without having much influence on general psychological thinking.

Research into inhibition has resulted in renewed interest in the relationship between temperament and physique. Arcus and Kagan (1995) tested the hypothesis that shy children have narrower faces than non-shy children. The study was undertaken with a sample of 462 infants, who were assessed for reactivity temperament at four months and for inhibition at 14 and 21 months. Measurement of facial width was made at 14 and 21 months. A calliper was used to measure the ratio of the width of the upper face to the height of the face and head. High reactive infants had narrower faces than low reactive infants at both 14 and 21 months (the effect sizes were moderate: at 14 months the ratios were 0.54 for high reactive infants and 0.57 for low reactive infants). There was a small but significant correlation ($r = -0.18$) between scores on the inhibition measure and facial width ratio when these were assessed at 14 months, although this was not significant at 21 months ($r = -0.10$).

Susceptibility to illness

A relationship between stress and susceptibility to allergies has been hypothesised for many years. For example Holmes *et al.* (1951) reported a series of case studies involving a sample of individuals whose ages ranged from 13 to 60 years. The participants' reactions were systematically monitored during the peak season for allergic rhinitis ('hay fever'). The study included some tests that were carried out in a controlled room where the atmosphere had a specified concentration of ragweed pollen (a known allergen), which was circulated in the air by an electric fan. During each of the tests observations were made of the nasal mucous membrane and measurements were taken of any swelling, nasal secretion and blood flow. In a series of studies, a combination of anxiety and environmental allergens was shown to be associated with intensification of symptoms. In one experiment an interview about a personally sensitive topic led to increased anxiety in a woman hay fever sufferer and her elevated anxiety level was associated with heightened nasal reactions and readily observable symptoms such as running nose, sneezing and irritation of the eyes. The researchers attributed the effects of anxiety to the influence of increased parasympathetic activity upon the nasal mucous membranes, which increased nasal hyperfunction until levels were reached that could not be sustained. They also argued that conflict and anxiety in the lives of individuals predisposed them to nasal hyperfunction and made them susceptible to hay fever.

Research drawing upon self-report data suggests that inhibited and shy individuals are more prone to suffer from allergies such as hay fever. Mothers of inhibited children in the Harvard study were more likely to report that their child suffered from hay fever and eczema. Kagan *et al.* (1991) report the findings of a telephone survey conducted with 528 close relatives (parents, grandparents, aunts and uncles) of a sample of inhibited and uninhibited children (these children were then about 12 years of age). The relatives were asked whether they had ever suffered from one or more of 63 medical symptoms, ranging from frequent headaches or stomach upset to serious illnesses such as cancer, stroke and heart disease. There were statistically significant differences for a small number of these disorders and illnesses, with relatives of inhibited children reporting a higher incidence of hay fever, eczema, stomach cramps, menstrual problems and high social anxiety. Thirty-two per cent of relatives of inhibited children had had hay fever compared with 23 per cent of the relatives of uninhibited children.

A second study with an independent sample of the relatives of a separate cohort of children replicated the findings for hay fever and high social anxiety, but not for eczema, cramps or menstrual problems. Thirty-two per cent of relatives of inhibited children had had hay fever compared with 14 per cent of relatives of uninhibited children. When attention was restricted to parents, 64 per cent of inhibited children had at least one parent who had suffered from hay fever; the comparable statistic for uninhibited children was 25 per cent.

Bell and her research team (Bell *et al.*, 1990) have obtained self-report data from shy people themselves. They surveyed a sample of 379 university students about their experience of allergic disorders, including hay fever, asthma, eczema, hives and reactions to specific environmental irritants such as house dust and pollen. The participants also completed a self-report shyness questionnaire. Students who had at some time been medically diagnosed as having hay fever had a higher shyness score than those who had not, but there was no evidence of any consistent relationship between shyness and any of the other allergies. Chung and Evans (1994) found a higher incidence of gastrointestinal illness among shy children, as assessed by the children themselves and their parents. They also found more signs of fatigue, as assessed by parents.

There is some evidence of a link between shyness and susceptibility to Parkinson's Disease. For example Bell *et al.* (1995) report that, among a sample of adults aged between 50 and 90 and living in a retirement community, those with high scores on a measure of shyness were significantly more likely either to have Parkinson's Disease or to have a relative with the condition. This was reported by 17 per cent of this group whereas indications of the condition were reported by only 2 per cent of those respondents who obtained extremely low scores on the shyness measure. Stein *et al.* (1990) found evidence of a high rate of social phobia among patients with Parkinson's Disease.

Explaining the findings

What do these differences mean and how are they to be explained? Do they require separate explanations or can they be related to some common underlying biological factors? In theoretical terms it would be advantageous if some common principles could be shown to be operative. Kagan (1994, p. 163) has speculated on the relationship between this pattern of differences and genetic factors that influence variation in the levels of norepinephrine, which, as we have seen, plays a central role in the regulation of sympathetic nervous system activity. The adaptive advantage of this gene would be providing efficient control of body temperature. As a secondary effect, the presence of high levels of this neurotransmitter would lead to greater reactivity in the limbic system sites involved in fear, particularly fear of the unfamiliar. Norepinephrine could also be implicated in the tendency to have blue eyes and a narrow face, if high levels of the neurotransmitter inhibit the production of melanin, including levels in the iris, and if increased levels of circulating glucocorticoids inhibit the production of melanin and the growth of facial bones.

Kagan (ibid., p. 163) refers to the observation that a combination of blue eyes, ectomorph physique and narrow face is more common among northern Europeans than among southern Europeans. He argues that the regulation of body heat was more significant for the ancestors of northern Europeans, who lived in much closer proximity to glaciated regions and endured low temperatures. This account is obviously speculative, but some indirect evidence is available that relates to differences between the northern and southern hemispheres. There is also a significant relationship between maternal exposure to short day length during pregnancy, particularly during the middle of the gestation period, and the likelihood that the child will have a shy temperament (Gortmaker *et al.*, 1997). This effect may be mediated by seasonal variation in concentrations of neurotransmitters or corticoids.

Susceptibility to hay fever may also be due to increased levels of neurotransmitters and glucocorticoids. High levels of serotonin and histamine are characteristic of both nasal hyperfunction and emotional reactions related to inhibition (Bell *et al.*, 1990). As Holmes *et al.* (1951) originally demonstrated, the reaction of the nasal membrane to environmental stimuli is mediated by the activity of the autonomic nervous system, so that heightened stress and anxiety leave the individual more vulnerable to these stimuli. Medications such as antihistamines, which control allergenic reactions, also affect the nervous system. Relationships between allergies and behaviour that seem to be mediated by neurochemical activity are not restricted to shyness. For example Marshall (1989) has constructed a model of the relationship between susceptibility to allergies and the uninhibited behaviour and lack of impulse control that is characteristic of children diagnosed with attention deficit disorder.

Some possible neuroendocrine links between shyness and Parkinson's Disease have been suggested. This condition is associated with dopaminergic dysfunction and its symptoms are alleviated by medication that is based on the synthetic production of dopamine; dopaminergic mechanisms have been proposed as explanations for the effectiveness of MAOI (monoamine oxidase inhibitor) treatment of social phobia. The peptide beta-endorphin and the catecholamines norepinephrine, epinephrine and dopamine are involved in generation of fear responses. Evidence of elevated beta-endorphin levels among shy elderly people may provide a link between shyness and Parkinson's Disease (Bell *et al.*, 1997). This peptide might also be related to the production of melanin and hence could influence eye colour. Coplan *et al.* (1998, pp. 41–2) note that it is one of two peptides derived from a common gene, the other (alpha-melanocyte stimulating hormone) being involved in the synthesis of melanin pigment.

In summary, there exist good psychophysiological reasons for believing that these phenomena are not just accidental findings but are interrelated and associated with temperament. Nevertheless this research is in its infancy and should be regarded as suggestive rather than conclusive. First, the evidence comprises only a small number of studies that have not fully explored the phenomena; for example scarcely any work has been carried out on physique or narrowness of the face. Second, the genetic origins and adaptive significance of this pattern of observations is highly speculative. Possible links at the level of activity of the sympathetic nervous system and the neuroendocrine system have been suggested, but precise models of these links have not been constructed or subjected to empirical tests. There have been no attempts to falsify hypotheses or to test competing hypotheses against each other. There have been no attempts to follow through the implications of the links to see if further predictions can be generated. Why should hay fever and not other allergies be associated with shyness? Why are the links merely probabilistic, so that many people with this allergy are not shy and many shy individuals do not suffer from the allergy? Melanin is involved in hair and skin colour as well as eye colour, so are there any contingent relationships between shyness, hair and skin? Why does the relationship between shyness and iris pigmentation depend on gender, and why are there not gender differences in physique or susceptibility to allergies?

The research has raised many questions. Nevertheless it does point to a biological basis for temperament, while the findings on the interaction between eye colour and gender imply that biological and environmental factors combine to influence ratings of children's shyness.

Summary

Research into inhibition has been a growth area in the study of shyness, and the longitudinal study led by Jerome Kagan and ﹒ based at Harvard has examined the biological basis of inhibition in considerable detail. This research has found evidence to suggest that inhibition does meet the criteria of appearing early in life, remaining stable over time and predicting behaviour. This evidence has also been found in other laboratories. It remains to be seen whether the origins of shyness and reticence are to be found entirely in early appearing inhibition. The number of adults claiming to be shy is much greater than would be expected on the basis of the proportion of the population who are inhibited in infancy. Core characteristics of shyness such as self-consciousness, self-evaluation and concern about the opinion of others develop later than infancy. It might be that inhibition predisposes an individual to adopt particular attitudes towards the self, but we do not have evidence of this. We shall consider this question in Chapter 4. Kagan's theory of the biological basis of inhibition emphasises structures and processes in the nervous system involved in fear and anxiety. Characteristics of shyness such as self-consciousness and, more controversially, blushing may be less straightforward to explain in terms of heightened activity of the sympathetic nervous system. We shall consider this issue in Chapter 5.

Chapter 4

Genetic and Environmental Factors in the Development of Shyness

Researching genetic influences

Studies of heritability

Studies of the heritability of traits have relied upon the analysis of family resemblance and 'natural experiments' that throw the contributions of genetic and environmental factors into relief. The degree of family resemblance is informative. Because a child receives half of his or her chromosomes from one parent and half from the other, the distribution of characteristics among members of a family can provide clues about the possible genetic origin of these characteristics. The genotype inherited by each child represents a random assortment of his or her parents' genes, so that on average children are expected to have 50 per cent of the genes of each parent. It is possible to predict the expected degree of similarity between different relatives, for example grandparents, aunts and uncles, cousins and so on. The correlations between test scores obtained by pairs of relatives can show whether the pattern of observed coefficients reflects the predicted degree of similarity. Thus the more distant genetically the pairs of relatives, the lower the predicted correlations. Such research is of course concerned with average degrees of similarity and requires large samples of participants. It is important to bear in mind that heritability estimates refer to averages, since, for example, two offspring from the same pair of parents can inherit different sets of genes and turn out to be quite different from each other purely for genetic reasons.

Nevertheless it is obvious that members of the same family are also like one another because of their shared environment. Factors that can influence psychological development – such as amount of disposable income, quality of housing, level of education, attitude towards child rearing and education, child rearing practices and so on – tend to be similar among close relatives. For the same reasons we might expect increasing differences in environment as family connections become more remote.

The study of identical twins has contributed enormously to understanding genetic factors. Identical or monozygotic (MZ) twins are produced when the fertilised egg, the zygote, divides to form two zygotes. This is a different phenomenon from fraternal or dizygotic (DZ) twins, where two ova have been fertilised: MZ twins have an identical genetic endowment; while DZ twins are genetically no more alike than any other pair of siblings. This distinction between the two types is manifest in physical appearance. MZ twins are physically very alike, indeed it may be difficult to tell one from the other, and they are, of course, of the same sex. DZ twins can look markedly different from one another and be of different sexes.

The existence of two types of twins suggests different comparisons. The frequency with which a condition that is true of one MZ twin is also true of the other can be examined, on the understanding that a condition that is genetic in origin should be present in both twins. A comparison of characteristics of MZ twins who have been reared in the same family with those who have been separated for some reason and brought up in different families is also informative about the relative importance of genetics and child-rearing practices. Alternatively one can quantify the genetic influence on a trait distributed throughout the population by analysing scores on the trait that are obtained by MZ twins (who share 100 per cent of their genes), by DZ twins or siblings (who share 50 per cent of their genes) and by adoptive parents and children who share none of their genes. These issues have been examined in large-scale studies of twins, in particular the Louisville Twin Study (for example, Matheny, 1989) and the MacArthur Longitudinal Twin Study (Emde *et al.*, 1992).

Nevertheless some of the limitations that apply to the study of family resemblance also apply to the special case of the study of twins. Not only do twins have a shared genetic endowment but they also share common environmental conditions. Indeed common sense suggests that the physical resemblance of MZ twins can lead to a specially close environment since parents and other members of the family may set out to treat them in similar ways, dressing them alike, taking them everywhere together, having equivalent expectations of them and so on. The environment shared by MZ twins may be much more similar than that shared by DZ twins, and indeed some of the studies of parental ratings that we shall review suggest that parents may exaggerate the contrast between DZ twins. The differences between the correlations of ratings of MZ and DZ twins are often much larger than predicted.

We must be careful to be specific about what we have in mind when we refer to the child's environment, since this is what the child inhabits from conception, not just from birth. Experiences that take place between conception and birth have to be considered, and twins have a distinctive experience since they share the mother's womb. Sharing limited space and a common supply of nutrients may result in competition for resources and the unequal distribution that ensues can produce physical and psychological differences. MZ twins frequently share a common chorionic membrane, which can give rise to an imbalance of placental circulation between them. Furthermore the establishment of a small advantage by one twin may lead to further advantages, as this twin will be stronger and more competitive. Some indication of these factors is given by the fact that markedly different birth weights are more prevalent among MZ than among DZ twins.

On the other hand, such competition might lead to disadvantages for both twins in comparison with a child who does not have to compete. This might contribute to the finding that on average, MZ twins are born nearly a month premature, and have birth weights about 30 per cent lower than the average (Emde *et al.*, 1992, p. 1451). It is not obvious what significance should be attached to this finding as many of the psychological differences between premature and full-term infants will have disappeared before the child begins school. On the other hand, shared adverse prenatal environments might result in a common predisposition to experience psychological or physical health problems later in life, and the high coincidence of these problems might lead to the erroneous conclusion that they are genetic in origin. Some of these influences may exaggerate genetic factors and others may underestimate them. In either case, making inferences from twin studies is not as straightforward as it might first appear.

Separation of a child from his or her natural (or biological) parents and being raised in a different family provides another 'natural experiment'. In the case of MZ twins who are separated, this seems the ideal experiment since any resemblance between them will be due entirely to genetic factors. Furthermore differences between MZ twins who have been separated and those who have been reared together are also informative about the role of the environment. For these reasons MZ twins have been eagerly sought out for research purposes. Although the separation of MZ twins is a relatively rare event some sizeable samples have been collected, for example the Minnesota Study of Twins Reared Apart (Lykken *et al.*, 1992). We shall see below that these twin samples have made a significant contribution to estimates of heritability.

Nevertheless this 'natural' experiment does not conform to the design requirements of a well-run experiment. The age at which the children have been separated is clearly a crucial factor to take into account, especially if early experiences are important for psychological development, yet this factor is outside the researcher's control and in practice twins will have been separated at a variety of ages. Moreover separation might not be a clean break and there might be continuing contact between families or between the twins. Notwithstanding these issues, there have been well-publicised cases where twins have been separated at an early age and do not become aware of the existence of their twin until much later in life. A well-designed experiment would also ensure that twins were assigned at random to different environments so that genetic–environment correlations could be avoided. Not only is this difficult to obtain in practice, but the preferences of families and the policies of placement agencies involved in arranging new homes for the twins might be opposed to this approach and seek to place children with families that are similar in important respects.

Finally, children who are not related to each other but are brought up in the same family also provide information about heritability. Children who have been adopted into a family provide the best known example of this, as there is no shared genetic endowment between adoptive parents and adopted child or between adopted child and the natural children of the parents. These studies can be used to examine correlations between unrelated children who are raised together and to compare parent–child relationships where there is a genetic relationship between parent and child and where there is not. Correlations of scores on measures of psychological characteristics provide an estimate of the contribution made by the shared environment, assuming that there were no selective placement procedures at work to find adoptive parents who were similar in important respects to the child's biological parents.

Estimates of heritability

A number of approaches have been taken to devise 'biometric' or mathematical models that apportion individual variation in temperament to genetic and environmental factors. Consider the relative similarity in the sets of scores obtained by samples of MZ twins and DZ twins where each pair of twins have been brought up in their own family. MZ twins have 100 per cent of their genes in common; DZ twins 50 per cent, on average. If it is assumed that the environments of MZ twins are no more similar than the environments of DZ twins of the same sex (because environmental factors such as child-rearing practices, parental attitudes, education and income are common to each member of the pair – but remember the caution mentioned above!), then it can be argued that because the MZ twins share 100 per cent and the DZ twins 50 per cent of their genes, the *difference* in the average correlation between the two types of twins reflects 50 per cent of the variability due to genetic factors. Thus doubling this difference would provide an estimate of the percentage of the variation in scores that is due to genetic factors.

Assume, for the sake of exposition, that the average correlation between the scores obtained by a sample of MZ twins on a measure of temperament is 0.50 and the average correlation for a sample of DZ twins is 0.30. According to this model the difference between 0.50 and 0.30 – that is, 0.20 – provides an estimate of 50 per cent of the variability due to genetic factors. Doubling this implies that 0.40 (40 per cent) of the variability in personality test scores is due to genetic factors, leaving 60 per cent for other factors, including environmental influences and measurement error. This result would assign a significant role to genetic factors but it would also imply that the larger part of the differences in scores in this test was not due to genetic factors.

This result does not imply that a proportion of any *individual* child's temperament can be explained in terms of genetic or environmental factors. The statistic applies to the population as a whole, and the correlations for any sample of children provide an estimate of the variation in that population that can be assigned to genetic or environmental influences. If the environment has a negligible influence on a particular characteristic then most of the variation in this will be due to non-environmental factors. If genetic factors are irrelevant to the trait then the observed variation will be entirely due to environmental factors. More complicated combinations of environmental and genetic factors can be envisaged, for example the environment might not have a constant effect on the population as a whole but affect only individuals with a particular genetic background. Therefore, an environmental factor may not affect all individuals in the same way, so that a simple additive model cannot explain the effects of genes and the environment.

It is possible to extend this simple mathematical model to distinguish two groups of environmental influences: *shared environmental factors* and *non-shared environmental factors*. The first term refers to influences that cause children in the same family to be like each other. The second refers to factors that make members of the same family different from one another. Family income provides an example of a shared factor, and the differential treatment of children – whether boys or girls, or first born versus later born children – is an example of a non-shared factor. A strong influence exerted by a shared environment can be inferred if there are similarities in personality between two unrelated children brought up together, for example an adopted child and a biological child of the family. A positive correlation between their test scores would imply that variation was due to their shared environment. A strong influence of non-shared environmental factors can be inferred if biological children brought up in the same family are markedly different from one another.

Shared environment (SE) can be estimated in various ways: from the correlation between unrelated children who are reared together and who have, across the sample as a whole, no genetic factors in common; from the difference in correlations between MZ twins reared together and MZ twins who have been separated, since the twins reared together have a common genetic make-up and a shared environment whereas those reared apart have only their genes in common. Several models have been developed to estimate the relative proportion of genetic, shared environmental and non-shared environmental influences upon temperament, personality and cognitive abilities.

The average values of correlations for different personality traits have been found to be about 0.50 for MZ twins and 0.30 for DZ twins, implying that 40 per cent of variation is due to genetic factors, 50 per cent to non-shared environment factors and 10 per cent to shared environmental factors. Identical twins are much more similar in personality than are fraternal twins. This is confirmed by studies of identical twins who have been separated and lived most of their lives apart (Lykken *et al.*, 1992). On the other hand non-twin siblings are not very much like each other at all – shared family environment has a negligible influence on personality development. The average correlation in personality test scores between siblings is only around 0.15. Similar results have been obtained in adoption studies: the correlation between pairs of siblings where one of the pair has been adopted is close to zero (Plomin and Daniels, 1987).

One complication in assigning variation in traits to different sources is that several studies of correlations between MZ twins and between DZ twins have found that the differences in correlations between MZ and DZ twins are much larger than predicted (the models assume that they ought to be twice as large). The correlations for DZ twins are very much lower than predicted, indeed they are often close to zero or even negative (Buss and Plomin, 1984; Emde et al., 1992). One possible explanation is that parental ratings, which often provide the data for correlation analysis, are subject to bias. Parents may minimise the differences between MZ twins but exaggerate those between fraternal twins, seeing them as more different than they actually are. An alternative, genetic explanation is that genetic effects are not additive; one gene might dominate another gene, and this would serve to reduce DZ correlations relative to MZ twins (where the set of genes is the same for each twin).

Heritability of inhibition and shyness

Table 4.1 summarises the findings of a selection of studies that have provided data for MZ and DZ twins on measures related to inhibition and shyness. For each of the studies, intraclass correlations are presented for MZ and DZ twins, together with an estimate of heritability. Because low DZ correlations have tended to be found in investigations using rating scales, the table also specifies whether the raw data used to compute the correlations were based on rating scales or other kinds of score, for example observations of behaviour in the laboratory.

A number of conclusions can be drawn from this set of studies. First, measures of shyness show a substantial genetic component. The MZ twin correlations are consistently high and where the heritability index could be computed it shows that genetic effects can explain a substantial proportion of variation. These findings are in line with those obtained for measures of temperament, which generally show a strong heritability component (Caspi, 1998), and support the claim by Boomsma and Plomin (1986, p. 143), based on earlier studies, that shyness is the most heritable of all personality traits.

Table 4.1 Studies of the heritability of inhibition and shyness

Study	Age	Sample	Data source	Measure	rMZ[1]	rDZ[2]	G[3]
Goldsmith et al. (1999)	3–16 months	121 MZ, 181 DZ	Psychologist ratings	Distress at novelty	0.59	0.28	0.62
				Negative affect factor	0.64	0.30	0.68
Goldsmith et al. (1997)	34–99 months	55 MZ, 64 DZ	Parent ratings	Shyness	0.60	0.01	1.18
		89 MZ, 95 DZ	Parent ratings	Social fearfulness	0.50	0.40	0.20
Emde et al. (1992)	14 months	100 MZ, 100 DZ	Observation	Inhibition	0.57	0.26	0.62
			Observation	Shyness	0.70	0.45	0.50
			Parent ratings (CCTI)	Shyness	0.38	-0.03	0.82
Matheny (1989)	12 months	33 MZ, 32 DZ	Aggregate of observations and ratings	Inhibition	0.71	0.25	0.92
	18 months				0.90	0.08	1.64
	24 months				0.81	0.11	1.40
	30 months				0.73	0.03	1.40
Boomsma and Plomin (1986)	7½ years	30 MZ, 28 DZ	Heart record	Resting heart rate	0.54	0.34	0.40
			Heart record	Heart rate during auditory task	0.58	0.35	0.46
			Parent rating (Conners)	Shyness	0.72	0.24	0.48
Spinath and Angleiter (1998)	2–14 years	184 MZ, 170 DZ	Mothers' rating (EAS)	Shyness	0.52	-0.05	1.14
			Fathers' rating (EAS)	Shyness	0.60	-0.06	1.32

Notes:
1. MZ = monozygotic twins, DZ = dizygotic twins.
2. r = correlation coefficient.
3. G = heritability estimate.

Second, the set of correlations replicates earlier findings that DZ twin correlations are too small relative to MZ correlations and are close to zero or negative. In 12 out of 16 comparisons the MZ correlations are more than twice the size of the DZ correlations. Six DZ correlations are either less than r = 0.10 or negative. It does not seem to be the case that these findings are restricted to ratings of children made by their parents or to any particular questionnaire since they are reported for different questionnaires and for behavioural data

(Matheny, 1989). Nevertheless ratings do seem more susceptible to this effect, and studies that have included more than one type of data have produced a more predictable MZ–DZ ratio for behavioural data than for ratings (Boomsma and Plomin, 1986; Emde *et al.*, 1992).

Spinath and Angleiter (1998) examined the ratings given by both mothers and fathers for their same-sex DZ twins on each individual item of the EAS questionnaire to determine whether the pattern of correlations was similar across all items. In fact this was not the case; when the set of 20 items was arranged according to the order of magnitude of correlations, this order was similar for fathers and mothers. Thus, for example, both parents regarded the twins as more similar to one another on the item 'Is very friendly with strangers' than on the item 'Is very sociable', even though both items are included in the shyness subscale. This demonstrates that parental bias in ratings is not consistent across all items but is sensitive to their content. This in turn implies that ratings are affected by parents' perception of their children rather than by genetic factors since these would be unlikely to distinguish between items represented on the same shyness factor. Nevertheless the perceived degree of similarity between twins is always very small, with correlation coefficients close to zero, and only 10 out of 40 items show coefficients greater than 0.20.

Third, this pattern of correlations makes it very difficult to obtain meaningful estimates of shared and non-shared environmental effects. Entering the correlations into the equations yields estimates of genetic effects and of total variation greater than 1.0, which is larger than the maximum specified in the model. Inspection of the estimates of these statistics suggests that non-shared environment has a much greater influence on shyness than shared environment and this is compatible with previous findings on temperament (Caspi, 1998). Where meaningful estimates have been derived, as in the shyness observation data reported by Emde *et al.* (1992) and the heart rate data reported by Boomsma and Plomin (1986), the proportions are of the order of 12–20 per cent for shared environment and 30–46 per cent for non-shared. The small contribution of shared environment is also apparent in studies that have compared the shyness scores of MZ twins reared together and apart, or compared adopted children with other members of the adoptive family.

Why are shared environmental effects so small relative to non-shared effects? This question continues to intrigue researchers, but no explanation has received general support. Common sense, not to mention theories of the effects of the environment on child development, suggests that shared effects ought to be important because it is widely believed that factors such as child-rearing practices and parental attitudes towards education have an important influence on children. It is not usually believed that they influence some children in the family but not others. However it has to be recognised that genetic factors also contribute to apparent similarities between members of the same family and these need to be controlled statistically before any effect of shared environmental factors can be fully assessed.

Little research has directly examined non-shared effects, again because it is difficult to do so with the available measurement techniques. However a study by Rodgers *et al.* (1994) suggests how this might be approached. They analysed the differences in scores between pairs of children in a checklist of behavioural problems. The pairs had varying degrees of relationship, being either twins, full siblings, half siblings or cousins. Information was also collected about the mothers' behaviour, including estimates of the time spent reading to their children and the frequency of physical punishment. For each pair of children, difference scores were calculated on these two measures and were regarded as providing an index of differential treatment, in other words, non-shared environmental effects. Analysis of the scores on the checklist found a very high heritability coefficient for all scales, including anxiety. It was also found that differential treatment was significantly related to differences between pairs on the checklist, after the genetic and shared-environmental effects had been controlled statistically. The member of the pair who received more physical punishment was rated as having more behavioural problems (of course it cannot be deduced from these data which was the cause and which the effect). This study shows that specific environmental effects can be analysed using models of genetic and environmental influences applied to kinship data.

Summary

The biometric approach to apportioning variation in psychological test scores to genetic and environmental influences has been widely applied to the analysis of personality. It has identified genetic influences, accounting for 22–26 per cent of variation, and non-shared environmental influences, accounting for about 50 per cent of variation. Contrary to expectations, shared environment has only a negligible influence, typically accounting for less than 10 per cent of variation in personality measures. Brothers and sisters within the same family can have very different personalities, and although this might not be surprising at the level of the individual family (the reader can possibly reflect on how different he or she is from other members of the family), it is surprising as an average effect over many families. Either there are systematic influences that have not been identified, or the genetic–environmental interrelationship is more complex than supposed.

Theories assume that there is a strong genetic component in temperament and this is supported by research into temperament in general, and into inhibition and shyness in particular. Meaningful interpretation of the application of biometric models to inhibition and shyness is limited by the finding that the correlations between DZ twins are much smaller than those between MZ twins. It is not understood why this is so. Bias in parents' ratings (exaggerating differences between DZ twins) is one factor but it does not provide the full explanation. Non-additive genetic effects are also a potential factor. Where the model can be applied, genetic and non-shared environmental influences are as strong for inhibition and shyness as they are for other temperaments and traits, and shared environment seems just as marginal an influence.

Estimates of heritability are based on trends identified in large samples of children, and they fail to reflect the interactions between temperament and environment that have been highlighted by other approaches. Nevertheless findings do support evidence of the early appearance of individual differences in inhibition. They offer support for the core assumption of the construct of temperament that these differences are innate.

The social origins of shyness

Shyness and attachment

Attachment theory draws upon concepts from psychoanalysis and ethology (the study of animals in their natural habitat). The British psychoanalyst John Bowlby was impressed with a finding from animal studies that there seems to be a critical stage in the young animal's life for bonding with its mother, and failure to establish a bond at this stage has damaging consequences for behaviour later in life. Bowlby attempted to integrate these observations with the fundamental tenet of psychoanalysis that the adult personality is formed in the early years, specifically during the relationship between the very young child and his or her parents. The development of a child's personality is mediated by his or her symbolic representation of early parent–child conflicts and the form taken by conflict resolution. Thus it is fundamental to attachment theory (for example Bowlby, 1988) that the establishment of emotional bonds between infant and caregiver plays a crucial role in human development.

Within this theoretical framework the quality of these bonds is assessed by means of observing a child's responses in the Ainsworth 'strange situation' test (Ainsworth *et al.*, 1978). This test involves a sequence of events involving the child, the mother and an adult stranger. The test begins with the child and mother together in a room, and then a stranger enters. Next the mother exits, leaving the child with the stranger; finally, the mother returns. Observation of the range of children's responses to the 'strange situation' suggests that children can be classified into one of three types on the basis of their willingness to explore the environment and the pattern of their reactions to separation from the mother and reunion with her. The child who is *securely attached* is confident in the new situation, does not necessarily stay close to the mother and reacts positively to the stranger. Although the child shows some signs of distress at separation and immediately seeks proximity to the mother on her return, he or she quickly becomes calm again and resumes playing confidently. There are two types of insecure attachment. The *avoidant* child pays little attention to the mother in the first phase of the test and is not distressed by her departure, being easily comforted by the stranger. When the mother returns to the room the child either ignores her or makes, at most, a tentative approach. The *resistant* child is fussy and wary while the mother is present and is reluctant to move away from her in order to play. Upon her return to the room the child seems ambivalent, seeking reunion with her but at the same time resisting it, and he or she finds it difficult to resume playing.

Although these three categories of attachment refer to qualities of the relationship between mother and child, Bowlby (1988) argues that a pattern of attachment tends to persist and becomes self-perpetuating. In line with the assumptions of psychoanalytic theory, the pattern becomes *internalised*, so that while it begins as a quality of the relationship it eventually becomes an enduring psychological characteristic of the child. The child constructs 'working models' of him- or herself and of the attachment figure. These models are based on the experience of the attachment relationship, and they function as templates for predicting and interpreting all subsequent close relationships, influencing the child's expectations of the self and other people. According to the theory, insecure attachments can lead to difficulty with forming and maintaining social relationships in later life. It is thus possible that shyness is produced by a particular working model of social relationships that is the outcome of early patterns of parent–child interactions. This thesis has some face validity if we note the similarity between the 'strange situation' as a measure of attachment and as a measure of the temperament of inhibition. The situation designed by Ainsworth shares several features with those designed for the Harvard, Maryland, and Cambridge longitudinal studies of inhibition (see Chapters 2 and 3).

Patterns of attachment are themselves influenced by the attitudes and behaviour of parents. Just as observations of behaviour provide the basis for classification of attachments, they can also provide the basis for classification of different styles of parenting. Ainsworth *et al.* (1978) found that an assessment of the mother's sensitivity to the needs of her child, based on home observations beginning when the infant was weeks old, could predict security of attachment at 12 months of age. This finding has had a profound influence on subsequent research and on explanations of the factors that influence attachment. Nevertheless these findings have not been consistently replicated and a number of studies have failed to find this relationship (Seifer *et al.*, 1996).

There are many reasons for failing to specify this relationship. Sensitivity is a broad concept that can be interpreted, and therefore measured, in different ways. It can mean that parents (including biological parents and foster parents, but also caregivers, guardians, elder siblings and all those who have a key role in caring for the young child) are flexible and responsive in their child care practices. It can refer to cognitive processes where the parent structures and interprets the tasks faced by the child in order to provide a framework for his or her learning. It can also refer to the parent's willingness to devote time to shared activities with the child. It can be defined in terms of the adult's alertness to the child's needs at any given time and the capacity to deal appropriately with these. It can imply that the parent is warm, encouraging and supportive.

The mother's authoritarianism, insensitivity to the child's needs, overprotectiveness, hostility, lack of warmth, passivity and a tendency to be overcritical of the child have all been suggested as potential factors in the development of a child's shyness. Research needs to establish which, if any, of these are significant, and what psychological processes mediate between parental style and a child's characteristics.

The relationship between parent and child is not only influenced by the parent's characteristics but also by those of the child. How are attachment and temperament related? The child's temperament might influence the parent–child relationship so that the pattern of attachment that develops for one child in a family might be different from the pattern that develops for another. A parent might be more sensitive in dealing with a child with some temperamental characteristics than with children with other characteristics. The child's temperament might influence his or her reaction to the parent's sensitivity or other characteristics that shape attachments. Attempting to test any of these possible relationships is problematic if one considers that the child's temperament might influence his or her behaviour in the 'strange situation' and affect classification into attachment status. For example an inhibited child might be less likely to be classified as having a secure attachment.

There is some evidence to suggest that shyness is positively associated with parental rejection and negatively associated with parental sensitivity and warmth. Seifer *et al.* (1996) report findings of relationships among measures of maternal sensitivity, infant temperament and attachment status from a longitudinal study of children that followed them from the age of three months to 12 months. The study incorporated a measure of shyness as a component of an approach scale, which assessed infants' tendency either to explore or to be reserved and shy. It was found that neither temperament in general nor shyness in particular was significantly correlated with attachment status, although shyness was related to maternal sensitivity; at both six and nine months the degree of tendency to approach was correlated with the quality and appropriateness of the mother's interaction with her child.

For a sample of adults with an average age of about 28 years, Schlette *et al.* (1998) found a correlation between self-reported shyness and a measure of the participants' recollection of parental rejection and lack of parental warmth. Duggan and Brennan (1994) found significant correlations between the Cheek–Buss shyness measure and attachment style categories derived from Bowlby's theory. Shyness correlated negatively with a measure of secure attachment and positively with a measure of fearful attachment.

Self-efficacy

There are other possible models of the relationship between a child's shyness and social development. One can ask how a child acquires confidence in his or her ability to undertake any activity. Albert Bandura has examined this question using the concept of *self-efficacy*. This is defined as 'people's judgments of their capabilities to organise and execute courses of action required to attain designated types of performances. It is concerned not with the skills one has but with the judgments of what one can do with whatever skills one possesses' (Bandura, 1986, p. 391). An individual bases his or her self-efficacy judgments on four sources of evidence: (1) personal experiences; (2) vicarious experiences; (3) labelling processes; and (4) inference processes.

When estimating the likelihood that they will act effectively in a particular social situation individuals refer to their past experiences in similar situations. A history of failure produces low self-efficacy beliefs, which are immune to the occasional success. This immunity is preserved by the kinds of explanation that the person has framed for these outcomes. For example a shy man might attribute a social success to the fact that no one had had an opportunity to get to know him as he really was. However in practice shy people may rarely 'fail' in a social situation as they develop strategies to guard against failure, but they do not credit the avoidance of failure to their own capabilities. Accordingly a history of situations that are 'survived' does not increase the individual's expectation that she or he will survive in the future. A lecturer may completely lack confidence in his or her public speaking so that each lecture is dreaded as the time to deliver it approaches. The talk itself may be of a satisfactory standard, nothing untoward happens during its delivery and the lecturer leaves the room with a sense of relief. Nevertheless the performance is not based on any foundation of self-belief, and as the occasion for the next lecture approaches, anxiety rises as before. In similar fashion, nervousness about dates, parties or social gatherings persists in the absence of any *faux pas* or experience of rejection.

An individual also acquires experience vicariously. He or she observes how others perform in comparable situations and notes the outcome of their performance. These observations can influence self-efficacy in various ways. The apparent poise of other people can be intimidating. Observing the failures of others can be frightening. Witnessing the countless criticisms and unkind or sarcastic comments that are part and parcel of everyday life enhances awareness of the costs that are potentially involved in social encounters and increases the individual's own fear of attracting negative evaluation.

Nevertheless observations are not simply made in a passive or automatic way. In their daily life people are not like psychologists who count the frequency of different actions. They interpret what they see in terms of their understanding of the situation. What can appear on the surface to be unkind remarks may often in practice be instances of a shared joke among people who know each other well or be affectionate references to a commonly understood experience. They can be instances of teasing. This form of verbal humour can serve positive ends in social relationships by increasing social cohesion and group members' enjoyment of interaction, or they can serve negative ends by expressing aggression. Nicknames can convey messages about friendship and affection, or else they can be sarcastic and critical. In the American television comedy *Cheers* the character Cliff Clavin (played by John Ratzenberger) illustrates how being called 'boring' is not entirely a negative evaluation. He is the regular butt of jokes about how boring he is, nevertheless he is regarded as good company, is accepted as a member of the group of people who meet regularly in the bar and shares in their activities just as much as anyone else. His 'character' has a valuable role to play in the group, facilitating a certain kind of humour and helping to sustain the life of the group by enhancing its members' enjoyment of each other's company.

These remarks are often embedded in relationships where teasing and shared references are more common than intentional negative evaluation. However teasing and the use of nicknames involve elements of both play and aggression and it may be difficult for someone at the receiving end to know how to respond appropriately. Someone who is unfamiliar with the role that is being played (for example, by Cliff) or who is not party to shared references, is likely to interpret the situation as more threatening than it actually is and may regard the risk of taking an initiative as much greater than it is. This could well be the case for a shy woman or man whose social repertoire might keep them on the periphery of the action, reluctant themselves to tease or offer a humorous remark and fearful of being the centre of attention. What is learnt through observing others is never independent of the personality of the observer.

One important form of observational learning is known as *modelling*. A child will take a parent or another significant adult as a model for his or her own behaviour. A parent who is sociable and outgoing provides a model for the child to imitate. In similar fashion, if a parent or significant figure in the child's life behaves in a reticent or non-assertive way in social situations this too might be imitated by the child. Furthermore an adult who behaves in this way fails to provide a model for confident or competent behaviour. Nevertheless, as suggested by our previous examples, a child's personality can also be a factor in the extent to which any model will be influential.

How children are labelled is also a factor. If parents have little confidence in their child they can undermine the child's belief in him- or herself. They can bring this about by reacting to the child's behaviour in subtle ways without necessarily being aware they are doing so. They can communicate the message more directly if they selectively praise and reprimand the child for his or her actions. Adults also attach verbal labels to a child's habitual ways of behaving, both when speaking to the child and when talking about the child to others. Terms such as shy, quiet, restless, naughty, disobedient, clever and bad tempered are common descriptions of children in everyday conversation. If adults label a child as shy the child may come to think of him- or herself as shy and begin to interpret responses to social situations as signs of their shyness, rather than attributing these responses to characteristics of the situations or considering that other people who are not shy respond in a similar way. We can appropriate the labels that are applied to us and make use of them to make sense of our behaviour. Zimbardo (1977, p. 52) provides an illustration of this, where a 57-year-old woman traces the onset of her shyness to a label supplied by her teacher when she was about 13 years of age: 'I consider myself to be shy. I wasn't until I was in the seventh grade when a teacher said I was "quiet". From that time on, I have felt I am below average in my conversational ability. I now have a fear of rejection.' We cannot tell from this quotation whether this experience was sufficient in itself to encourage the woman's view of herself, or whether other kinds of evidence about herself had already predisposed her to think of herself along certain lines. These beliefs might have been given shape and a label by the teacher's attribution.

Finally, people can infer expectancies from their physiological reactions. Through past learning, cues that are associated with situations such as meeting new people or public speaking can become stimuli that directly elicit symptoms of tension or fear. People may take these reactions as indications of their own inadequacy. There is evidence that people do come to label themselves as shy, at least partly on the basis of their physiological reactions to social situations (Cheek and Watson, 1989). If they become aware of an increase in their heart rate or become conscious that they are blushing they regard these as evidence of their shyness. Thus their interpretation of events within a specific situation is framed in terms of a more enduring psychological trait. This can of course be an erroneous interpretation, since these reactions may be more informative about the properties of the specific situation than of any qualities of the individual. Challenging situations of many kinds (giving a speech) can raise the heart rate, and finding oneself the focus of attention (being congratulated) can elicit blushing; these situation-response contingencies are widespread and are not experienced solely by shy or anxious people.

Self-efficacy theory has generated an extensive body of research, including on the causal connections between self-efficacy beliefs and behaviour. It is believed that processes of self-regulation and goal setting influence these connections. In academic settings, positive self-efficacy beliefs are predictive of high achievement, and one of the factors mediating this relationship are the goals that an individual sets for him- or herself. Setting high goals is correlated with successful performance whereas setting low goals is correlated with less success. Little research has looked directly at the role of these beliefs in shyness, although there is considerable conceptual overlap between these constructs. Self-efficacy beliefs are relevant to specific domains, rather than being generalised, so that an individual has expectations about particular classes of social situation. Shyness, too, can be highly specific to certain kinds of situation. The notion that individuals set low goals for themselves surely has its equivalent in the self-protective strategies that shy people adopt to cope with situations that make them apprehensive.

The development of shyness

Developmental pathways

Research into inhibition has provided evidence of its relative stability through the childhood years. Nevertheless there remain questions about the relationship between inhibition and shyness later in life. One important issue is whether there are people who were inhibited in childhood but are no longer inhibited as adults and, conversely, whether there are shy adolescents or adults who were not inhibited at a young age. The population of shy adults might comprise some individuals who have an inhibited temperament and others who do not. This suggests that there might be turning points on the path from infant temperament to adult personality. The concept of developmental pathways has proved fruitful in the analysis of the continuities and changes that are revealed in longitudinal studies of development. For example Rutter (1989) has shown that while adverse circumstances in early family life can predispose a woman to experience difficulties in her own adjustment when she becomes a mother, this outcome is by no means inevitable. It is possible to identify events and experiences that lead to more positive outcomes. These events include success at school, avoiding an early pregnancy, positive reasons for choice of partner and good quality support offered by the partner. It is possible by means of longitudinal studies to trace various pathways to different outcomes. These pathways can be traced forward in time by means of prospective studies, or backward in time by retrospective studies. This conceptualisation of development raises several interesting questions about shyness:

- What kinds of event function as turning points to direct a child along a pathway to shyness?
- Is the type of shyness that is reached at the end of a pathway from inhibition to shyness different from the type that is the end-point of a pathway that begins with non-inhibition?
- Are there other dimensions of temperament or later emerging personality traits that predispose an adult to be shy?
- Are there early socialisation experiences that influence either the particular pathway that is taken or the type of shyness that is reached?

Little evidence is available to help answer these questions. The last question has attracted most attention and was addressed earlier in this chapter. The concept of developmental pathways has been applied in order to relate temperament to properties of the parent–child relationship. For example Rubin (1993) proposes a route that leads from inhibition to later problems of adjustment. Inhibited children find it difficult to deal with novel situations, and in turn, their parents find the child difficult to soothe and placate. Parents might respond to their child with insensitivity or hostility, or by attempting to control the child's behaviour. The pattern of insecure attachment set up in this way may become internalised by the child to form his or her 'internal working model' and contribute to subsequent unsatisfactory relationships with peers and at school.

Mills and Rubin (1993) have compared the beliefs and attitudes about social competence held by mothers of socially withdrawn children with those held by mothers of children who were either aggressive or 'average', that is, neither aggressive nor withdrawn. The initial sample comprised 122 mothers of four-year-olds; 45 of the mothers participated again when the children were six. The mothers of the withdrawn children were more likely to emphasise the explicit instruction of social skills – telling the child what to do, and using rewards and punishments to encourage more skilled behaviour – and believed that directive action should be taken to help children overcome their difficulties. They were more likely to attribute the child's behaviour to a trait rather than to his or her age. Finally, they were more likely to be disappointed, embarrassed or guilty about their child's behaviour.

However these findings could not be replicated with a fresh sample of mothers of older children, so it remains an open question whether these relationships changed with age or whether there were other differences between the two samples that might have confounded the results. Moreover it cannot be established whether the mothers' beliefs and behaviours influenced their children's withdrawn behaviour or whether they were a response to it. Nevertheless the findings are, at least in some respects, compatible with Rubin's theory that temperament and caregiver–child relationships influence shyness.

Shyness and development of the self

The most common distinction between types of shyness is between early appearing, fearful shyness and later appearing, self-conscious shyness. It is possible that that inhibition predisposes a child towards fearful shyness, since this is defined in terms of wariness about novel situations and apprehension about strangers, and these are also the defining properties of the inhibition temperament. The self-conscious form of shyness, which relates to concern with how one is regarded by other people, might only emerge when children acquire a self-concept sophisticated enough to incorporate awareness of how they are viewed by others. Perhaps developments in self-awareness constitute a significant factor in the recruitment of new children to the 'ranks of the shy'; we shall consider this issue now.

Some general principles should be kept in mind. First, the growth of the child's self-understanding is a gradual process, not a 'once and for all' matter nor a sequence of discrete stages. Thus a male child identifies himself as a boy and not a girl from the age of two to three years, but it is only later, when he is about four, that he believes that he will always be a boy as he grows up and that he would remain a boy even if he wore a dress or played 'girls' games' (Szkrybalo and Ruble, 1999). Any indications of the age at which changes take place refer only to trends and cannot be exact. Second, this growth is associated with other cognitive, emotional and physical changes, and it is misleading to regard it as a process that can be treated separately from these other changes. Third, developments are embedded in the social world of the child. The self is a *social construction*, accomplished through the child's relationships with caregivers; relationships that are themselves embedded in a larger social world of cultural practices. It is easy to lose sight of this crucial dimension when analysing development at the level of the individual child.

Outlined below are some stages in the development of self-awareness by a hypothetical child:

- Ann becomes aware that she is a distinct entity with identifiable characteristics.
- Ann becomes aware of normative standards for behaviour and she evaluates herself relative to these standards.
- Ann realises that other people have a cognitive or emotional representation of events that differs from her own.
- Ann realises that this can be a representation of her. Others have a view of her, which can be different from her own view of herself.

- Ann realises that this view is evaluative of her character or her conduct; she is good or bad.
- This view influences the view that Ann holds of herself; she refers to it when evaluating herself.

Self-awareness

According to most experts the young infant initially makes no differentiation between aspects of the self and aspects of the environment – a state labelled by Piaget as *ontological egocentrism* and by Freud as *primary narcissism*. There is agreement between cognitive and psychoanalytic theories that there can be no awareness of self until the infant becomes aware of the existence of objects. Gradually the child comes to extract invariances from her experience and to achieve some understanding of the permanence of objects and their separate existence beyond her own activities. This achievement gives rise to the realisation that she is just one object in a world of objects. Egocentrism begins to break down, but this is a gradual process and it persists in various forms for some time to come.

Development during the first year of life is largely concerned with the organisation and integration of perceptual and motor systems. There are only the rudiments of self-awareness as the infant begins to make a distinction between self and mother and to experience the self as an agent who can produce changes in the environment. Nevertheless the infant seems to be biologically programmed to engage in social interactions, and in the second half of the first year there are significant developments in communication that have implications for self-awareness. The infant demonstrates a capacity to imitate the mother's behaviour. Also, from about the age of two months she can adjust her line of gaze to follow the mother's line of sight, or can follow a gesture (such as pointing) to look at a target. There is also evidence of early forms of communication (*protoconversation*) where the infant shares her experience with the mother. The infant distinguishes the mother from other people, and looks for her and shows distress when separated from her.

Nevertheless careful analysis of these achievements reveals the strong pull of egocentrism. For example in the first year the infant is remarkably accurate at following the mother's line of sight, indeed she can ignore one target in the visual field to follow the line of sight to another, correct target. However if the mother looks to a target *behind* the infant, the infant still searches in the visual field in front of her. As Butterworth (for example Butterworth and Jarrett, 1991) has shown, the child shows signs that she is both egocentric and not egocentric, since she can follow the line of sight but nevertheless takes the other point of view as if it were her own. Recognition that she and her mother have different viewpoints comes later.

The second year is regarded as crucial in the acquisition of self-awareness. Developments during the year are rapid and take place on many fronts. As locomotion skills develop the child becomes more autonomous and is able to explore the environment. She shows greater tolerance for separation from the mother, which implies that she has the ability to form and maintain a stable mental representation of the mother. And of course there are dramatic developments in the child's comprehension and use of language.

Some of the implications of these developments are evident in children's performance in visual recognition tasks, which are investigations of children's responses to seeing their own mirror image or seeing a video recording of themselves. In the first year the infant typically shows interest in, and seems to derive great enjoyment from, the mirror image but does not respond any differently to her own image and the image of someone else. In the second half of the first year she enjoys playing with the reflected image, for example waving at it and making it move, and this behaviour provides an illustration of her emerging sense of agency. Also, she seems to recognise herself in *contingent* situations, when her action produces a corresponding change in the mirror image.

Significant changes in response take place during the second year. From about 15 months old the child is able to recognise herself in non-contingent situations as well, that is, in a photograph or video recording as well as in the mirror. The course of this development has been examined more closely by means of the visual self-recognition paradigm. In the baseline condition of the experiment, infants observe themselves in a mirror. Following this stage, and when a criterion number of glances at the mirror have been reached (to establish that the child is actually attending to the image), a mark is made on the child's nose by surreptitiously touching it with a dab of rouge make-up. In the follow-up condition the infant is again placed in front of the mirror and any reactions to the mark – such as laughing or crying, changes in facial expression, or touching or pointing at the nose or face – are noted. These reactions are never exhibited by infants younger than 15 months, but there is some evidence of reactions between 15 and 18 months, and after 18 months there is a dramatic increase in the frequency of mark-related behaviours (Brooks-Gunn and Lewis, 1984, pp. 223–4). This trend is also found when steps are taken to control for alternative explanations of the infant's behaviour, for example to control for the fact that the infant's nose is touched when the rouge is applied and this touch sensation might trigger the reaction.

Elaboration of this research by Lewis and Brooks-Gunn (1979) aimed to distinguish between contingent and non-contingent cues for self-recognition: is the child relying on the movement of the image or is she or he recognising her or his own features? The study involved three conditions: (1) self-contingent feedback, provided by immediate ('live') presentation of the filmed child on a television monitor; (2) self-non-contingent feedback, where the monitor showed a film of the child recorded on a separate occasion; (3) other non-contingent feedback, where another child of the same age and gender had been filmed previously. The difference in the child's reactions to the image in conditions (2) and (3), the self versus other noncontingent conditions, first became substantial at 21–24 months, implying that visual self-recognition based on features is only established at this age.

On the basis of these visual recognition studies, Lewis and Brooks-Gunn summarised the changes that occur in self-knowledge during this period in terms of a transition from the *existential* self to the *categorical* self (they subsequently revised this to a distinction between the 'I-self' and the 'me-self'). This implies that, for the older child, self-knowledge is beginning to be organised around categories (such as age or gender). This process of categorisation is facilitated by developments in language during this period, since verbal labels can be attached to the categories. Bertenthal and Fischer (1978) have found that, from about 24 months of age, a child is capable of responding with his or her name or with an appropriate personal pronoun when the mother points to the child's image in the mirror and asks, 'Who's that?' Kagan (1981) has found that the frequency of self-descriptive utterances and the use of words referring to psychological states increase towards the end of the second year. Utterances that accompany actions and refer to 'I', 'me', 'my', or the child's name are absent before 19 months but show a sharp increase at around 24 months. Psychological words such as 'want', 'hurt', 'feel' and 'think', first appear between 19 and 22 months.

There is evidence of a parallel development in another species, for example in a lowland gorilla, Koko, who was taught sign language at a young age and was closely observed as she grew up (Patterson and Cohn, 1994). Koko was taught sign language from the age of one year and was continuously exposed to spoken English. The ability to use and understand personal pronouns ('me', 'mine') and her own name emerged at 34–35 months. Koko also participated in a visual self-recognition experiment, and she exhibited self-directed behaviours to her mirror image from 42 months. The connection between visual self-recognition and the emergence of self-referent pronouns is seen in both human infants (by the end of the second year) and young gorillas (by the middle of the third year).

There are other similarities in the course of development. Koko began to use words referring to internal states, including emotion words like 'sorry', 'good', 'kiss', 'smile', and 'stupid', from 31 months. There was a rapid increase in their acquisition in the fourth year, again approximately one year later than her human counterparts. Koko also showed signs of embarrassment. On one occasion at the age of five she was signing to herself while playing with her dolls, but when she noticed that she was being watched she immediately stopped this activity and looked away. Around the age of six Koko began to make utterances that attributed an emotional state to someone else.

Self-evaluation

The acquisition of a categorical self together with developments in language converge to provide the child with the symbolic means cognitively to represent rules and standards and to evaluate his or her own ability to meet standards. During the second year the child begins to demonstrate awareness of adult standards for behaviour and to show signs that he or she is evaluating him- or herself relative to standards. At this age children become concerned with deviations from normative standards, pointing to a small hole in clothing, a missing button or a cracked toy (Kagan, 1981). Words referring to standards, such as 'bad', 'good', 'broken' or 'dirty', also appear in their vocabulary. Children's sense that things are 'bad' may be based on their anticipation of adults' reactions, since these flaws are the kinds of deviation from normal that an adult will disapprove of and comment upon.

There is also evidence of children's capacity for self-evaluation. Kagan (ibid.) has found that two-year-olds show signs of distress when they watch an adult demonstrate a difficult task. These signs first appear at 15 months, are infrequent before 18 months and reach a peak at around 24 months; this trend is interpreted as children's growing awareness of their inability to perform the task. Further support for the notion that self-evaluation and the attainment of standards play an increasing role in children's performance at this age comes from the observation that that they can be resistant to offers of help from an adult, determined to persevere and try to complete the task themselves. Furthermore smiles of mastery, which accompany the successful completion of a challenging task, emerge at around 18 months and reach a peak at around two years of age (these smiles are observed when the child is working alone, and the smile is not directed at anyone else).

However the pleasure manifested by the child might reflect her or his enjoyment of practising the activity or the satisfaction that is derived from exercising agency – doing it by her- or himself – rather than an indication that she or he has reached a certain standard. Furthermore the pleasure might be transient and have few implications for the child's self-concept. Stipek (1995) reports the findings of a project similar to that conducted by Kagan. There was little evidence that the rates of smiling were any different when an adult completed the task from when the child completed the task. This suggests that such smiles are expressions of pleasure rather than reflections of a sense of personal achievement.

Stipek has also found that children begin to look to adults for recognition of their achievements and to anticipate adult reactions to their success or failure from around 22 months. At this age children show characteristic bodily reactions to failure: looking away, avoiding eye contact and adopting a more closed posture. Evidence that self-evaluation is influenced by the nature of the task, which implies that children's reactions are related to their expectation of success or failure and not just to disappointment or frustration, is provided by Lewis et al. (1992). They found that, among a sample of children aged between 33 and 37 months, a pattern of gaze avoidance, body closure, turning down the corners of the mouth, and withdrawing from the task was more likely to be elicited by failure at an easy task than at a difficult task.

Pride and shame are emotions that typically accompany experiences of personal success and failure in older children and adults.

Several theorists have proposed that shame and embarrassment both emerge during the second year. Some evidence of this has emerged from visual self-recognition studies. According to Amsterdam and Levitt (1980), embarrassed, coy or shy responses to the mirror image emerge at 14 months and are evident in 75 per cent of children after the age of 20 months. Brooks-Gunn and Lewis (1984) report the same age trend in the children in the no-rouge (control) condition of their experiments. A parallel development is also evident in children who are coaxed by their mother or a researcher to dance for them; signs of embarrassment at having to do this are only shown by those children who show self-conscious-ness in response to their image in the mirror (Lewis *et al.*, 1989).

A similar age trend has been proposed for the emergence of shame. Amsterdam and Levitt (1980) argue that this emerges in the second year, when behaviours that until then have been pleasurable are proscribed by the mother/caregiver. The sudden change from positive to negative affect induces shame (we shall look at this par-ticular explanation of the origins of shame in Chapter 5). Specifically, the opportunities to explore the environment that are afforded by the child's greater locomotive ability bring him or her into contact with dangerous or otherwise forbidden objects, and the mother will react to this with disapproval or disgust. Similarly, pleasure in playing with the genitals, which can be observed from about six months in boys and 10 months in girls, becomes prohib-ited and masturbation becomes a secret activity for both sexes from about 18 months.

Schore (1998) also proposes that shame emerges at around 14–16 months and agrees with Amsterdam and Levitt that it is induced by the sudden inhibition of positive affect. However he provides an alternative account of this process, one that refers to the maturation of the nervous system during the first two years. Schore argues that early communication between mother and infant is sustained by the mother's facial expressions and the 'tuning' of her expressions with those of the infant. Her positive emotion produces excitement in the infant by altering the circulating levels of catecholamines and opi-oids, and this process plays a significant role in the growth of pre-frontal cortical and limbic brain structures. However during the sec-ond year the mother's role changes from an entirely supportive one to a more controlling one. Her disapproval of, say, her child's mas-turbation is shown in her facial expression, and this in turn leads to 'misattunement', which produces the sudden, unanticipated removal of positive affect. Schore suggests that this experience of shame is mediated by parasympathetic activity that inhibits excitement and slows down heart rate, and argues that this requires a state of development of the frontal region of the cortex that is not in place until the second year. Thus according to this theory, shame results from an interaction between socialisation practices and maturation of the brain and central nervous system.

Awareness of other perspectives

It is not clear whether the above developments in self-awareness are in themselves sufficient to produce the painful self-consciousness of shyness, embarrassment or shame. Other theorists argue that this involves a shift in perspective taking so that not only does the child feel that he or she is not reaching a standard but is seeing him- or herself as if through the eyes of another. For example Tangney *et al.* (1996, p. 1257) write: 'In shame, the self is both agent and object of observation and disapproval, as shortcomings of the defective self are exposed before an internalised observing "other".' In their account of embarrassment, Semin and Manstead (1981) make a distinction between the self-image and the 'subjective public image'. They argue that an emotional reaction is produced by an individual's awareness of a discrepancy between the two images occasioned by the recognition that some action unfairly reflects poorly on his or her subjective public image. The kind of thinking involved in this form of self-awareness is complex and presumably demands a level of cognitive development that has not been reached by the end of the second year. Stipek (1995, p. 249) makes a similar point about the processes involved in children's self-evaluation. She argues that these develop through a series of stages, from their simple pleasure in their ability to produce changes in the environment, to looking to the adult for his or her reactions to their performance, and to their internalisation of adults' standards, so that these will influence the children even in the adults' absence.

Lewis (1995) approaches this issue by distinguishing between *exposed emotions*, which depend on the kind of self-consciousness that can be seen in two-year-old children's emotional reactions to their mirror image, and *self-conscious evaluative emotions*, which appear from the third year. Embarrassment is an example of both types, and Lewis distinguishes two types of this emotion. The first, which Lewis (ibid., p. 211) suggests is closer to shyness, requires

Figure 4.1 Example of smiling with gaze aversion in an infant

Infant (11 weeks, 6 days) interacting with Self in mirror, carried by Mother

Intent gaze to self; brows raised.

Smile starts; cheek raise.

Smile widens, eyes and head
turned up and left

Smile widest; eyes and head
further averted

A shy or coy smile can be elicited in infants as young as two months by a greeting from a familiar adult or when they see their mirror image. It is typically accompanied by an ambivalent pattern of looking and looking away at the peak of the smile (Reddy, 2000).

only self-consciousness and can occur whenever one is simply conspicuous, finds oneself the focus of attention, or is praised or complimented – it is not related to negative evaluation of the self by others. The second type does involve self-evaluation of behaviour relative to standards and is closer to the emotion of shame. According to this approach, early signs of coyness or embarrassment are different from later forms, and the difference is that the later form makes significant cognitive demands on the child, who has to be able to appreciate that his or her actions are subject to evaluation by another person. It is not enough for the child to know that there are standards for behaviour that are set by other people, that he or she is failing to reach these standards and that other people are aware of this failure. Rather the child has to view his or her own behaviour from another perspective.

A prerequisite for the capacity to do this is children's awareness that other people may have views that are different from their own. This emerges in the third year and has been studied under the rubric of 'theory of mind', research that was stimulated by the 'false belief' paradigm (Wimmer and Perner, 1983). An experiment is arranged as follows. Ann watches as Maxi, a puppet, puts away a bar of chocolate. After Maxi goes off his mother comes in and moves the bar of chocolate to a new place. Ann is then asked where Maxi will look when he returns – in the place where he put it or where it is now. Three-year-olds respond that Maxi will look in the new place, whereas by the age of five most children say that Maxi will look in the place where he originally put the chocolate, where he believes it to be. If Ann can answer the question correctly, this shows that she realises that Maxi's behaviour is guided by a belief that he holds, and that his belief is different from the knowledge that she has about the situation. The ability to think in these terms represents an important step in the growth of a child's social understanding, and possibly in the development of shyness.

The question arises of whether this ability is sufficient for the experience of self-conscious shyness, where the self is the focus of attention. If this state entails taking the perspective of another person, then Ann has to be aware that she can be the object of another's thoughts and that the other person can hold beliefs and attitudes about her that may be different from her own. Writers on shame imply that a further step is necessary, that is, the ashamed person takes a 'higher-order' perspective on the self. A man who realises that he is being observed as he rummages in an unattended handbag feels shame because he can imagine what his behaviour might look like. He does not have to share this evaluation – he might have a legitimate reason for doing so. It is not essential that that another person is actually present to see him or that the interpretation is attributed to anyone who is present. He compares this interpretation with his own understanding of the reason for his actions. In shame people do not have to speculate about what any particular individual thinks of them, rather they adopt the perspective of a 'generalised other'. This implies the capacity to coordinate different perspectives. The person can take a third-order perspective of events, that is, see him- or herself and the other participants as if from an outside viewpoint. (We often adopt this viewpoint in hindsight when we make an assessment of how we behaved in a particular situation, for example when we think about how shy we were on a first date or how we misinterpreted someone's action – we are like a character in our own story.) Selman (1980) argues that the ability to do this develops somewhat later than four years, at about the age of seven to eight years.

Perhaps shyness does not require this level of sophistication in perspective taking. The preoccupation in shyness differs from that of shame in that it involves adverse judgments of the self; also, these judgments are attributed to specific others who are present. For example Bronwen and Delyth are preoccupied with the adverse impression they think they are making on the others present. Bronwyn believes she is failing to live up to the expectation that she will be the 'life and soul' of the party, that her answers to questions are inadequate, that she is expected to be good in conversation, and that others keep looking at her. Delyth feels that nothing she says will be of interest to the other tennis players. Perhaps the capacity for this kind of self-evaluative thinking is attained prior to the ability to adopt a third-order perspective.

However we know scarcely anything about perspective taking, particularly the processes by which children become aware that other people have an attitude towards their character or conduct and they come to internalise that view. Children gain extensive experience of adult attitudes in the approval and disapproval that draw attention to the social value of their accomplishments, for example in toilet training. Not only do caregivers tell children what they ought to be able to do – 'I shouldn't have to remind you at your age' – they also tell them what other people will think of them – 'What will they think if you can't tell them you need the toilet?' or 'What will they say if you wet the bed?'. The children learn what distinguishes the acceptable from the unacceptable and also that what other people think is important. Furthermore the recognition that they do things that are evaluated by other people influences their view of themselves.

Developments through childhood

Self-image continues to change throughout the childhood years. The social world of children itself changes markedly and often rapidly during this period. Interactions with adults and other children outside the family expose the child to a wider social environment. The experience of school is also significant. Removed from the home and surrounded largely by strangers, children have to measure themselves against a range of unfamiliar tasks and all this takes place within a climate of evaluation. The child is compared with his or her peers and with the standards expected by the teacher. A significant proportion of the feedback that is provided by the teacher is negative. Comparisons are not simply in the scholastic domain – Harter (1990) has identified a number of different domains in early childhood: scholastic competence, athletic competence, social acceptance, physical appearance and behavioural conduct.

These changes in the demands and opportunities provided by the social world are accompanied by several broad developments in children's thinking about themselves. First, children tend to think of themselves increasingly in terms of psychological characteristics rather than in terms of their age, gender or physical characteristics. This trend is demonstrated in responses to tests that ask children to provide self-descriptions, to 'say who they are'. Second, children increasingly draw upon a trait vocabulary to describe themselves and other people. By the age of four they respond reliably to a measure of self-esteem (Harter, 1990).

Children also begin to adopt different kinds of explanation for their performance. They can attribute their success or failure to their own ability or effort, or they can attribute these outcomes to external factors such as the difficulty of the task. They realise that ability is highly valued by the school and is regarded by their peers as a positive attribute. Furthermore they realise the implications for the self-image of explanations couched in terms of ability and effort. Success that is attained despite little effort implies high ability whereas failure after an investment of effort implies low ability. Carol Dweck and her associates (for example, Mueller and Dweck, 1998) have investigated the consequences for children's attitudes and performance of their espousal of trait explanations for their behaviour. There are individual differences in children's tendency to adopt trait explanations. Some children regard ability as a fixed personal quality and hence they tend to approach tasks in terms of how diagnostic they are of their abilities, and avoid those that are difficult and would show them up. Other children regard their ability as an attribute that can be developed, so that they perceive difficult tasks in terms of the challenges they pose and they tend to persist even when they initially fail.

This combination of environmental demands, perceptions of how they are evaluated by parents, teachers and peers, and a tendency to think of themselves in trait terms sets the scene for children to form an image of themselves as social actors. They see themselves as children who are liked or disliked, popular or neglected, confident about meeting people or lacking in confidence. Individual differences in shyness do emerge in childhood and are correlated with measures of self-esteem. The significant correlation between measures of shyness and self-esteem that is found among adults is also evident among four-year-olds (Kemple, 1995). In one study, American children in the fourth to sixth grades who were nominated by their peers as shy had lower self-esteem than children who were not nominated as shy (Hymel *et al.*, 1993). Crozier (1995) found that in a sample of children aged between nine and 12 years, a self-report measure of shyness correlated significantly with Harter's measure of self-esteem across four of the five domains (the exception being behavioural conduct).

Studies of children's conceptions of shyness also show a growing relationship between shyness and evaluation of the self. During the course of individual interviews Crozier and Burnham (1990) asked children what shyness meant. There were clear age trends: the youngest children associated shyness with concern about meeting new people whereas older children also related it to being evaluated, and a strong element of embarrassment was apparent in the older children's responses. Younger and his associates used two tasks – a peer nomination procedure and a test of memory for information about hypothetical children – to examine developments in children's schemas for withdrawn behaviour. Children were asked to give their reasons for nominating classmates as withdrawn, and their answers were categorised as referring either to a child's shyness or to a child's rejection by others. Even the youngest (first grade) children were able to make a clear distinction between the two reasons for withdrawal (Younger and Daniels, 1992). Research using memory tasks (for example Younger and Piccinin, 1989) has shown clear age improvements in recall and recognition memory for descriptions of withdrawn behaviour.

Adolescence, in particular, is characterised by heightened self-consciousness. A number of theoretical positions have been adopted on the reasons for this, notably Erik Erikson's (1968) theory of personality development, which regards adolescence as a key stage in the formation of the individual's sense of identity (Reimer, 1996, provides a valuable overview of these theories). Here we outline some empirical findings to illustrate this surge in self-consciousness. Simmons et al. (1973) conducted interviews with a large sample of young people and their parents. They interviewed approximately two thousand young people aged between nine and 18 years. The sessions included self-rating scales assessing self-consciousness, self-esteem and the perceived stability of the self (a typical item measuring self-consciousness referred to nervousness about giving a talk in front of the class). Participants between 12 and 14 years exhibited higher self-consciousness, lower self-esteem and a less stable self-image; they were also more likely to believe that their parents, teachers and peers had an unfavourable view of them. Scores on the self-consciousness scale were close to zero among eight- and nine-year-olds, but they increased dramatically between the ages of nine and 14 and then reached a plateau.

Although these age trends imply the significance of puberty for changes in self-image, the scores were also influenced by the children's social environment, specifically the type of school attended. Thus twelve-year-old children who were in elementary school were more self-conscious than children of the same age who had moved on to high school; 43 per cent of those in high school had high scores in self-consciousness compared with 27 per cent in elementary school. Nor was this difference in self-consciousness simply due to reduced self-esteem in the new environment. Simmons et al. (1973) reported no differences between schools in self-image scores, and other evidence (Crozier et al., 1999) suggests that children can gain in self-esteem after the transition from junior school to high school.

The increase in self-consciousness has been demonstrated empirically by Tice et al. (1985). Their sample of participants, aged between seven and 35 years, participated in a computer game. In one exercise they were unobtrusively observed and in another the researcher stood just behind the players and watched their per-

formance. Children aged seven to 12 years improved their performance while being watched, whereas players over 14 years showed a
decrement; closer analysis of the older group's results showed that
those aged 14 to 19 performed most poorly of all.

Summary

Children's capacity for self-awareness and self-evaluation grows
rapidly from the second year. They become aware of the standards
of behaviour expected by others and they begin to internalise these.
We have summarised some evidence to suggest that caregivers are
alert to their children's social behaviour, react to it in different ways
and differ in their attitudes towards how children's social competence can be developed. Perhaps these factors set the scene for children to evaluate their own behaviour in terms of internalised standards for appropriate social behaviour, which they have picked up
from their caregivers' responses. They begin to form self-efficacy
beliefs about themselves as social actors that will shape their future
expectations about for social interaction.

We can interpret this process in terms of a dynamic interaction
among a number of factors. People's observations of their behaviour, its apparent effect on others and their responses to it, shape
their expectations about future social encounters. They draw upon
these expectations when deciding which social gatherings or groups
to join. These beliefs also influence the kinds of behaviour they
exhibit there, for example they adopt cautious and defensive styles.
Such styles will tend to produce less successful outcomes.
Individuals' experiences in these situations feed back into their
expectations and affect their beliefs about themselves. Self-appraisal
plays a key role in this process and individual differences in self-
evaluation may have a key role in influencing whether a child sets
up the kind of expectancy that leads to shyness, or an alternative
one that leads to greater social self-confidence.

Individuals may have a bias towards generating certain kinds of
expectations, because of either temperament or their early relationship with their parents, or because of the interaction between temperament and early relationships. The strongest evidence about the
nature of shyness in childhood comes from studies of inhibited temperament. Yet there is some way to go before we can chart the development of shyness from infancy to adulthood.

Chapter 5

Shyness and embarrassment

Shyness is not the only form of discomfort experienced in social situations. In this chapter we shall consider embarrassment, one of the most common reactions to social difficulties. There are several reasons for devoting attention to embarrassment in a book on shyness. First, it can be very difficult for people to distinguish between the two experiences, and many have wondered if there is in fact any real difference between shyness and embarrassment. For example most people are self-conscious about changing their clothes in the presence of others, but are they being shy or embarrassed? Are these just different words for describing the same psychological state? If they are different states, how can they be distinguished?

Second, the question of the relationship between shyness and embarrassment has presented challenges to psychological theories and a number of competing positions have emerged. Some influential approaches to social anxiety have offered explanations that can be applied to both shyness and embarrassment, for example the theories developed by Buss (1980) and Schlenker and Leary (1982). On the other hand, some theories of shyness have paid very little attention to embarrassment, for example those accounts of temperament that emphasise fear of the unfamiliar and anxiety about interaction with strangers. Psychological trait theories have tended to concentrate on shyness and have paid much less attention to the identification and measurement of any predisposition to embarrassment.

Two perspectives on embarrassment

In general terms there are two approaches to the analysis of embarrassment. The sociological perspective takes the social encounter as the unit of analysis and considers embarrassment as a disruption of the smooth running of an encounter. This way of thinking about embarrassment reflects the derivation of the word, which relates to notions of a barrier or an impediment. Disruptive events usually happen during social exchanges that have some reason to take place and where there is an incentive to continue, so that escaping the situation is not always an option. Therefore embarrassment obliges the participants to take some action to overcome their current difficulties and retrieve the situation.

The 'self-presentation' account of embarrassment offered by the American social psychologist Erving Goffman has been very influential. Goffman developed a framework not just for the analysis of the management of social encounters, but also for the investigation of people's attempts to create a good impression on others and to deal with any threats to that impression. Because this framework draws heavily on the theatre as a metaphor for social interaction processes, and analyses these processes in terms of actors, props and settings, front stage and backstage, it is often labelled a *dramaturgic* approach.

Goffman (1956) analysed embarrassment in terms of its function in facilitating the smooth running of encounters and explained it in terms of a breakdown in the presentation and acceptance of social identities, which, he argued, provide the basis for successful social interaction. Gross and Stone (1964) also define it in terms of a barrier to further participation in a social encounter that occurs because an individual's identity cannot be sustained in the prevailing circumstances.

From this perspective, embarrassment is not merely an unpleasant experience to be avoided, it also serves valuable social functions. It does this by providing a 'brake' to stop problematic social encounters before the problems become too serious. The penalty it provides for untoward behaviour is severe enough to restrain behaviour but not so harsh that it permanently incapacitates the person in terms of future involvement. A society where embarrassment was unknown would be a harsh place with few restraints on aggression; likewise an individual without the capacity for embarrassment would be unpleasant to know. Embarrassment also permits flexibility of social interaction since it enables individuals to move beyond rigid categories and allows them to test the boundaries of acceptable behaviour without excessive risk.

The second perspective focuses on the experience and behaviour of an individual who is facing a predicament. This perspective is the focus of this chapter, since this type of embarrassment is closer to the experience of shyness, although – as we shall argue below – it is essential to recognise the inherently social nature of such experiences. The flavour of this approach is captured in the definition offered by Miller (1996, p. 129): 'Embarrassment is the acute state of flustered, awkward, abashed chagrin that follows events that increase the threat of unwanted evaluations from real or imagined audiences.' One advantage of considering the individual's psychological reaction to embarrassment as well as its role in the management of encounters is that embarrassment has psychological consequences that cannot be understood solely in terms of the properties of any particular encounter. Although it seems to be merely a temporary interruption of events and is often even a source of humour, it can be an intensely unpleasant state and people are often strongly motivated to avoid it. This can have serious consequences for themselves and other people. For example many people are not sufficiently assertive about their rights, because of the potential embarrassment of coping with a conflict with a shopkeeper or official. Likewise many fail to seek the medical advice they need, particularly if this relates to more private parts of the body. Also, educating young people about sexual matters is widely regarded as crucial for tackling problems such as unwanted pregnancy and sexually transmitted diseases, yet it is a task surrounded by embarrassment and one that sometimes proves very difficult for parents or teachers to undertake. While writing this chapter I noticed two headlines in the press: 'Private Matters: Health issues you're too shy to talk about' (*The Mirror*, 2 October 1999); and 'Red-faced parents' course in sex talk', 'Parents who are too embarrassed to tell their children about the facts of life are to receive help from a pioneering course' (Mark Woods, *The Independent*, 2 October 1999).

Finally, the analysis of embarrassment is important for attempts to understand the nature of social phobia and the design of techniques to help people cope with or overcome their fears. The fear of being embarrassed is central to the anxieties expressed by many people suffering from this condition, and chronic blushing is a very common presenting problem among social phobics. We shall consider the relationship between embarrassment and blushing below, and examine their implications for social phobia in Chapter 6.

Causes of embarrassment

There have been several attempts to classify the enormous number of events that can induce embarrassment. Gross and Stone (1964) solicited recollections of embarrassing incidents from a sample of 880 students. They identified three types of embarrassing situation:

- *Inappropriate identity*, where the person fails to confirm the self-image that is presented, or fails to present the image that is required, for example someone wears the wrong colour tie at a formal dinner, or a professor makes a spelling error on the blackboard.
- *Loss of poise*, where the individual loses control of the 'props' and 'setting' that are required for effective performance; the countless examples of this include slips of the tongue, spilling drinks or stumbling over furniture, exposing the body, smiling when it is inappropriate to do so and laughing uncontrollably.
- *Disagreement over the definition of the situation*, where an erroneous assumption is made about the roles that are required or are being played, for example a student doctor fails to recognise a consultant physician on his rounds and patronises him as if he were a patient.

Further attempts at classification have been made, where large samples of people are questioned about a recent incident (Buss, 1980; Edelmann, 1987; Miller, 1992). A problem with soliciting recollections of incidents in this way is that people might tend to recall the more vivid events and hence the small embarrassments that are a feature of everyday social life might be underrepresented. Also, people try to cope with their embarrassment and attempt to remedy the situation by adopting various 'facework' strategies. These might not be reported if people focus on more dramatic events where these strategies were not attempted or are not be recalled because they were ineffective. In order to circumvent some of these limitations, Stonehouse and Miller (1994, described in Miller, 1996, pp. 50–70) invited a sample of individuals to keep a diary for several weeks. They asked them to note how often they were embarrassed during each week, and to describe the most recent incident. Virtually all the participants (94 per cent) claimed to have been embarrassed at some point during the week. Incidents were coded into categories.

Some consistency has emerged from such studies. In addition to the categories devised by Gross and Stone, further ones have been proposed. *Breaches of privacy* include revealing confidential information about yourself, being caught behaving in public as if you were in private, being an inadvertent witness to a private event, buying items of an intimate nature or participating in an interaction with sexual overtones. A typical example is the scene in the film *Annie Hall*, where Woody Allen attempts to buy an 'adult' magazine by placing it between two respectable journals before handing the bundle to the shop assistant, only for him to shout the name of the magazine across the shop to check its price with a colleague.

Being praised or congratulated is regularly identified as a source of embarrassment. This perhaps belongs to a more general category of being singled out for attention; thus simply walking across a room filled with people or across a stage at a prize-giving ceremony can be embarrassing even without any loss of poise. However, over-praise might be a distinct cause in its own right. For example we say that we spare someone's blushes by not praising them too much. 'Gwen' recalled receiving a 'student of the year' award on stage: 'I felt that the Principal made me out to be better than I actually am, and in front of all these people in the audience that I knew. When I eventually stepped on the stage to receive my prize I'm sure I was bright red and I was very hot. I was very, very embarrassed.'

Vicarious embarrassment occurs when an individual is embarrassed even though it is someone else who is, or is expected to be, embarrassed. This phenomenon has been submitted to empirical investigation. Miller (1987) studied it as an instance of *empathic* embarrassment. Empathy is the sharing of another person's emotion (in contrast to sympathy, where one feels a complementary emotion, such as feeling compassion for someone who is grieving rather than grieving with them). Perhaps you are embarrassed for someone else because you can imagine what it would feel like to be in his or her position. Miller predicted that greater familiarity with the embarrassed person (the 'actor') and more pronounced signs of the distress he or she was experiencing would make an onlooker's empathic embarrassment more likely. These would make the actor's situation more salient and thereby enhance the onlooker's capacity to imagine him- or herself in the actor's position.

This hypothesis was investigated in an experiment where an actor performed a series of embarrassing activities: singing, dancing and acting the part of a child throwing a tantrum. The observers were more embarrassed watching the actor's predicament than were those in a control situation who watched an actor perform innocuous tasks. Nevertheless there were no straightforward influences of prior acquaintance on the observers' rating of their own embarrassment. Also, although the observers rated themselves as embarrassed, they tended to be less embarrassed than the actors themselves, implying that empathic embarrassment is a milder form than that occasioned by performing the task.

There are individual differences in the tendency to feel embarrassed for someone else. Empathic embarrassment is generally more pronounced among women. This might be because they tend to be more susceptible to embarrassment, but also because they are good at identifying emotions in other people (Miller, 1995). Marcus and Miller (1999) also found that characteristics of the observer influenced the degree of empathic embarrassment experienced. They asked students to rate the embarrassment of their fellow students as they made classroom presentations and also their own embarrassment when it was their turn to be the speaker. It was found that ratings of empathic embarrassment were influenced predominantly by characteristics of the observer (39 per cent of variation in empathic embarrassment could be attributed to the observer, but only 8 per cent to characteristics of the speaker). More empathic embarrassment was reported by students who had been embarrassed by their own talk, although analysis revealed that this trend was not just a matter of greater general susceptibility to embarrassment. This finding may reflect the influence of familiarity with the task. Awareness of your own chagrin may make you more sensitive to that experienced by others when they perform the same task.

Of course in everyday life the onlooker is often connected in some way to the actor because of prior acquaintance or a shared social identity. It is hardly surprising when a mother is just as flustered if her child spills his or her drink over the host's furniture as she would have been if she had spilled it herself. Heider (1958) proposed the concept of a *cognitive unit* to apply to this extension of the self to other actors with whom the individual feels a sense of belonging. The formation of a cognitive unit is sensitive to its context (Ortony *et al.*, 1988, p. 78). If we are abroad we can become embarrassed about the behaviour of our compatriots, say, football supporters, if, as they often seem to be, they are involved in misbehaviour. Their behaviour reflects on us even though we do not know any of them personally and even if nobody else knows that we are their compatriots. Yet if we were at home these football supporters would not be part of our cognitive unit. We can form cognitive units about our forebears, and feel shame or embarrassment about their treatment of indigenous peoples or slaves, or their behaviour in wartime.

Empathic embarrassment is not the only form of vicarious embarrassment. For example 'Elin' was performing in a comedy produced by her local amateur dramatic group. The play involved a series of misunderstandings and mistaken identities; one of these called for Elin to appear in one scene in her underwear. The audience reacted with surprise and laughter when she came on stage, but there was also an element of embarrassment. Some will have been embarrassed *for* her as they could readily imagine their mortification if everyone were to see them in their underwear. However some will have been embarrassed *by* her, as they would be uncertain about how to respond appropriately and no one wanted to be seen to stare; her family might not have been able to look. Elin might have felt no discomfiture playing the scene, thinking of herself as an actress in costume; nevertheless the audience could still blush on her behalf. Embarrassment can 'spread' when a person's position creates a disturbance in a social situation and obliges others to take some form of remedial action, thereby creating a predicament for them.

The recording and classification of such situations provides a valuable step towards understanding embarrassment, but it is only a first step. For one thing, all social situations have meanings within a particular set of cultural conventions. This is particularly clear in the case of clothing and the difficulty of keeping it in place, which occupies a high position in any list of recalled incidents. Standards of propriety of dress vary across cultures, and in Western society they have changed enormously over a relatively short period of time.

Moreover lists do not inform us about the processes that give rise to embarrassment, nor do they permit tests of hypotheses about the causes or consequences of this emotion. Yet theories of the processes involved ought to be able to account for the kinds of situation where embarrassment is experienced and explain what distinguishes them from the kinds of situation where a different emotion is experienced. With this in mind, we shall consider the application of one general theory of social anxiety to the explanation of embarrassment and then consider two more specific accounts, one based on the dramaturgic approach and one that relies on the notion of threats to esteem.

Theories of embarrassment

Self-presentation theory

Schlenker and Leary's theory of social anxiety proposes that the anxiety experienced in a social situation is a function of two processes: the degree of motivation to create a desirable impression on other people and the subjective probability of being able to make that impression. These two processes are in a multiplicative relationship, in that higher scores for either will tend to increase the level of social anxiety. Conversely, if motivation is zero, or if the person feels certain of attaining his or her self-presentation goal, then there will be no social anxiety. A desired impression is not synonymous with 'making a good impression', but relates to the individual's self-presentation goals at any particular time. It might be enough to avoid creating a poor impression or even to remain unnoticed, the goal of many students when the teacher is looking for an answer to a question or seeking volunteers for an onerous chore!

The theory also encompasses embarrassment, although here it is less a matter of judging the likelihood of things going wrong in the future, since the predicament has already arisen to challenge the individual's self-presentation goals. As Leary and Kowalski (1995, p. 83) define it, embarrassment is '*reactive*, in that it is a response to a self-presentational failure that the person believes has already occurred' (emphasis in original). The theory predicts that embarrassment is more likely when the motivation to create a desired impression is more powerful. How embarrassment relates to the second component of the model – the subjective probability of creating a good impression – is less clear since the predicament has already risen. However these difficulties create a new situation for the individual since he or she has a new self-presentation goal, or a goal that has hitherto been dormant is activated, and anxiety might now be a function of the importance of reaching this new goal and the likelihood of achieving it.

Thus the sequence seems to be that some disruption of a social encounter has implications for the identity of the actor, and awareness of the discrepancy between this identity and the desired identity creates anxiety. The actor now faces a dilemma and her or his continuing anxiety will be influenced by the belief that she or he can achieve the desired identity, which may simply be that of a competent actor. It is an important feature of any response to a situation that it extends over time, and hence it may consist of a sequence of cognitions and physiological changes. To label it 'embarrassment' or to suggest that it is invariably accompanied by overt responses (smiling, avoidance of eye contact) and physiological reactions (high arousal) is to neglect this important aspect.

Could embarrassment be predicted in advance if the individual's standing on the two parameters of the self-presentation theory were known? A problem with making predictions is that embarrassing events are by their very nature sudden and unforeseen. Nevertheless it is possible to contrive situations in the laboratory so that embarrassment is likely to ensue. For example Edelmann and Hampson (1979) arranged for a confederate to ask participants to give their opinions on a set of paintings, after which he unexpectedly announced that he was the artist of a picture that had been criticised. In a post-experiment questionnaire 15 of the 22 participants reported embarrassment at this revelation and subsequent analysis of videotapes of their behaviour revealed that their reported embarrassment was accompanied by avoidance of eye contact and increases in speech errors and body movements. Manipulation of self-presentation goals by means of descriptions of the setting and instruction or judicious selection of participants for an experiment along these lines should enable predictions of the model to be tested.

One of the strengths of self-presentation theories has been their attention to how people try to manage their embarrassment. Goffman introduced the concept of *facework*, defined in terms of the strategies used to cope with difficulties. Two broad strategies can be distinguished: *preventive practices*, where the actor takes some action to avert threats to identity; and *corrective practices*, where remedial action is taken after a disruption. Thus a doctor forestalls embarrassment by adopting a good 'bedside manner' – friendly but distant, interested but objective – and uses technical terms to refer to parts of the body. The patient tries to suppress any signs of embarrassment, and the doctor tactfully ignores these, or perhaps gives the impression that he or she has interpreted them as anxiety or slight pain.

Detailed taxonomies of self-presentation practices have been offered (see for example Shepperd and Arkin, 1990). Particular attention has been paid to apologies, excuses and justifications (Semin and Manstead, 1983) as each of these can play a key role in repairing an encounter that has gone awry. For example a person who apologises for his or her behaviour is recognising that rules of social conduct have been infringed, that these rules are valuable and ought not be broken, and that he or she takes responsibility for his or her part in this and expresses remorse. If the apology seems sincere and is commensurate with any harm that has been caused, it helps the individual to reestablish identity and also assists the other participants get the encounter on course again. It is incumbent on the others to accept the apology either explicitly, or implicitly by reaffirming the individual's identity in the situation.

Alternatively an actor can offer an excuse or a justification for her or his conduct. In making an excuse she or he admits that a transgression has taken place but minimises her or his responsibility for it: 'I did not let you know I was going to be late because I couldn't get to a phone'. In offering a justification she or he accepts responsibility but plays down the transgression: 'I didn't let you know I was going to be late but we are still in time for the show'.

Humour can also prove an effective way of managing an awkward situation. Smiling and laughter are frequent reactions of onlookers, and the embarrassed individual can take advantage of the potential for humour to cope with the predicament. It is not known whether the effectiveness of humour depends on the nature of the predicament, the characteristics of the person or the wittiness of the joke. It might work in various ways, by filling the embarrassed gap in the encounter, by shifting the focus of attention by introducing a fresh topic or train of thought, or by inducing somatic changes, as spontaneous laughter may involve physiological processes incompatible with embarrassment.

There are empirical studies of facework practices. Semin and Manstead (1982) found that a target person who knocked over a pile of cans in a supermarket was regarded more favourably if signs of embarrassment were shown. A survey of students' responses to predicaments (Miller, 1996, p. 173) indicated that the most common were evasion (28 per cent), making amends (17 per cent) humour (17 per cent) and an apology (14 per cent). Escapes, excuses, aggressive acts and justifications comprised fewer than 10 per cent of accounts.

Self-presentation theory provides a framework for understanding social anxiety in all its facets and it facilitates the integration of findings from many research studies. It assumes that embarrassment is a form of anxiety, but there are some difficulties with this as the physiological concomitants of embarrassment are not always associated with anxiety and some embarrassing situations seem to pose little threat to the individual's self-presentational goals. However these create problems for other theories as well, so further discussion will be postponed until they have been introduced.

Esteem theories

Some explanations emphasise the implications of the predicament for the individual's esteem, either in his or her own eyes or in the eyes of others. Modigliani (1971) proposes that embarrassment is produced by a temporary, situation-specific loss of self-esteem that results from a failure in self-presentation. Babcock (1988, p. 459) also relates embarrassment to self-esteem, arguing that it ensues 'when an individual finds herself acting in a way that is inconsistent with her *persona* or conception of herself'. The individual fails to live up to her own standards; embarrassment is not produced by a preoccupation with failure to meet the expectations of others.

There are difficulties with this explanation when accounting for embarrassment caused by conspicuousness, overpraise or when the individual is congratulated or complimented. The explanation also has difficulty accounting for empathic embarrassment. Furthermore an individual's persona is tied to particular social contexts, and hence what other people think must be important. Behaviour that is appropriate in one set of circumstances can be embarrassing in another, for example realising that your priest has heard you make a risqué joke, or being seen by your teacher when you are dressed up for a night club. School sports days are a rich source of embarrassment for children whose parents visit the school, when there can be a clash between their identity in the eyes of their parents and that in the eyes of their peers. These predicaments seem to belong to the category of 'inappropriate identity' rather than of low self-esteem. Finally, it is not clear from this theory how embarrassment is to be distinguished from, say, a feeling of disappointment, since this too accompanies our sense of failing to act in accordance with our personal standards and does not involve any preoccupation with what an audience might think.

The emphasis on self-esteem runs counter to the majority of esteem theories, which emphasise a discrepancy between the self-image and the image one wishes to present. The self-presentation theory of embarrassment (Leary and Kowalski, 1995) emphasises the discrepancy between performance and standards and assigns a central role to the possibility of being negatively evaluated by others.

Semin and Manstead (1981) point out that because many disruptions of role performance are accidental and outside the actor's control, they have no implications for the actor's self-image. However actors also have a sense of how they are seen by others, their *subjective public image*, and Semin and Manstead argue that it is a discrepancy between their self-image and the subjective public image that produces embarrassment. Castelfranchi and Poggi (1990, p. 238) offer the example of a man who has saved a woman from drowning and is giving her mouth-to-mouth respiration when he realises that he is being observed by a passer-by. He becomes aware that it might look to the other person as if he is taking advantage of the woman and he feels ashamed. He knows he has nothing to be ashamed about but appreciates that his subjective public image is a negative one. He has acted in good faith; what creates his predicament is the presence of the spectator. Nor is it necessary that the passer-by actually holds an adverse view of the actor's behaviour. What is critical is the actor's recognition and endorsement of the fact that his conduct *can* be seen in a negative light.

On the face of it, these explanations have difficulty accounting for embarrassment arising in incidents where there do not seem to be any implications for the individual actor's esteem, for example where the actor is conspicuous or is an observer of someone else's plight. Can they explain those situations where both self-esteem and public esteem are high, as when someone is complimented, congratulated or the recipient of a prize? Or those where public esteem is high but self-esteem is not, as in the case of overpraise? An adherent to the self-esteem position could argue that being conspicuous invariably makes you aware of your failure to meet personal standards, since most people fail to do this most of the time, and being conspicuous highlights this non-fulfilment. Receiving excessive praise can also make this discrepancy salient. It also raises the possibility that the individual may have deceived others into a view of him- or herself that is undeserved, a deceit that is incompatible with personal standards.

Theories that emphasise loss of esteem in the eyes of others can refer to the person's anxiety about creating a desired impression, since being conspicuous or receiving excessive praise influence the subjective probability of achieving this goal and also increase the cost of failure to do so. To be conspicuous is to run a greater risk of negative evaluation. Being overpraised increases the likelihood that one will fall short of the standards expected by others (inevitably so, because one knows that the praise is excessive).

Dramaturgic theory

Silver *et al.* (1987) argue that a more parsimonious explanation of these causes of embarrassment is available. Their approach is strongly influenced by Goffman's dramaturgic account, with its emphasis on a disruption that occurs because the consensus on the identities of the actors has been broken. In their view 'Embarrassment is the flustering caused by the perception that a flubbed (botched, fumbled) performance, a working consensus of identities, cannot, or in any event will not, be repaired in time' (ibid., p. 58). This account does not require that the embarrassed person has brought about the botched performance, or that this is the responsibility of anyone present, since the disruptive event can be purely accidental. It also highlights the difficulty of restoring the working consensus, and one of the features of embarrassment is that it results in an individual being uncertain about what to do next, unable to carry on a role.

Certainly many embarrassing incidents involve being at a loss for what to say or do. I recall walking along a path that runs beside the large windows of the ground-floor classrooms of my school when I absentmindedly kicked at a stone on the path. It flew up and struck a window, and the teacher and the whole class turned to look at me. I could not think of anything to do to extricate myself from the situation, my behaviour was simply inexplicable, and I hurried away, feeling – and no doubt looking – very foolish.

The dramaturgic account can explain well-established features of embarrassment, for example it suggests that the reason why precipitating incidents are often sudden and unexpected is that it is more difficult to find an appropriate part to play when there is little time to think about it. The theory can also be applied to many of the cases that trouble esteem theories. Thus praise can be embarrassing because it is difficult to know how to respond to a eulogy, particularly if the recipient is conscious that a modest response is called for. The winner of a competition, whether sporting, political or literary, should not look too pleased and should express regret at the outcome for the defeated rival, often a difficult act to bring off – punching the air when your opponent's backhand lets her down is 'bad form'.

The case of vicarious embarrassment is problematic for esteem theories unless they extend the notion of a cognitive unit to cover *any* relationship, however tenuous, with the person who is facing the predicament. It is not a problem for the dramaturgic account since this defines embarrassment in terms of the *perception* of a botched performance, but this raises a different problem in that it explains too much. Do you need to be present in order to be embarrassed by someone's predicament, could you experience it simply by reading about it in a book? Presumably it is possible to describe an event so vividly that the reader does feel embarrassed (and I suspect that this is usually a matter of empathy), although most people seem to find descriptions of embarrassing incidents humorous. Such incidents are the stock-in-trade of situation comedy. We laugh at someone who slips on a banana skin, more so if the victim is a dignitary or pompous person, but in real life we are obliged to suppress our laughter while we help the victim to get up.

However in most instances of vicarious embarrassment the observer does participate in some way, even if it is only as an inconspicuous member of a large audience, and the outright failure of a performance might place the observer in the difficult position of knowing what to do next.

Comparing theories

There have been attempts to assess the relative merits of these theories. In one study Parrott and Smith (1991) requested each participant to provide a description of a typical embarrassing incident and one of an actual embarrassing incident. Each resident was rated on a set of items. These items were intended to be representative of five theories: dramaturgic, self-presentation/social anxiety, situational self-esteem, personal standards and shame. Whereas typical incidents received high ratings on all five sets of items, showing that each theory captures something of people's common-sense notion of embarrassment, the dramaturgic and self-presentation/social anxiety items were more characteristic of participants' accounts of actual embarrassing incidents than the other three sets of items.

It is difficult to test the dramaturgic and esteem theories directly against each other because in many situations they cannot be disentangled, since situations where you are flustered and uncertain about what to do often lead you to believe that you will be evaluated negatively by others. Parrott *et al.* (1988) arranged a clever experiment to try to disentangle situational self-esteem and the effect of the disruption of an encounter. They made use of a *pretext*, that is, a fictitious reason for an action that is given to conceal the real reason in order to spare the feelings of the recipient – for example a woman declines a date by explaining that she is washing her hair that evening. The researchers presented the participants with three versions of a story in which Fred asks Jane for a date. In the 'credible pretext' condition Jane says that she does not date co-workers; in the 'transparent pretext' condition she gives the same reason, but Fred knows that this is not true; in the 'no pretext' condition she simply declines the invitation.

The prediction is that the credible pretext allows Fred to maintain his self-esteem and also enables the encounter to proceed. The transparent pretext poses a threat to his self-esteem but it does allow the interaction to proceed without disruption. The straightforward rejection is a blow to his self-esteem and also makes it difficult for both parties to know what to do to continue the conversation. If embarrassment is produced by a loss of self-esteem then the credible pretext should produce less embarrassment than either the transparent or no-pretext condition. On the other hand, if disruption is the cause of embarrassment, the transparent and credible pretexts should be comparable since neither pretext disrupts the encounter. It was found that ratings of embarrassment were significantly larger in the no-pretext condition relative to the two pretext conditions. These did not differ from each other, thus supporting the dramaturgic hypothesis.

Yet all three scenarios were rated as at least moderately embarrassing, and even the credible pretext condition attracted a mean rating of 3.39 on a seven-point scale of embarrassment, implying that there was some degree of situational self-esteem in the students' assessment of the situation. Miller (1996) extended the design of this experiment to include a condition where the message declining the invitation was not given directly by the woman but was brought by a messenger. The messenger's view of whether the refusal was transparent or genuine could also be manipulated into different versions of the story. Box 5.1 provides a summary of the

Box 5.1   Design of an experiment to compare esteem and dramaturgic theories of embarrassment

Amy brings Bill a message from Anne, turning down his invitation. There are four conditions: Amy either believes the reason given for the rejection is genuine or she knows it is false (an excuse); Bill believes the reason to be either genuine or false.

	Amy believes Anne's reason for declining date is genuine	Amy believes Anne's reason is an excuse	
Bill believes Anne's reason is genuine	(A) Low	(B) Low	Threat to Bill's esteem
	Smooth	Awkward	Interaction
Bill believes it is an excuse	(C) High	(D) High	Threat to Bill's esteem
	Smooth	Awkward	Interaction

Source: Based on the design of the study reported by Miller (1996).

design of the study, the implications of each condition for the target person's self-esteem and the potential awkwardness of the encounter between him and the messenger. Miller found that there was more embarrassment when the social encounter was more awkward (scenarios B and D), but the greatest embarrassment was reported when the date was declined without a credible pretext, whatever the beliefs of the messenger (C and D). These results offer support to both models, although they imply that a threat to self-esteem is the more potent source of embarrassment. Nevertheless, clever as these studies undoubtedly are, they do involve ratings of hypothetical situations and it remains to be seen which model is more successful in predicting actual cases of embarrassment.

Embarrassed reactions

We now turn to the nature of responses to embarrassing incidents. As in the case of shyness, it is useful to think of these in terms of cognitive, behavioural and somatic responses. This section briefly considers cognitive and behavioural reactions. The subsequent section concentrates on blushing, because this remains little understood and it may have a role in shyness as well.

As implied in our description of embarrassing incidents, cognitions accompanying embarrassment are feeling surprised, flustered, awkward, uncomfortable and nervous. Nevertheless self-consciousness is at the heart of the experience of embarrassment, just as it is for shyness. Buss (1980) argues that embarrassment starts with acute public self-awareness, and Semin and Manstead (1981) and Edelmann (1987) see *individuation* (awareness of being the focus of others' attention) as the crucial link in the chain between disruption of a routine event and embarrassment. There is empirical evidence for this. In the study by Parrott and Smith (1991) outlined above, a substantial proportion of the participants rated actual embarrassing incidents as involving 'being the centre of attention', 'feeling the centre of attention', 'everyone noticed', 'desire less attention', 'subjected to ridicule, humiliation, or laughter' and 'worry what others think'. Of course such concerns are often exaggerated and we are less the object of scrutiny than we imagine.

On one occasion, when I was thinking about this chapter, I was travelling on a crowded train in Manchester. Sitting alongside me were three students who were talking about their experience of sharing accommodation. One was being teased about her untidy habits and she forcefully rejected the accusation. However the effectiveness of her denial was undermined by a very embarrassed smile. She looked downwards and away and I also noticed that she brought her hand up to her face and began to rub with her index finger a place just between her eyebrows, effectively covering her face. Likewise 'Heini' recalls the time when her shoe fell off her foot and landed on the track between the platform and the train: 'When I told the guard I remember repeating how sorry I was to have caused so much trouble and how embarrassed I felt. I'm sure I blushed and I definitely put my hands up to my face in an attempt to cover it up and I screwed my face up behind my hands.'

These are examples of an *emotional display*, a pattern of facial expressions, gestures and posture that typically accompanies an emotion. Such displays have been carefully analysed and classified. Ekman and his research team carried out cross-cultural studies that resulted in an 'atlas' of the emotions (Ekman and Friesen, 1978). The expression of emotion is governed by *display rules* and modified by the attempts of individuals to control the expression of their feelings. The spontaneous expression of strong emotion tends to be met with disapproval and when it does happen, for example in the case of grief, it can be embarrassing to others. Young children are encouraged to moderate their displays of emotion. For these reasons the expression of emotion can vary among individuals, across situations and across cultures with different display rule systems (Asendorpf, 1990a, provides a thorough analysis of these issues for shyness and embarrassment).

Embarrassment does seem to have a distinctive emotional display, including gaze aversion, touching or covering the face, smiling and a stiff posture (Keltner and Buswell, 1997, p. 254). Blushing is not included as reddening of the face is not unique to embarrassment and occurs with other emotions, such as anger. The prototype of embarrassment based on the ratings of typical incidents reported by Parrott and Smith (1991) includes redness of the face, perspiring, gaze aversion, hiding the face, a lowered head, a nervous laugh or smile and fidgeting. In cross-cultural survey of embarrassment Edelmann (1990a) reports the incidence of various overt signs in Britain and five other countries (Greece, Italy, Japan, Spain and Germany). The frequency of the signs mentioned by British respondents was blushing, 55 per cent; averted gaze, 41 per cent; smiling, 37 per cent; laughing, 19 per cent; and touching the face, 16 per cent. Overall there was considerable consistency among countries in the frequency of these signs, although there was more blushing, looking away and touching the face in Britain compared with the other five countries.

These reactions have also been examined in natural settings and in the laboratory. For example in the study by Edelmann and Hampson (1979) discussed above, when the interviewer suddenly announced that he was the artist of the criticised painting the subjects made more body movements, had more speech disturbances and looked less at the interviewer. According to Asendorpf (1990a), embarrassed smiles can be distinguished from non-embarrassed smiles. He carried out a detailed analysis of the smiles that had been videotaped during a social encounter arranged to include incidents likely to provoke embarrassment. Smiles were coded using the

Facial Action Coding System (Ekman and Friesen, 1978) to identify the facial muscles involved. Smiles that were judged as embarrassed could be distinguished on the basis of the timing of gaze aversion. This occurred one to one-and-a-half seconds before the apex ends (the apex of a smile is defined as that part of a smile when the corners of the mouth are pulled up to the maximum, that is, when the smile is at its most intense). This contrasts with smiles judged as not embarrassed, where gaze aversion typically occurs immediately after the apex finishes.

Keltner (1995) also carried out a detailed analysis of responses to embarrassment using the Facial Action Coding System. She identified a sequence of events lasting some five seconds after an embarrassing event: (1) gaze aversion, (2) smile control, (3) a non-Duchenne smile, (4) a second smile control, (5) head turned down and (6) touching of the face. (A non-Duchenne smile is not a full smile and only involves the major muscle action that pulls the corners of the lips upwards.) This pattern of smiling is quite distinct from a smile of amusement.

One problem with the identification of a specific display is that embarrassment can coincide with other emotions. Since predicaments typically arise when they are not expected, embarrassed reactions can be accompanied by expressions of surprise or dismay. This is perhaps one reason why a sudden loss of poise can give rise to a shriek of laughter. It might also explain the frequent occurrence of smiling in embarrassment.

The identification of a facial display that is distinctive of an emotional reaction is of interest for a number of reasons. First, distinctive facial expressions have provided a basis for taxonomies of the basic emotions, thus the identification of a characteristic display provides support for the notion that embarrassment is a distinct emotion. It also raises questions about the functions of this display. Why does embarrassment produce this specific pattern of reactions? One answer to this question is that the display functions as a signal, more specifically a signal of appeasement.

Embarrassment and appeasement

Keltner and Buswell (1997) argue that the display of emotion in embarrassment operates as a sign of appeasement. They offer several lines of argument. Different species have quite distinct appeasement displays and many of these involve behaviours that have some resemblance to the human display of embarrassment: gaze avoidance, turning and lowering the head, a smile-like grimace and a submissive posture that makes the animal look smaller. The situations that give rise to these displays are similar across species, for example encounters with individuals of higher social rank, or else they are equivalent, for example the threat of physical aggression in non-human species and the threat to identity and self-esteem among humans. The outcomes can be similar too. In non-humans the appeasement display placates the dominant individual and diverts attention away from the submissive one. In humans, blushing can embarrass others or cause them to look away (Leary and Kowalski, 1995, p. 155). Finally, the display serves a similar function across species by contributing to the restoration of social relationships after some form of disruption or some change in circumstances that needs to be accommodated.

This account has the advantage of offering a plausible integration of evidence about the causes and functions of embarrassment and the facial expressions and posture changes that accompany it. Nevertheless the role of blushing in Keltner and Buswell's account is uncertain. Although reddening of the bottom can form part of an appeasement or sexual display in other species there seems to be no non-human counterpart of reddening of the face. Furthermore the implications of those circumstances where blushing is unwanted need to be examined.

There are different causes of embarrassment – inappropriate identity, loss of poise and so on – and there are various unwanted interpretations of a person's conduct (one is seen as brazen, boorish, incompetent, insensitive or undignified), but it is not known whether these elicit different emotional displays or types of reaction. One can speculate that the risk of appearing boorish or thoughtless might elicit an apology, that looking foolish might lead to laughter, and that seeming immodest might lead to blushing. There is evidence of differences in reaction tendencies. Cupach and Metts (1990) have found that humour is most likely after an incident involving loss of poise or control, whereas apologies are more likely after the violation of a rule. However there are exceptions. Humour is possible even with a rule violation; 'Rhodri' might be able to interject something funny about his tactless relative that will diffuse embarrassment (see p. 168). These findings raise the question of whether there is a single emotional display that is elicited whenever embarrassment is experienced or whether different elements are evoked in different circumstances, and what is the contribution of display rules to this.

I recently observed a quite different emotional display when joining the 'express' queue in a supermarket. A woman in front of me (on her lunch break from work, judging by her black suit and tights) was queuing to pay for a personal item. She had gone red in the face. Whenever she looked around her she made no eye contact with anyone, and her eyes were often cast down. She had a serious, tight-lipped expression. Eventually she handed the item to the woman assistant without smiling or looking at her. Although she blushed she did not exhibit the nervous smile or other facial signs of embarrassment. It is possible that she was experiencing a different emotion, for example shame. Perhaps it is relevant that she was on her own and not interacting with anyone. However her predicament can be analysed in terms of the impression she feared she was making. She was not at risk of seeming foolish, and no element of surprise or a *faux pas* was involved. Her embarrassment related to being exposed and to a breach of privacy of the body, and this gives rise to the notion that there are different displays for different threats to identity. We shall consider this in the context of blushing.

Blushing

'This is one of the occasions when one could do with being married,' said Treece with a bright smile to one of the girls, the enthusiastic Miss Winterbottom. 'Can I help?' asked Miss Winterbottom. The man with the beard burst into fresh laughter. 'I mean, like getting something from the kitchen,' went on Miss Winterbottom, blushing to a full shade of red (Malcolm Bradbury, *Eating People is Wrong*, 1978, p. 82).

Blushing is a very common response to situations that create social discomfort, particularly when the person makes an unintentional gaffe like the eager Miss Winterbottom. Buss (1980) regards the blush as the hallmark of embarrassment, nevertheless there is considerable disagreement about its involvement in the self-conscious emotions. Keltner and Buswell (1997) do not consider it an essential part of the distinctive embarrassment display on a number of grounds. It occurs significantly later than the rest of the display – some 15–20 seconds after the trigger event, in comparison with the five seconds or so taken by the pattern of gaze aversion → smile control → smile. One can be embarrassed without blushing, and reddening occurs with other emotions as well. On the other hand, gaze aversion and an embarrassed smile often accompany a blush. Buss (1980) and Edelmann (1987) argue that blushing characterises embarrassment but not shame. However a number of studies have found that shame does involve blushing (for example Keltner and Harker, 1998, p. 78). Furthermore research participants have reported that they blush when they are shy. When describing a situation where she felt shy, 'Eleri' wrote: 'I was feeling a bit shaky, hot and could feel my face having a permanent blush. The pressure of everyone's eyes penetrating, as if into my body, was overpowering at specific moments'.

A substantial proportion of the respondents to the Stanford shyness survey reported that blushing was part of their shyness (Zimbardo *et al.*, 1974). In an investigation of children's conceptions of shyness Crozier (1995) provided children with a target word or phrase, and asked them to write down the first things that came into their mind. Both 'blushing' and 'going red' were frequent responses to the target phrase 'being shy'. Crozier (1999) interviewed a sample of adults about the effect that shyness had had on their adjustment to university. Content analysis of the interview protocols revealed frequent mentions of blushing, particularly when respondents reported feeling self-conscious.

Notwithstanding these findings, there is only limited evidence that blushing is a typical reaction to shyness, whereas there is a substantial amount of evidence that it is characteristic of embarrassment. In the cross-cultural study reported by Edelmann (1990a), blushing was frequently mentioned as a symptom of embarrassment; this ranged from 21 per cent of Spanish respondents to 55 per cent of British respondents. A rise in body temperature was also mentioned, ranging from 4 per cent (Italy) to 25 per cent (Spain).

In addition to these controversies, there are two problematic aspects of blushing: its relationship to anxiety, and its visibility in social situations where drawing attention to oneself is unwanted.

Physiology of blushing

Blushing and the associated rise in skin temperature are caused by an increased blood flow to the subcutaneous capillaries, which lie close under the skin in the face, ears, neck and upper part of the chest. An essentially hairless species such as ours relies heavily on the circulation of blood close to the skin, particularly in the case of the face, hands and feet, in order to adapt to changes in environmental temperature. This flow of blood is regulated by centres in the hypothalamus responsible for the control of body temperature. When the body temperature rises, for example as a result of physical exertion, the capillaries are opened (a process called vasodilation) and a larger volume of blood is moved close to the surface of the skin, allowing cooling of the blood and consequently a reduction in body temperature. When the body temperature needs to rise the capillaries are narrowed by a process of vasoconstriction, and less blood travels close to the skin. The face may be the prime site for reddening because it has a greater density of capillaries below the skin and the skin is thinner than at other sites. Also, there is a greater density of beta-adrenergic receptors in the facial veins, the significance of which we shall consider below.

The neurobiological mechanisms involved in blushing are as yet little understood. The picture is complicated by the fact that reddening of the face has a number of different causes, including the influence of alcohol and other drugs, menopausal 'hot flushes' and certain tumours. About 50 per cent of women undergoing the menopause suffer from flushes, and this is associated with higher blood flow and greater vasodilation following mental or physical exertion (Stein and Bouwer, 1997). It is also simplistic to imply that there is only one form of blushing. Leary and Kowalski (1995, p. 150) distinguish between the *classic* or *embarrassed blush* and the *creeping blush*. The latter spreads slowly, over a period of perhaps several minutes, and is 'blotchy' rather than an overall reddening. I have noticed that some people engaging in a conspicuous activity, for example leading an academic seminar or working with equipment in front of an audience, begin with no signs of reddening but over a period of twenty minutes or so a blush gradually creeps up from the neck. However there seems to be no research into the circumstances in which each type of blush occurs.

Changes in skin colour and temperature, and their role in embarrassment, were demonstrated in an experiment reported by Shearn *et al.* (1990). The participants watched either a videotape intended to induce embarrassment (a recording of themselves singing 'Star Spangled Banner') or a control videotape (the shower murder scene from Hitchcock's film *Psycho*, which would elicit a clear autonomic response, but not one of embarrassment). These recordings were watched in the presence of other people. Several physiological meas-ures were taken. Skin colour was measured by means of photo-plethysmograph probes attached to the cheek and ear, a thermome-ter recorded skin temperature and skin resistance was measured by means of electrodes attached to the fingers. Redness of cheek and ear as well as measures of skin conductance were significantly greater in the condition expected to induce blushing. There were changes in facial temperature but this tended to depend on the gender of par-ticipants. Women showed a large increase in temperature, whereas the increase among men was small relative to the no-blush condition.

A detailed analysis of the time course of reactions showed that visual signs of blushing, as assessed by the ability of observers to detect it in a video recording of the participant's face, coincided with the peak of measured colouration but not with maximum facial temperature; this occurred a few seconds later. Shearn *et al.* (ibid, p. 691) speculated, 'We suspect that the perception of one's own blushing is the detection of a rise in facial temperature, and not the more immediate blood flow or volume responses, which are scarcely detectable. If this is so, then others will see our blushing before we detect it. The perception of one's own blushing may, of course, occasion further blushing.'

This distinctive pattern of reactions causes problems for those theories of embarrassment which assume that it is a form of social anxiety since it appears to be a reaction to social difficulties associ-ated with self-consciousness but is *not* associated with heightened arousal mediated by the sympathetic nervous system. Vasodilation is a function of parasympathetic nervous system activity. In the clas-sic fear reaction, vasoconstriction occurs as blood is diverted to those muscles where it is most needed for action of one kind or another. Blushing tends to be associated with a reduction in heart rate in embarrassing situations (Keltner and Buswell, 1997) imply-ing inhibited sympathetic and increased parasympathetic nervous system activity. Stein and Bouwer (1997), also make the point that lower heart rate and blood pressure accompany blushing. However Cutlip and Leary (1993) argue that when an embarrassing event is *unexpected* there tends to be an increase in heart rate and blood pres-sure whereas this increase has not been found to occur when an embarrassing incident is anticipated.

Some research suggests that blushing may be mediated by sym-pathetic rather than parasympathetic activity. Sympathetic arousal of beta-adrenergic receptors can produce vasodilation, and there is a high density of these receptors in the facial veins. Although the release of norepinephrine elicits a vasoconstrictive effect, at lower levels it can also elicit a vasodilation effect. Some of the implications of these physiological findings have been studied empirically. Drummond (1989) reports that blushing in response to an embarrassing situation can be detected in individuals who have a lesion in the sympathetic pathway to the face, but such blushing only occurs in the unaffected region of the face, not in the damaged region, where blushing is inhibited. Drummond (1997) has examined the effects of blocking beta-adrenergic receptors in the blood vessels on one side of the forehead by means of local administration of an antagonistic drug (propranolol; the effect of the drug is temporary, lasting less than one hour). The participants were selected on the basis of their scores in a blushing propensity questionnaire and they undertook two tasks: singing 'Old MacDonald had a Farm' with suitable animal noises, and performing a mental arithmetic exercise under stressful conditions. The results are not straightforward to interpret. Nevertheless the drug inhibited (although it did not prevent) increased blood flow during the singing condition. This occurred whether the participants had a high tendency to blush ('blushers') or little tendency ('non-blushers'). It inhibited increases in blood flow during the mental arithmetic exercise in the group of non-blushers, although the blushers did show an increase during this exercise. Blocking the beta-adrenergic receptors had no effect on blood flow responses in two further conditions: an intensive workout on an exercise bicycle, and being subject to heat treatment.

These findings show that the causes of blushing are complex and imply that there is a small, but detectable, effect of sympathetic activity on blushing. Of course peripheral measures of nervous system activity are 'noisy'. They are affected by the limitations of measurement devices and subject to many influences, including temporary fluctuations of mood and other physiological states of the participants. Furthermore our conception of blushing is itself imprecise and our common-sense notion of blushing (and embarrassment) may reflect various psychological states, never mind patterns of physiological reaction. Individual differences in the meaning of situations are a further complicating factor, for example Shearn *et al.* (1990) note that one participant in their experiment sang the American national anthem without any sign of blushing and she turned out to be an accomplished singer, experienced in performing in public.

Nevertheless it is clear that blushing is not simply an anxious response. It seems to involve a mixture of sympathetic and parasympathetic activity. Clearly there is much more to be learned about blushing, for example whether the two kinds of autonomic reactivity are related to different kinds of eliciting situation or to different patterns of reaction. It is possible that the timing of reactions is crucial. The type of event that creates a predicament for the individual might begin to elicit an aroused or sympathetic reaction, but this is interrupted by increased parasympathetic activity while a decision is reached about the appropriate action to take. Embarrassing incidents might not directly evoke a complete programme for a flight or fight response. This is compatible with the notion that embarrassment entails uncertainty about what to do next in circumstances that are potentially threatening to the individual's identity but do not signal a risk of physical attack.

Unfortunately the parasympathetic system has been much less studied than the sympathetic system, and there exists no body of research comparable to that devoted to fear and anxiety.

Blushing and conspicuousness

A second problem for theories of blushing is that colouring of the face makes the individual conspicuous. Other elements in the display of embarrassment – gaze avoidance, smile control and lowering the head – seem to be related to concealment rather than drawing attention, and people in embarrassing situations often wish that they were not the objects of others' attention. Indeed drawing attention to him- or herself can be the last thing the embarrassed person wants as this can intensify his or her embarrassment. An example of this comes from the time when I was a student on a developmental psychology course, part of which was concerned with the topic of sexual development. We were a very large class, and when the lecturer devoted part of a session to discussing masturbation some of us could see Stephen, a friend from our old school, turning bright red, and afterwards he was teased a lot about this. I am not sure why he did blush. He was probably not the only one to do so, since in those less enlightened times this was not a topic that young men had heard discussed in a serious way, and they had never heard it mentioned in front of hundreds of young women. Of course it had been a topic of endless fascination at our boys' school, with much teasing, name calling and tricking boys into blushing. Also, Stephen had the very clear complexion that makes a blush highly visible.

Whatever the reason, his red face produced the very outcome he would have wished to avoid at almost any cost, since it gave the impression of guilt. His awareness that he might be seen in this way would in itself have intensified his discomfort and deepened his blush. This episode involved embarrassment at the public airing of a topic that was seen as taboo. Mention of such topics is usually a source of blushing, indeed it can be incumbent on an individual to show signs of modesty on such occasions, especially people whose social position or role is incompatible with any reference to a taboo topic in company.

Nevertheless disclosure can be of more personal or idiosyncratic information. In *Your Lover Just Called* (1980 pp. 23–4), John Updike describes a couple who are holding a rather tense 'post-mortem' on a party they have attended. Richard had danced throughout the party, not with his wife but with another woman, Marlene. He makes fun of his wife for the attention he claims she had paid to another man. She ripostes: '"You're too absurd," she said ... "You're not subtle. You think you can match me up with another man so you can swirl off with Marlene with a free conscience." Her reading of his strategy so correctly made his face burn.' Richard blushes because his gambit to deflect attention from his conduct has turned out to be transparent. He could, of course, try to deny the allegation, but the blush makes it very difficult for him to do so. If he had not blushed, it would surely have been easier for him to sustain his strategy. We learn from the continuation of Updike's narrative that Richard attempts to escape from his predicament by making a joke of the situation. However his attempt at humour falls flat, and only makes matters worse – 'Plunged fathoms deep in the wrong, his face suffocated with warmth, he concentrated on the highway and sullenly steered.'

Elizabeth Gaskell provides another literary example in *Ruth* (1853/1967). The heroine has given birth to an illegitimate son and has been abandoned by the father (a scandal for a respectable woman at the time – the mid 1800s). She keeps the circumstances of the birth a secret and claims to be a widow. Thereafter any reference, however oblique, to her marital status or to the age of her child causes her to blush.

This notion that blushing is associated with the threat of disclosure is compatible with the self-presentation theory of social anxiety. Cutlip and Leary (1993) argue that blushing occurs when the individual finds him- or herself the object of undesired social attention. The notion that any scrutiny is unwanted is not intended to imply that the secret is concerned with anything blameworthy. For example a young woman might not wish it to be known that she is engaged to be married or is pregnant even though she is happy and excited about this event, but simply because she does not believe that the time or place is propitious for sharing this 'news'. Not only will she colour if someone asks her outright, she may blush at any reference to weddings or motherhood.

This hypothesis contrasts with the classic view expressed by Darwin in his seminal account of blushing. Although he argued that self-attention elicits blushing, he went on to emphasise the adverse judgment potentially made by others: 'Whenever we know, or suppose, that others are depreciating our personal appearance, our attention is strongly drawn toward ourselves, more specifically to our faces ... whenever we know, or imagine, that any one is blaming, though in silence, our actions, thoughts, or character; and, again, when we are highly praised' (Darwin, 1872/1965, p. 344). He qualifies this emphasis on negative evaluation by including praise as a cause of blushing.

Blushing as communication

We have noted in our discussion of embarrassment that people can be embarrassed even if they are not responsible for the disruption to a social encounter and it is parsimonious to assume that this holds for blushing as well.

This does not explain why the desire to keep a secret is associated with a reaction that makes it more likely that the individual will be the object of attention or why it occurs alongside an embarrassed display aimed at making the individual less conspicuous. Castelfranchi and Poggi (1990) argue in answer to this question that blushing is not merely expressive, but also has a communicative function. More specifically, an individual is signaling to others that she or he is sensitive to their judgments, shares their values and is apologising for her or his role in bringing about the awkwardness. It does seem to be the case that blushing is an effective response in many situations. It can serve to diffuse an aggressive reaction to your conduct – if, say, you have made a rude or insensitive remark or bumped into someone – by indicating that you did not do this deliberately. It can head off an erroneous judgment about your character. On the other hand, if you do not blush you may be seen as thoughtless, or even brazen or shameless (*Roget's Thesaurus* gives 'unblushing' as an alternative to brazen, shameless, impenitent and unabashed).

One objection to this interpretation of blushing is that it is an involuntary response and its onset cannot be consciously controlled. Therefore it could not be an element of a self-presentation strategy, since the concept of strategy implies something deliberate, the selection of one action over another in pursuit of a goal. Although the blush might be similar to offering an apology or excuse in its *effects*, it differs from these in the matter of the actor's control. However Castelfranchi and Poggi (ibid.) take a contrary stance, and argue that its involuntary nature makes it a particularly effective gesture of appeasement; since a blush cannot be conjured up at will, it is more likely to be judged as sincere. (I suspect that if actors blush on stage it is because they have been successful in feeling themselves into the part and the situation – they are experiencing the emotion and the blush comes with the emotion. On the other hand they could simply learn the head and eye movements and posture that will make them appear abashed or embarrassed whenever they wanted.) In comparison, lowering the head and casting down the eyes can be just a formal acknowledgement of shame where no genuine emotion is experienced, or it can be the wily act of an unscrupulous person who is prepared to manipulate the reactions of others.

There remains the issue of the intentionality of blushing. It is advantageous for 'Rhodri' to blush when his elderly relative makes loud remarks about other diners in the restaurant. By acknowledging to them that he recognises that his companion's behaviour is rude, that the lapse is unintentional and that he is sorry if this has embarrassed them, he can begin to reassert his claim to be well mannered. It is also beneficial for the others present, as his reaction assures them that he shares their values about acceptable conduct and this allows them to interpret the person's conduct in a way that requires no remedial action on their part. But although his blush reaps all these benefits it hardly makes sense to say that Rhodri *means* to send the signal. Indeed people's self-presentation goals are often attained more effectively if they hide their embarrassment or shame, in these circumstances their blush can give them away. Stephen's experience in the lecture room is one example, but there are many others. If you are falsely accused of some misdemeanour you will not want to blush when you are defending yourself against the charge; if you wish to keep a secret, then you should not blush at every allusion to it. Likewise people are often reluctant to show signs of the fear they are feeling, but the shakiness of their voice or their body movements give them away. Indeed signs of fear might act as signals in particular circumstances, to a mother to protect her frightened child, or a nurse to reassure an anxious patient. The fact that these signs produce benefits does not mean that they are expressed in order to communicate. Castelfranchi and Poggi (ibid., p. 246) address this issue:

> Of course, the communicative goals we listed probably are not intentional in the expression of shame, nor, perhaps, are they interpreted by a receiver on a completely conscious level; in fact they might not be represented at all in [their] individual minds. Yet they function as subgoals to some social and biological functions, that is, to some advantages for the group and for the individual.

In these terms, blushing does serve a communicative function, whether or not an individual intends it to do so. Questions remain as to whether it invariably does so, or even whether there are different kinds of blush.

The predicament of the woman in the supermarket queue, discussed earlier, shares features with our other examples of instances of blushing. When Miss Winterbottom accepted Treece's 'proposal', Stephen heard mention of masturbation, Richard's motive was exposed and Ruth's 'marriage' was alluded to:

- The person is the object of attention.
- Something normally hidden is revealed or brought into the open.
- This is connected to sexual activity or private parts of the body.
- A hidden motive is inferred or alluded to.
- It is difficult for the person to know how to cope with the exposure.

Such circumstances might not be the only triggers of blushing but they characterise many of the situations where it occurs. One can speculate about the physiological processes that accompany this state. The person is aroused but no action is called for: he or she is 'barred'. This state might produce a balance of the sympathetic and parasympathetic systems, but one that is maintained at a higher level of reactivity than a resting state and requires a continuing process of adjustment.

There is a need to discover which factors have causal properties. Are revelations of a secret or allusion to sexual matters merely instances of unwanted attention, or are they fundamental to the blush? Many of the situations in which blushing occurs have sexual connotations (some children blush if they are asked if they have a boyfriend or girlfriend). One explanation of this is that shame becomes associated with sexual pleasure when the child is forbidden to touch the genitals (Amsterdam and Levitt, 1980). Even if this particular explanation is not found to be convincing, it is plausible that socialisation pressures link shame and embarrassment (and hence blushing) with public references to sexual activities. These activities are only one example of the kinds of thing one can be ashamed about.

However in an evolutionary context the blush might not be a sign of shame. It may have originally been a sexual display, perhaps an individual signaling to another person that he or she was aware of being an object of sexual interest. This display has subsequently become associated with occasions on which the individual is conspicuous or the object of attention, is admired or praised, or is uncertain how to act. This would imply that the connection between shame and blushing is that prohibition of sexual activity associates shame with the sexual blush, not sex with the blush of shame. This account is frankly speculative, although it might be open to empirical examination since it implies that members of societies with few inhibitions about sexual activities will blush when they are admired or complimented but not when they are ashamed.

We now turn more directly to the question of the relationship between shyness and embarrassment. One approach considers these as emotional experiences, as reactions to specific social events. A second approach considers whether trait shyness is related to a predisposition to embarrassment.

Embarrassment and shyness

Differential emotions

Whether shyness and embarrassment are different emotions is con-troversial, but there is very little direct evidence on the issue. A number of theorists stress their similarity. We shall first consider the contribution of Silvan Tomkins, a 'grand theorist' in the tradition of Freud and Piaget. His work has been neglected, in large part because he devoted his working life to the production of a four-vol-ume, densely-written exposition of his theory (the final two vol-umes were published shortly after his death in 1991), rather than publishing in the academic journals. He is also distinctive in his argument that the face is the site of the emotions.

Tomkins proposed that a small number of primary affects consti-tute the major motives of human behaviour. He argued that these affects are first and foremost facial behaviours and that awareness of affect is based on awareness of these facial responses. This is a radically different approach from most theories of emotion, which, as we have seen in the case of fear and anxiety, emphasise visceral responses and overt behaviour. Shame–humiliation is one of the pri-mary affects (although Tomkins also described it as an *affect auxil-iary* because it arises in the context of other affects, namely interest-excitement and enjoyment–joy). Shame has a distinct facial display involving lowering the head and eyes, and blushing. According to Tomkins (1963, p. 133):

> Shame turns the attention of the self and others away from other objects to this most visible residence of self [the face], increases its vis-ibility and thereby generates the torment of self-consciousness.... Blushing of the face in shame is a consequence of, as well as a further cause for, heightened self- and face-consciousness.

Shame is first experienced when there is an obstacle to the full expression of interest or joy. Shyness, shame and embarrassment are identical as *affects*. They 'feel' different because the same affect is evoked by different circumstances and produces different conse-quences: 'Shame is experienced as shyness when one wishes to be intimate with the other but also feels some impediment to *immediate* intimacy. That impediment may be located either in the self, the other, or in the dyad, or in a third party who intrudes' (Tomkins, 1995, p. 404, emphasis in original).

The child's excitement and happiness are impeded by the strangeness of the other, whether this is the strange behaviour of the mother who begins to socialise her child, apparently withdrawing the love that was hitherto given unconditionally. They can also be interrupted by the arrival of a strange person. The shyness experienced by a daughter upon the return of her father from war duties to a family which has developed its own routines without him provides a clear example of this effect of the strangeness of another on the child's happiness (see Chapter 1). More prosaically, a child can become shy if a parent brings home a work colleague or comes home with a new hairstyle.

Although Tomkins' theory is not widely known, it has influenced Carroll Izard's differential emotions theory (see for example Abe and Izard, 1999). This, too, proposes that there is a small set of fundamental, discrete emotions, and that these emotions have three components: a neurophysiological component; a distinctive pattern of expressive behaviour, including facial responses; and an experiential quality. Izard draws upon evidence from studies of facial expression to determine the set of fundamental emotions. Shame–humiliation is expressed in wrinkling of the forehead, the inner corners of eyebrows are drawn down, there is lowering of the eyes or glancing, the lips are drawn in and the corners of the mouth depressed, and the head is lowered. These expressions are characteristic of shame, shyness and embarrassment, and were visible in the woman in the supermarket queue. However there are phenomenological differences between these emotions.

Theories that adopt a cognitive approach to the classification of fundamental emotions tend to emphasise the similarities between shame and embarrassment and neglect shyness. Discrepancy theory (Higgins, 1987) proposes that emotions can be distinguished on the basis of the type of discrepancy that exists between the individual's self-concept and his or her standards of behaviour. Discrepancies can be classified in terms of the domain of the self (the actual self, the ideal-self and the ought-self) and the perspective that is taken on the self. Shame and embarrassment are conceived of as dejection-related emotions contingent upon a discrepancy between one's actual self and the ideal state that some significant other hopes that one will attain. People believe that they have lost esteem in the eyes of others.

Ortony *et al.* (1988) classify shame and embarrassment as 'self-reproach' emotions; both involve the person's disapproval of his or her own conduct. Both are intensified by public awareness of this conduct. Embarrassment often coexists with shame because the breach of a standard often leaves the individual uncertain about what to do next in the situation. Also, the inability to respond suitably can lower the person's esteem in the eyes of others.

An analysis of emotions undertaken by Scherer (1984) reveals that shame and embarrassment are similar in important respects; they are both responses to unpleasant or obstructive situations, where the person is unable to cope because of lack of control or low self-confidence, and where the person's own behaviour is central. The difference between them is that shame is reactive, that is, it follows an action, and it involves a failure of that action to conform to social norms. Embarrassment is both reactive and anticipatory: an event has happened and the person is uncertain what to do next. This uncertainty is associated with lack of self-confidence and difficulty in defining the role requirements of the situation.

Alternative positions are taken by theorists who specialise in the 'self-conscious emotions'. They emphasise the differences between shame and embarrassment, and some argue that embarrassment is a fundamental emotion in its own right (Keltner and Buswell, 1996; Miller, 1996). Miller argues that it meets all the criteria for identification as a basic emotion:

- Quick onset.
- Brief duration.
- Involuntary.
- Relatively automatic appraisal process.
- Universal antecedent events.
- Distinctive physiological responses.
- Distinctive emotional display.
- Found in other species.

However the question of interest here is whether it is also a discrete emotion, distinct on these criteria from shyness. Research has tended to concentrate on distinguishing embarrassment from shame, and less attention has been paid to the shyness–embarrassment distinction. According to Crozier (1990) they are similar in that each entails self-consciousness, uncertainty about what to say or do, and lack of self-confidence. There are also quantitative differences between them: shyness is rated as less unpleasant and more passive and individuals believe it is unlikely that they could have acted differently. In their study Mosher and White (1981) found that shyness and embarrassment attracted different descriptions. Embarrassing incidents were rated high in shame, surprise and anger, whereas those that elicited shyness were rated as high in interest and fear. Shyness was found to be closer to embarrassment than to shame, a finding replicated by Tangney *et al.* (1996).

Nevertheless empirical studies of ratings of situations that elicit shyness or embarrassment cannot establish that they are separate emotions, however large the differences in ratings. These descriptions are influenced by common-sense conceptions of the two emotions, and these may or may not be a valid guide to the underlying processes. The question can only be decided by the construction and testing of theories that specify the processes that take place between characteristics of situations and emotional responses. The current theories are not specified in detail and there remains uncertainty, for example, about the contribution of the sympathetic and parasympathetic nervous systems to these emotions.

Correlates of blushing and embarrassability

An alternative approach is to consider whether individual differences in shyness are associated with a greater tendency to experience embarrassment. Research has examined the relationship between blushing propensity and the subscales of the self-consciousness scale (SCS) (Fenigstein *et al.*, 1975). Several studies have shown that social anxiety is significantly correlated with blushing propensity but the relationship with the two self-consciousness subscales is at best moderate. This pattern has been found among samples of chronic blushers (Edelmann, 1990a, 1991) and among samples drawn from a broader population (Bögels, *et al.*, 1996; Crozier and Russell, 1992; Leary and Meadows, 1991). Bögels *et al.* (1996) have also found that social anxiety is correlated with a measure of fear of blushing.

Modigliani (1968) constructed an embarrassability scale (MES) as a measure of individual differences in the susceptibility to experience embarrassment. The 22 items refer to situations that commonly elicit this reaction and respondents rate how embarrassed they would be in each situation. Edelmann (1985) reported that scores on the MES correlated with the SCS subscales social anxiety and public self-consciousness but not with the private subscale. Miller (1995) distributed the MES, the Cheek–Buss shyness scale, the SCS, the interaction anxiousness scale and self-report measures of sensitivity to social evaluation, social skill, self-esteem and positive and negative affect to a sample of 310 students. Embarrassability was significantly correlated with shyness but the moderate size of this coefficient ($r = 0.37$) implies that they are distinct scales. Factor analysis of the scales showed that shyness and embarrassability were represented on different factors. Shyness was represented by a factor that could be interpreted in terms of social self-confidence; other scales on this factor were social anxiety, low self-esteem and poor skills in social discourse, self-presentation and interpreting non-verbal signals. Embarrassability was represented by a factor labelled 'social evaluation', which permeated scales measuring fear of negative evaluation, sensitivity to the appropriateness of behaviour, motivation to avoid social rejection, motivation to be approved by others and public self-consciousness.

In summary, shyness is most closely associated with a lack of social self-confidence, expressed in low self-esteem in social situations and concern about lack of social skills. Shy people lack confidence about their ability to know what to say to people or how to manage a social situation. This is much more important for their shyness than fear of being negatively evaluated by others, although this is obviously also a concern. People who are prone to embarrassment are highly sensitive to social norms of conduct, and are concerned about the appropriateness of their behaviour and whether it will lead to being rejected or disapproved by others. Concerns about social skills are much less salient.

Thus there is an overlap between shyness and susceptibility to embarrassment. Self-consciousness and concerns about self-presentation are common to both. Nevertheless the constructs differ. The shy person focuses on a perceived lack of social competence, whereas the embarrassed person focuses on the rewards and punishments afforded by situations. It is tempting to construe these emphases in terms of the *self-presentation equation*. Social anxiety is high for the shy person because his or her confidence about attaining goals is relatively low; it is high for the embarrassed person because the motivation is relatively high. Nevertheless it should not be forgotten that both elements of the equation are needed: the shy person is motivated to create a desired impression and the embarrassed person lacks confidence, even if this lack of confidence is perhaps more rooted in the properties of social situations than in low self-esteem.

Shyness might also elicit embarrassment, either by producing some form of difficulty in the situation, such as lengthy silences, or because the shy person is ashamed of his or her shyness. Therefore a shy person's reactions to a social situation might include a mixture of emotions. I have found support for this in a content analysis of students' recollections of situations where they were shy, as their descriptions included terms related to embarrassment as well as shyness (Crozier, 1999).

Summary

Embarrassment is a common form of psychological discomfort in everyday social situations. Despite its ubiquity, its investigation has uncovered many puzzles, and it remains problematic at the psychological and physiological levels. Events happen to interrupt the smooth running of a social performance. They give rise to an unpleasant emotional experience. Although people normally go to great lengths to avoid embarrassment, it is often associated with humour and laughter. Embarrassing incidents are a frequent source of jokes, whether in everyday social situations or in comedy. A common theme in research is that, like shyness, it results from a threat to social identity. However the notion of identity has to be extended to situations where embarrassment is caused by someone else's discomposure and there seems to be no threat to the observer's self-esteem. Many people in a situation can experience embarrassment and it can spread, as in the example given earlier in this chapter of Elin's performance.

Embarrassment and shyness share many features. Self-consciousness is common to both. They also involve uncertainty about how to behave; however with embarrassment the focus is on the difficulty of meeting the demands made by the specific situation, whereas with shyness it is on the individual's sense of his or her own abilities. Research into this relationship has found that measures of shyness, public self-consciousness and embarrassability are correlated with each other, but there do seem to be distinct factors involved. Once more, shyness is more closely linked to a sense of personal inadequacy.

Embarrassment seems to have a distinctive emotional display, one that seems quite different from the visible signs of anxiety. There is dispute as to whether it is an emotion in its own right or simply a form of anxiety that is experienced in social situations. If it is distinct, this raises questions about the status of shyness. Does it belong with embarrassment or with anxiety? In Chapter 4 we noted that some writers have postulated two forms of shyness (Buss, 1980), two sources of shyness (Asendorpf, 1989) and two forms of embarrassment (Lewis, 1995). In each case, one form or eliciting situation relates more closely to self-consciousness and to the individual's concern about how he or she is perceived by others. Further research needs to consider the nature of this duality.

Blushing remains a puzzle. At the physiological level it seems to involve activity by both branches of the autonomic nervous system. It cannot be controlled, and awareness that one is blushing maintains the blush. Simply being told that one is doing so may be sufficient to induce a blush. It makes people conspicuous in situations where they do not want to be the centre of attention. Most researchers agree that it is a sign of embarrassment, but it is not induced by all embarrassing situations and it is reported as an element of shyness and shame. Some have disputed that blushing is experienced in shame. There is little evidence of this, but it would be stretching credulity to believe that Shakespeare was describing embarrassment in the following scene from Richard III (Act I, Scene II), where Lady Anne addresses Gloucester who has murdered her father and her husband:

If thou delight to view thy heinous deeds,
Behold this pattern of thy butcheries.
O, gentlemen, see, see! Dead Henry's wounds
Open their congeal'd mouths and bleed afresh.
Blush, blush, thou lump of foul deformity,
For 'tis thy presence that exhales this blood
From cold and empty veins where no blood dwells;

The embarrassed person runs the risk of being seen in a poor light. However there are several forms of unwanted social image and a range of circumstances in which discomfiture can arise. Future research could examine whether this variation gives rise to different cognitions or to distinct emotional displays.

Chapter 6

Overcoming social anxiety

This chapter examines some approaches to help people overcome their problems with shyness and social anxiety. The examination is based on our conception of shyness as comprising a number of components: lack of self-confidence; feelings of self-consciousness, anxiety and embarrassability; reticence; and difficulty dealing with social situations. Before we introduce these approaches we shall consider the notion that shyness is in fact something that ought to be overcome. There are several problematic issues. Some derive from continuing uncertainty about the definition of shyness and the value of the construct for identifying a category of people who have much in common with one another, while others draw upon scepticism about medical approaches to psychological conditions. Several positions can be identified:

- People are often shy in the same way as they are often flustered, sad or angry, and they have no more reason to overcome their shyness than to overcome these other states of mind.
- Shyness is the norm. Contemporary social life is complex, overly individualistic or alienating, and many of the certainties previously provided by clearly defined status and role have been eroded – 'not being shy' is a mythical state.
- Everybody is shy; if 'shy' people have a problem at all, it is that they are simply too self-absorbed.
- Shyness is a personality trait that is a stable, possibly innate characteristic of an individual, therefore it cannot be 'overcome'.
- Many of the problems of daily living have been appropriated by a self-seeking medical establishment and turned into an 'illness'; shyness is simply another example of this process.

- Shyness has positive qualities that should be respected not derogated by making the assumption that shy people have to change – people say they want to overcome their shyness but they are pressured into this belief by the prevalence of the myth of 'not being shy', and by the marketing expertise of the medical profession and pharmaceutical companies that have a self-serving interest in fostering this attitude.
- Shyness is too imprecise a concept to form the basis of any effective intervention.

I think it is important to establish at the outset that many individuals do have severe problems with facing social situations. They often describe these problems as 'crippling' or a 'nightmare' and refer to them as having restricted their life in distressing ways, for example they are unable to retain employment because of the emotional exhaustion of summoning the effort to travel to their workplace every day by public transport. Furthermore, many people only realise that their problem is shared by others or even has a name when they encounter discussion of shyness in the media. It may well be that the label they attach to their problem is one that also refers to experiences that most people have, or at least some of the time. Furthermore the situations that cause their problems are also difficult for many other people. In these circumstances the label 'shyness' is only a rough guide to the social anxieties that are experienced. Many of those who do not experience the severe problems faced by such individuals nevertheless believe that they too have a problem with social situations since they use the term 'shyness' to describe themselves. However, even if the difficulties experienced by most people are relatively trivial, this should not be a reason to ignore the problems faced by the minority who do face social situations with dread.

It is also arguable that psychologists have been unsuccessful in developing robust concepts or an adequate framework for understanding these kinds of difficulty. Imprecise concepts lead to confusion and hinder attempts to find effective interventions to help people with their problems. Nevertheless the difficulty of grasping these issues should not form a basis for claiming that severe social anxieties are not meaningful or that people should not or cannot be helped with suitable forms of treatment.

It is easy to go along with these claims if one accepts arguments such as those vigorously put forward by Michelle Cottle in an article with the provocative title 'Selling Shyness: How doctors and drug companies create the "social phobia" epidemic', which appeared in the journal *The New Republic* in August 1999. In this article she argues that researchers exaggerate the incidence of social phobia in the general population when they claim that it is a disorder that will affect one in eight Americans at some time in their life. She claims that the magnitude of the incidence of this disorder is a consequence of adjustments that have been made to its definition, so that it no longer applies to a small number of individuals with extreme problems but refers to a much broader range of social anxieties that are widely shared in the general population. She further argues that these definitions are not scientifically neutral but are influenced by an acquisitive medical establishment, which includes clinicians, researchers and pharmaceutical companies. As a consequence of this, she continues, the large number of people who have anxieties about meeting new people, attending social gatherings and so on come to believe that medication will provide an answer to their problems.

This line of argument is not specific to shyness or social phobia, and similar positions have been advocated with reference to a range of psychological conditions as diverse as depression and dyslexia. The 'medical model' of psychological states and conditions has been heavily criticised for a number of years. However Cottle does raise issues that are problematic for research into shyness. Her article poses two questions. First, what is the relationship between shyness construed as a temperament or personality trait, shyness as an emotional reaction to social situations, and social phobia as a diagnostic category? Second, is social phobia a medical matter, appropriate for treatment by pharmaceutical techniques? Before we try to address these questions we need to look at the concept of social phobia and its relationship with shyness.

Social phobia and shyness

Box 6.1 sets out diagnostic criteria for social phobia published by the American Psychiatric Association (1994, p. 416). The first criterion refers to a range of fears about social situations – unfamiliar situations, being scrutinised by others, appearing anxious to others and acting in a way that will be humiliating or embarrassing. These fears are persistent and are recognised by the individual as 'unreasonable'. As it stands, this description does not seem

Box 6.1   Diagnostic criteria for social phobia

A. A marked and persistent fear of one or more social or performance situations in which the person is exposed to unfamiliar people or to possible scrutiny by others. The individual fears that he or she will act in a way (or show anxiety symptoms) that will be humiliating or embarrassing. **Note:** In children, there must be evidence of the capacity for age-appropriate social relationships with familiar people and the anxiety must occur in peer settings, not just in interactions with adults.

B. Exposure to the feared social situation almost invariably provokes anxiety, which may take the form of a situationally bound or situationally predisposed Panic Attack. **Note:** In children, the anxiety may be expressed by crying, tantrums, freezing, or shrinking from social situations with unfamiliar people.

C. The person recognizes that the fear is excessive or unreasonable. **Note:** In children, this feature may be absent.

D. The feared social or performance situations are avoided or else endured with intense anxiety or distress.

E. The avoidance, anxious anticipation, or distress in the feared social or performance situation(s) interferes significantly with the person's normal routine, occupational (academic) functioning, or social activities or relationships, or there is marked distress about having the phobia.

F. In individuals under age 18 years, the duration is at least six months.

G. The fear or avoidance is not due to the direct physiological effects of a substance (e.g., a drug of abuse, a medication) or a general medical condition and is not better accounted for by another medical disorder (e.g., Panic Disorder With or Without Agoraphobia, Separation Anxiety Disorder, Body Dysmorphic Disorder, a Pervasive Developmental Disorder, or Schizoid Personality Disorder).

H. If a general medical condition or another medical condition is present, the fear in Criterion A is unrelated to it, e.g., the fear is not of Stuttering, trembling in Parkinson's disease, or exhibiting abnormal eating behaviour in Anorexia or Bulimia Nervosa.

Specify if:

Generalized: if the fears include most social situations (also consider the additional diagnosis of Avoidant Personality Disorder).

Reprinted with permission from the *Diagnostic and Statistical Manual of Mental Disorders,* 4th edn. Copyright 1994 American Psychiatric Association.

markedly different from the conceptions of shyness described in this book. To understand how the difference between them has been construed we need to look more closely at the source and function of these diagnostic criteria.

Much effort in psychiatry and clinical psychology has been directed towards the issue of diagnosis. There have been a number of attempts to construct diagnostic systems to mark off different conditions, for example the diagnostic and statistical manuals of the American Psychiatric Association or the International and Statistical Classification of Diseases and Related Health Problems. There are obvious benefits to this, for example in tracing the origins and causes of psychological problems and for developing and evaluating effective intervention techniques. These systems have identified a number of different anxiety disorders, including social phobia.

A clinical syndrome of social phobia has been recognised as a diagnostic category since its inclusion in the third edition of the *Diagnostic and Statistical Manual* (hereafter *DSM-III*) of the American Psychiatric Association, published in 1980. This edition identified three types of phobia: agoraphobia, social phobia and simple phobia. Social phobia was described as a persistent fear of finding oneself in a situation where one is subject to scrutiny by others and that one's behaviour might lead to embarrassment or humiliation. This causes a significant amount of distress because the sufferers of such fear recognise that their fear is excessive. *DSM-III* identified a separate disorder that shows some overlap with the concept of shyness: *avoidant personality disorder*, which was defined in terms of hypersensitivity to social rejection, low self-esteem, social withdrawal and reticence.

Diagnostic systems are intended to be modified in the light of gains in understanding of the various conditions and problems, and two subsequent editions of the *DSM* presented somewhat different definitions of social phobia and criteria for its diagnosis. The diagnostic criteria in Box 6.1 come from the most recent edition, *DSM-IV*. Hazen and Stein (1995) point out that one criticism made by researchers was that the *DSM-III* definition restricted the category to fear of a *specific* situation, with the contingent exclusion from the category of a more generalised fear of a range of social situations. Subsequent editions have adjusted the definition to refer to 'one or more social or performance situations'. Further changes are references to the individual's fear that embarrassment or humiliation can also result from showing signs of anxiety as well as from his or her actions; to the tendency to avoid situations or to respond to them with intense anxiety; and to the significant interference with the individual's everyday life produced by this anxiety or distress. Extending the category to include fear of a range of different situations has produced further problems. It is not clearly established whether there are two types of social phobia – a generalised type, which involves fear of a range of situations, and a specific type where the phobia is of a particular class of situations, for example eating or drinking in front of other people. Second, the extension of the category to incorporate a wide range of situations brings it closer to the avoidant personality disorder category and to shyness. Empirical studies have shown that a considerable number of people do attract diagnoses of both social phobia and avoidant personality disorder, although the numbers in question vary from study to study. One view of this relationship is that there are quantitative differences, with avoidant personality disorder being a more severe form of social phobia (Hazen and Stein, 1995, p. 18).

How is social phobia to be distinguished from shyness? We must bear in mind that these are *concepts* that have been developed to try to make sense of social difficulties. They are not states that have been shown to have an existence independent of our concepts. It is open to us to adjust our concepts in order to describe what is happening in the world. This is more difficult in the case of shyness since this concept has evolved in natural language and it has robustness and a broader range of connotations and implications than the concept of social phobia. Given this, it does not make sense to frame the question in terms of the way in which shy people really differ from social phobics without being more precise about how we are applying the two concepts.

Second, these concepts serve different functions. The term 'social phobia' was produced in an attempt to identify a discrete clinical or medical condition. Because it is intended to form a basis for intervention, its definition must be precise enough for different clinicians to apply it without too much ambiguity. It is also used as a basis for choosing among alternative forms of treatment, allocating resources to medical departments and settling health insurance claims. It is a quasi-legal term, indeed it sometimes functions as a legal term. Shyness does not have the restrictions imposed by this usage. Different researchers are free to use it in various ways.

One obvious candidate for specifying the difference is the intensity of the emotional reaction: social phobia refers to a more extreme

Figure 6.1 Two models of the links between shyness and social phobia

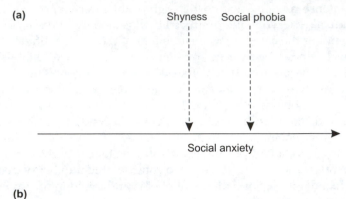

form of anxiety (Figure 6.1a). I can perhaps illustrate this with a personal example. I am often nervous and can feel self-conscious about speaking up in front of a group of people, whether this is at a committee meeting or a social gathering. I am sure that I am not alone in this, but I often wish I could be more effective in such situations. Nevertheless I also enjoy social gatherings and I am motivated to attend them, even though I could endorse many of the items in a social anxiety checklist. I also have a fear of heights, which is most evident when climbing a ladder or standing on the roof of a high building. Fortunately I can avoid most situations that necessitate this – I can hire people to fix my television aerial or clear my guttering. When I do try to climb a ladder, after a certain point I become frozen with fear and I grip the sides of the ladder while I ease myself back to a comfortable height. I have no doubt whatsoever that this is a different order of experience from my social anxiety. I cannot conceive of enjoying any aspect of it. If I was in different circumstances and climbing was a necessary part of my life I would be forced to seek help. If I wish to imagine someone with a social phobia, I only have to summon up an image of myself in this predicament.

Striking as this difference is to me, it is questionable whether intensity of reaction could provide a basis for defining two categories. For one thing I do not know whether other people make such a sharp distinction between these states as I do. There may be a continuum of levels of fear from mild to extreme, and this leaves the clinician with the decision of where to draw a cut-off point between category boundaries. Furthermore there are individual differences in the manageable intensity of emotional reaction. A similar problem arises if the reasonableness of the fear is used to define the category, as this too varies from person to person and is also influenced by social attitudes about appropriate reactions to different kinds of event. For example someone might put up with greater anxiety in social situations relative to fear of high places, because it is not 'mature' or 'manly' to admit to the former anxiety. Finally, there are also problems with the criterion of disruption to everyday life. My fear of heights can be contained because of my social circumstances, not because of anything inherent in the eliciting situation or the fear. In addition the definition would exclude those people who have a very intense level of fear but nevertheless try to cope with it, while including other individuals who experience less fear but have a lower tolerance threshold for it. It is almost as if people are penalised for coping with their fears, and indeed they might well be penalised financially if an insurance settlement rests on the assignment of the category.

An alternative conceptualisation is that social phobia is a distinct condition. An individual's shyness might predispose him or her to social phobia, either directly or mediated by other personality dimensions (Figure 6.1b). Shyness might make people more likely to encounter the kinds of experience that make them susceptible to the condition.

Empirical studies

Turner *et al.* (1990) reviewed the relationship between social phobia and shyness. They adopted the definition of social phobia in what was then the latest edition of the *DSM* (*DSM-III–R*), but acknowledged the absence of a clear definition for shyness. The most striking difference concerns estimates of the prevalence of shyness and social phobia in the community. As we have seen, shyness, as assessed by the Stanford survey, is widespread in society and up to 50 per cent of the American population seem prepared to label themselves as shy. Data from parental ratings of children's shyness also suggest that the prevalence is high among children. On the other hand estimates of the prevalence of social phobia are much lower. In the National Comorbidity Study (NCS), a survey of a large national sample (over 8000 respondents) in the United States, structured interviews were carried out by trained staff (see Kessler *et al.*, 1994). The diagnostic interview included social phobia items reflecting the *DSM-III-R* criteria. The survey found a 12-month prevalence of 7.9 per cent and a lifetime prevalence of 13.3 per cent. That is, nearly 8 per cent of the population met the criteria for the disorder during the previous year, while some 13 per cent would meet the criteria at some time in their life. These data imply that social phobia is the third most common psychiatric disorder in the United States after major depression (17 per cent lifetime prevalence) and alcohol dependence (14 per cent).

While it is reasonable to assume from these data that the prevalence rates for shyness are substantially higher than the social phobia rates, one should be cautious about drawing more definite conclusions. For example the NCS data are not based on actual psychiatric diagnoses – that is, statistical information collected from medical or insurance records or psychiatric units – but on self-reports about social difficulties. To the extent that the items in the NCS interviews were similar to the shyness items, then the prevalence rates would be similar for the two 'conditions'. Inspection of the items, as presented by Walker and Stein (1995, pp. 61–2), does suggest considerable conceptual overlap. Although the participants' answers to the interview questions were also assessed for the persistence and degree of distress caused by the condition, equivalent responses have not since been obtained in surveys of shyness. This inevitable dependence of the statistics on the nature of the items included in the surveys has presumably contributed to the varying rates of prevalence reported in different studies (ibid.).

Turner *et al.* (1990) conclude that there is empirical evidence of similarities in cognitive, somatic and behavioural features. Both shy individuals and social phobics are characterised by a fear of negative evaluation, a high frequency of negative thoughts and a low frequency of positive thoughts during social interactions. Both groups show high systolic blood pressure and heart rate. They also share a tendency to avoid social situations and to display reticence during interactions. One possible area of difference is in occupational and social functioning. There is evidence that both groups have difficulty making friends, forming intimate relationships, being assertive and speaking in public or in group settings. However social phobia is associated with considerable distress in and impairment of everyday life, whereas the shy people in the Stanford survey reported difficulty with rather than severe impairment of everyday functioning. Social phobics also often take extreme steps to avoid routine social situations, with a disruptive effect on their social life.

A further potential difference concerns the chronic and persistent nature of social phobia in contrast to shyness; many respondents in the Stanford survey reported that they were once shy but no longer considered themselves to be so. DeWit *et al.* (1999) collected retrospective accounts of social phobia from a sample of more than one thousand respondents. While 50 per cent of the participants reported that they had recovered from this phobia, its average (median) duration was 25 years and in some cases had lasted up to 45 years. The authors conclude that social phobia is a 'chronic and unremittent disorder' (ibid., p. 569). There is also evidence that people diagnosed with this condition are at greater risk of developing other psychiatric conditions. Schneier *et al.* (1992) have found considerable comorbidity with the abuse of alcohol and other substances. For example 19 per cent of a sample of social phobic patients also had an alcohol abuse disorder. In an analysis of the NCS, Kessler *et al.* (1999) also found significant rates of comorbidity between lifetime social phobia and major depression and mood disorders.

The comparison of shyness and social phobia by Turner *et al.* (1990) revealed that shyness may have an earlier onset, as it can be seen in childhood whereas social phobia tends not to appear until adolescence. Epidemiological studies have shown that the typical age of onset of social phobia is late childhood or early adolescence, although other research has established that social phobia is prevalent in childhood (Beidel and Turner, 1998, pp. 59–62).

Social phobia in childhood may also be associated with a relatively rare condition known as *selective mutism* (Black and Uhde,

1992). This is defined in terms of total lack of speech in one type of situation but the ability to speak in other situations. This was originally called *elective* mutism, guided by the notion that affected children were choosing not to speak, but current practice reflects a move away from an emphasis on the child's 'refusal' (influenced by psychoanalytical interpretations in terms of underlying unconscious conflicts) towards an emphasis on anxiety. Obviously it is important to rule out other reasons for speech problems, including developmental delays or neurological conditions. Accounts of selective mutism regularly mention the child's shyness, inhibition and anxiety (Dow *et al.*, 1995).

A further approach to examining possible relationships between the constructs is to investigate whether scores on a measure of shyness at one time in life serve to predict whether a person will attract a diagnosis of social phobia at another time. This relationship is confounded by the many factors that influence the likelihood of a diagnosis being received, such as the extent of provision, the individual's awareness of the available provisions, differences among doctors in their knowledge of and attitude towards social phobia, and the individual's willingness to seek medical help. Nevertheless it can give some indication of whether shyness predisposes social phobia. Van Ameringen *et al.* (1998) have found significant correlations between a questionnaire measure of social phobia and both the Cheek–Buss shyness scale (r = 0.56) and the respondents' retrospective reports of inhibition in childhood (r = 0.50).

Turner *et al.* (1996) provide a review of the findings of studies examining the relationship between inhibition and anxiety disorders among samples of children. Inhibition, particularly stable inhibition, is associated with a greater tendency towards anxiety disorders and phobic disorders, including fear of public speaking, fear of strangers, fear of crowds and fear of being called upon in class. However they argue that the studies in question have several limitations that caution against confident generalisation from the findings. The studies involved small samples rather than an epidemiological approach and tended to group a number of anxiety disorders together to provide an index of propensity to disorders, so that it is difficult to tease out any specific links between inhibition and social phobia.

The relationship between these constructs is clearly in need of further conceptual analysis and empirical research. One plausible notion is that there is a continuum of social difficulties, ranging from situational shyness, where an otherwise confident person might find him- or herself experiencing discomfort in a difficult or unfamiliar situation, to the other extreme, where a routine event such as eating a meal in a public place produces a panic attack and severe disruption of behaviour, or where even the anticipation of such an activity produces intense fear. The distress caused by such difficulties will lead many individuals to seek help; the more extreme their location on this hypothetical continuum, the more likely it is that they will seek help and the more likely it is that they will be diagnosed as socially phobic. Nevertheless there will be many people suffering from extreme fear who do not seek professional advice, and others who do seek help but do not receive this diagnosis.

In equivalent fashion, one can imagine people endorsing items in the Stanford shyness survey or obtaining high scores on a self-report shyness measure. Some of these respondents might have been diagnosed as social phobics; others might well attract this diagnosis if they presented themselves for assessment. Their scores on the shyness measure might predict the likelihood of attracting a diagnosis of social phobia. To be sure, alternative measures, such as the EPI neuroticism scale, would also be able to predict the likelihood of diagnosis but, we would suggest, with relatively less success because of the clear overlap in content between assessments of shyness and social phobia. Certainly, it should be possible to improve the measures of shyness in order to make better predictions.

On the other hand, shyness measures should be sensitive to social difficulties along a broad band of the hypothetical continuum. There will be individuals who are not diagnosed as having social phobia but who nevertheless experience problems in their social relationships. When these individuals think or talk about their difficulties shyness is the word that is most likely to come to mind, although, depending on the circumstances, other descriptions will do, such as embarrassed, lacking self-confidence, nervous and so on.

One problem with this approach arises if we consider individuals obtaining a high score on a shyness measure who subsequently experience fewer social difficulties following some form of intervention. Have these people become less shy? If their scores on the trait measure are now lower, does this call into question the conception of shyness as a stable trait? One step towards answering these questions is to make a distinction between an underlying trait and its measurement at any given time. Another is to distinguish between a surface trait and a source trait, and to recognise that the surface trait of shyness may be influenced by source traits and environmental factors.

There is evidence that people can become less shy over time, perhaps because their self-concept alters, they attach less importance to being evaluated by others or they gain more experience in the kinds of situation that elicit shyness. In terms of self-presentation theory, there are changes in people's motivation to create a desired impression and in their subjective probability of doing so. Significant life events can also modify people's shyness; for example becoming a mother can make a woman more assertive because meeting the needs of her child outweighs the cost of any embarrassment. An empirical example of this capacity for change is provided by the finding, reported in Chapter 4, that self-consciousness declines after adolescence.

Is social anxiety an illness?

We now turn to our second question on the status of shyness and social phobia as conditions that can be treated by clinical interventions, including pharmaceutical treatments – is either of them an illness? If social phobia cannot be distinguished from 'ordinary' shyness and if shyness is nothing more than one of life's routine difficulties such as feeling sad sometimes, then, the argument goes, it is unwarranted and perhaps dangerous to treat it as an illness.

Of course there is another way of looking at this issue. Given that shyness can be modified and that people can become less anxious about social interaction, it is ethical to try to identify the factors that can produce these changes and to make them available to people as techniques for personal development. Individuals have the right to apply these factors or not, as they see fit. Although this is close to my position, I can see that there are counterarguments. First, people may be pressured to change, either directly or indirectly, because of cultural expectations about appropriate behaviour, media influences and so on. Second, some might accept the argument in principle but be unwilling to extend it to pharmaceutical interventions. Yet we are happy to accept this position for, say, smoking. There are pressures on people not to smoke, difficulties are put in the way of people who wish to smoke in public places, and there are techniques to help people to give up smoking if they choose to do so. Although we do not talk of treating smoking as an illness, we would, I imagine, be prepared to endorse pharmaceutical interventions to help people give up their habit.

A more general issue is that people seem to want to restrict the term illness to physical conditions. I do not believe this is justified. One reason is that it is difficult to maintain a distinction between physical and mental problems. For example, regarding schizophrenia as an illness has led to progress on several fronts. It has reduced the stigma associated with this condition, removed the attribution of blame that was attached to many of its characteristic behaviours, and opened up the possibility of change. If it could be shown that particular chemical imbalances occur in the brains of people suffering from this condition, and that these could be corrected by pharmaceutical means, I would imagine that schizophrenia would be regarded as indistinguishable from 'physical' forms of illness.

Diagnosis is an attempt to impose order on the complexities of mental life and behaviour. Although many distinct clinical conditions have been recognized, such as schizophrenia and autism, it has taken a lengthy period of time and a substantial amount of research to reach a degree of consensus on their status as conditions and that status is still not without controversy. Other conditions, such as depression, share with social phobia the lack of a clear boundary between the diagnostic category 'depression' and the feeling of 'ordinary depression' experienced by people who have never been diagnosed as having the condition or received any clinical attention. It is a matter for conceptual analysis and empirical enquiry whether depression is a continuum upon which people can be located at different positions (and there is some fairly arbitrary cut-off point separating individuals who are clinically depressed from those who are not) or whether there are qualitative differences between these individuals. A questionnaire measure such as the Beck Depression Inventory (Beck, 1989) can yield a distribution of scores in the same way as the Cheek–Buss shyness scale does. Investigations of depression are undertaken with both clinical and non-clinical samples. Effective pharmaceutical treatments are being developed to relieve the symptoms of depression.

There are striking similarities between the progress of research into social phobia and that into *attention deficit hyperactivity disorder* (ADHD). Both have attracted a large amount of research attention in a short period of time. Both are included as diagnostic categories in the *Diagnostic and Statistical Manual*, but their definition and diagnostic criteria are not yet settled and have varied in successive editions. The components of ADHD – hyperactivity, impulsivity and attention problems – have been intensively studied without agreement being reached on how they relate to each other or whether they constitute one or more categories. Researchers suggest that there is a neurological basis for at least some forms of ADHD and, as with social phobia, the neurotransmitters serotonin and catecholamines have been implicated, as well as activity in the frontal lobes. Finally, pharmaceutical treatment appears to have been effective in controlling some of the overactive behaviour that has been problematic to parents and schools. If the stimulant drug methylphenidate (Ritalin) is administered on a regular basis, that is, a number of times each day, it produces short-term improvements in concentration and the ability to restrain impulsive reactions.

Although these improvements provide relief for those who regularly spend time with a child who has these problems, reliance on drug treatments to control children's behaviour has created widespread unease. In part this is because of side effects of the drug and the return to problematic behaviour when the effects of the medication wear off. But there is a more general moral issue that arises because the condition is poorly defined. From one perspective, the education system can be seen as controlling children who behave in ways deemed unacceptable by having recourse to drug control. People feel a similar unease about psychiatric patients being managed by keeping them permanently on medication. Finally, there are equivalent anxieties that those who are simply shy might be pressured to be more extraverted, or whatever the ideal for social success might be.

It seems clear that the pattern of difficulties exhibited by children who are regarded as having ADHD is complex and, at least in part, a reaction to the pressure imposed by the education system. It is improbable that problems of this complexity can be resolved simply by medication. If such treatment does provide temporary relief in less tractable cases then this creates an opportunity for making educational and social interventions. In similar fashion, medication that alleviates the panic attacks brought on by social situations should be regarded as providing an interval in which to address the precipitating circumstances and their control. We shall now examine some of these approaches to social anxiety.

The cognitive–behavioural approach

Behaviourist approaches to anxiety

The psychoanalytical perspective on anxiety is that it is invariably produced by subconscious conflicts. It follows from this that any attempt to remove the symptoms directly would be ineffective since the essential causes of these symptoms would remain untouched. Any success would only be temporary at best; or else fresh symptoms would be substituted for those removed. Only a systematic analysis of the nature of the underlying conflict could bring about improvement. The specific approach taken to this analysis would depend on the particular psychodynamic theory adhered to by the therapist, but whatever model was adopted, therapy would inevitably be a difficult and time-consuming task. The behaviourist approach rejects this theory and argues that the origins of anxiety are to be found in learning experiences. Since anxiety has been acquired through a process of learning it can also be 'unlearned', and symptoms can be removed by means of a process of conditioning.

The seminal study was the demonstration by John Watson, one of the founders of the behaviourist approach in psychology, of the acquisition of a phobia by an infant, who is known to posterity as Little Albert (Watson and Rayner, 1920). A loud and unpleasant sound (the unconditioned stimulus) was made whenever Little Albert came into contact with a rat (the conditioned stimulus). After exposure to this pairing of stimuli he avoided the rat and showed distress at seeing it. It seemed as if an animal phobia had been conditioned into the child, and just as a fear could be acquired in this manner, it could also be removed through a process of extinction. This could be achieved by repeatedly presenting the conditioned stimulus in the absence of the unconditioned stimulus until it eventually no longer elicited the fear response. The findings of the original study by Watson and Rayner (1920) were controversial, for example it proved difficult to replicate the findings, and even in the original experiment the conditioned response proved resistant to extinction (Eysenck, 1982, p. 213). However the approach has been highly influential and a number of similar techniques have been developed to reduce anxiety.

Subsequent laboratory-based research has examined the role that conditioning plays in the development of anxiety. For example

Ohman and Dimberg (1978) paired an unconditioned aversive stimulus (an electric shock) with a neutral stimulus (the presentation of an angry face). Subsequently a measured fear response was elicited when the angry face was presented without an accompanying shock; that is, the angry face now acted as a conditioned stimulus that elicited a conditioned response. The experiment also compared the relative effectiveness of three kinds of facial expression – an angry face, a happy face and one with a neutral expression. It was found that the angry face was associated with greater resistance to extinction of the conditioned response and this was potent when the gaze of the angry face was directed at the person (Ohman *et al.*, 1985).

This research illustrates a number of points. First, it is possible to demonstrate the acquisition and removal of a specific fear in the laboratory using standard conditioning procedures. Second, quite specific circumstances – not simply any facial expression, or even an angry face, but an expression that seems to be targeted at the individual – elicit the conditioned response. Finally, it implies that some kinds of stimuli are more likely to elicit conditioned fear responses than others. It is easier to condition a response to an angry face than a happy one, and this is in line with the finding that some kinds of stimuli are more 'prepared' (Seligman, 1971) for conditioning than others. In Watson's original experiment it might have been easier to condition the child to be frightened of the small animal than of another arbitrarily chosen stimulus, and there could well be a biological basis for this tendency. Animal phobias do tend to be centred on particular species, for example spiders, rodents and snakes. Seligman (ibid., p. 312) makes this point succinctly about phobias: they

> comprise a relatively non-arbitrary and limited set of objects; agoraphobia, fear of specific animals, insect phobias, and fear of the dark, and so forth. All these are relatively common phobias. And only rarely, if ever, do we have pyjama phobias, grass phobias, electric-outlet phobias, hammer phobias, even though these things are likely to be associated with trauma in our world.

Ohman and Dimberg (1978) have proposed that there is also a biological basis for fearing certain facial expressions, notably those that signal the possibility of the individual being rejected by the group. It is argued that a species that depends on group living for its survival will evolve a sensitivity to signals of social rewards and punishments.

Gilbert and Trower (1990) have put forward a similar argument, that social phobia has a biological origin related to dominance relationships within the group.

According to the conditioning model, fear of encountering a social situation can be extinguished by repeated exposure to the situation in the absence of the unconditioned stimuli. This has provided the basis for a number of approaches to treating social phobia. If circumstances can be arranged so that the individual experiences the feared situation – for example eating a meal in public – without any embarrassment or humiliation ensuing, then the situation will come to lose its aversive quality. One method relies simply on repeated *in vivo* exposure to the feared situation (this means that the client faces the actual situation, not a simulation of it or a less frightening version). It is crucial for the individual to confront the situation rather than adopt the typical response of avoiding it. An avoidance response can be conditioned so that it is maintained even though the individual rarely comes into contact with the aversive stimuli that led to the phobic response in the first place. The shy person who does not make a contribution to the conversation avoids the humiliation of saying something foolish but becomes trapped in reticence because he or she foregoes the rewarding experiences that can be found in conversation.

One potential limitation of this method is that the phobic individual may become so overwhelmed with anxiety as soon as he or she enters the restaurant that there will be no possibility of experiencing the situation in a non-aversive way. Behaviourists have developed supplementary techniques to deal with this problem. The first technique involves teaching the individual how to relax. People can be taught to tense and flex combinations of muscles in a systematic and progressive way in order to enhance their awareness of what it feels like to be in a relaxed state and to enable them to relax the muscles at will. Muscles in the arms, legs, trunk, head and neck can be tensed and flexed in a systematic procedure. With practice, for example by following a programme of repeated exercises while listening to taped instructions, the individual will gradually acquire this control. The rationale for this training programme is that relaxation and anxious reactions are incompatible responses. By deliberately relaxing in a stressful situation the individual will not be able to make anxious responses.

The second technique is called systematic desensitisation. Rather than face the feared situation in its entirety, the elements of the situation are analysed and presented to the individual in a progressive way, one step at a time. For example, before an actual restaurant is entered the therapist might ask the client to imagine the prospect of going out for a meal and gradually work towards imagining the details of sitting down, reading the menu, ordering a meal, eating it and so on. The client might be asked to imagine that he or she is alone during these events, or is with company, or is in a busy restaurant. The client can also practise relaxation while imagining these scenes, so that eventually few signs of distress accompany the mental images. Eventually the therapist will set the client the task of going to eat a meal in an actual restaurant. This, too, would be approached in a systematic, step-by-step fashion.

The behaviourist paradigm was an important element in the development of psychology as a scientific discipline, specifically the application of experimental methods to the study of mental life. Accordingly its approach to treatment included the use of empirical methods to evaluate intervention techniques. Concepts such as 'cure' or 'improvement' were regarded as imprecise, subjective and influenced by many factors over and above any treatment effects. Researchers, it was argued, should concentrate on observing and measuring behaviour. Baseline measures should be taken prior to treatment and compared with post-treatment measures. While single case study interventions could be studied systematically, the use of samples of clients and their assignment either to a treatment or to a control group was regarded as sound scientific practice. Thus the behaviourist approach has always been associated with a body of research literature that compares the effectiveness of different interventions. We shall review some of this research after introducing two other techniques: the teaching of social skills, and cognitive–behavioural therapy.

Social skills training

The rationale for this approach is that people might experience social anxiety because they lack the confidence to contribute effectively to social interactions or because their lack of poise produces difficulties. Even if exposure or systematic desensitisation could reduce their anxiety, their lack of social skills would leave them vulnerable to embarrassment or humiliation. One way of boosting their confidence is to help them become more effective social performers, and several techniques have been designed to accomplish this.

These techniques begin by making systematic observations of the individual's social functioning to identify the situations in which he or she behaves in an inept or unskilled way, and this information is used to design training programmes to increase skilled behaviour. A range of different skills can be identified. Van der Molen (1990, pp. 272–5) draws upon an analysis of conversation as an exchange of messages, where the participants take turns to play the roles of speaker and listener. He distinguishes between *sender skills* and *receiver skills*. Sender skills can be further classified into *active* skills, where the individual takes the initiative in conversation (making requests, giving opinions, criticising, expressing emotions such as anger or affection, disclosing information about oneself), and *responsive* skills, which help the individual to respond to others (refusing, responding to criticism, responding to expressions of emotion). Receiver (or listener) skills include listening appropriately, asking different kinds of question and reflecting on feelings.

The approach involves a number of specific techniques. These can be illustrated by outlining some of the core elements of the social skills training in Van der Molen's programme. An early step in the procedure involves *modelling*, where an instructor demonstrates the skill, perhaps on videotape. Both the 'wrong' way to behave and a more effective way can be presented. The instructor draws the client's attention to key points in the sequence, as this helps the client form a conceptual model of how the components of the skill fit together. The skill is practised in short role-play exercises and these are recorded on videotape for subsequent analysis. The therapist and the client talk through the role-play, identifying effective behaviour and showing where performance could be improved. The instructor then provides a summary of what has been learned and draws attention to aspects needing additional practise. The approach emphasises the importance of practise, and clients are set homework assignments. These are not only used for rehearsing skills, but also for applying what has been learned to fresh situations, a process that is known as transfer of training. As the programme progresses clients are encouraged to try to implement their skills in the kinds of situation that previously induced anxiety.

These techniques raise a number of issues. The notion of a skill is a complex one. It refers at one level to the 'micro-level' of social interaction, that is, the timing of responses, making eye contact, showing the other person you are listening, being sensitive to signals about whose turn it is to speak, knowing when there is an opportunity to speak. These can perhaps be acquired in a mechanical way without the individual being skilled at another level: the ability to contribute effectively to the topic of conversation, to shape it in ways that meet his or her goals, to be sensitive to the needs of the other person, to synchronise one's own behaviour with that of the other person, and so on. Social interactions contribute to the development of mutually rewarding relationships and they serve other life goals of the individual, they are not simply exercises in sending and receiving messages. Furthermore a skilled person can reflect on his or her social behaviour and is able to adjust this in the light of altered circumstances. He or she can choose from a range of equivalent responses, rather than pursue well-rehearsed moves. Effective behaviours are strategic rather than the sequencing of isolated components of behaviour. All the elements of skill can perhaps be learned, but I am not convinced that they are learned from the kinds of exercise involved in social skills training. Reservations such as this have played a part in the development of the cognitive approach to interventions.

A second issue is that people who are shy or are diagnosed as having social phobia might not be deficient in skills. Elsewhere we have noted evidence that many such people underestimate their skill levels relative to observers of their behaviour. Also, it may be difficult for shy people to draw upon their repertoire of skills if they are experiencing anxiety or intense self-consciousness. Shyness seems to be situation specific, so that an individual is able to perform more effectively in some situations than in others. The difference between situations may be their implications for negative evaluation of the self, rather than one situation requiring more 'skills'. Failure may be judged more likely in some situations or the perceived costs of failure might be very high. For example I might be able to deliver an excellent presentation on shyness but go to pieces if I find out that an authority on the topic or a future employer is in the audience. Nevertheless an emphasis on skills can augment self-confidence, and an additional advantage of this approach is that research has established that well-practised habits are more resistant to the disruptive effects of anxiety. Also, this technique necessarily provides opportunities for exposure to the feared situations so that it can draw upon the benefits of simple exposure methods.

Before considering studies that evaluate the effectiveness of anxiety-reduction and social skill techniques, we shall describe cognitive behavioural therapy, since many evaluation studies have compared these techniques with cognitive approaches.

Cognitive processes in social anxiety

The behaviourist approach to the treatment of social phobia was originally based on a research paradigm that concentrated on the measurement of overt behaviours. As the central paradigm in experimental psychology shifted towards recognition that it was essential to analyse the cognitive processes that mediate between the presentation of a stimulus and an overt response, behaviourist approaches to therapy began to focus on the possibility of producing systematic changes in cognition. Rather than regarding anxiety as an acquired habit, it was seen as the result of aberrations in thinking, therefore therapy should be directed at correcting or challenging the bias and distortion involved in the assumptions and beliefs of anxious people. Research into anxiety was also moving towards recognition that worrisome and intrusive thoughts are not only core components of this emotion but also have effects on overt behaviour. For example they divert attention away from task-relevant activities and towards the self, or sustain an emotional state in the absence of an eliciting stimulus. As seen in Chapter 2, research into shyness has revealed that this too has a strong cognitive component, and that shy individuals are prone to self-focused attention and forms of thinking that interfere with their effective performance in social situations.

Although thinking processes cannot be observed, they can be inferred from measures such as thought-listing procedures and think-aloud protocols. Beck (1989) explored ways of encouraging clients to report on 'automatic thoughts', which frequently accompanied the more salient thoughts reported to the therapist in response to prompts about the nature of their problems, but of which they were scarcely aware. With sensitive probing, the contents of this thinking became accessible and Beck found them to have common properties that could be identified in different patients. They were specific rather than vague in content and negative in tone. They often involved patients' self-critical monitoring of what they were planning to say to the therapist and their concern about the impression they were making on him. They were autonomous in that they 'just happened' and were difficult to stop. What patients say about themselves and their articulation of their beliefs play an important role in cognitive–behavioural approaches to therapy.

The effects of cognitive processing can also be assessed by experimental techniques such as priming methods, the Stroop paradigm and comparison of performance in tasks that make varying demands on the working memory system by making different demands on the central executive and storage processes. Clark (1999) reviews a number of such studies carried out in his own laboratory. For example individuals who were selected as either high or low on a measure of social anxiety rated the descriptiveness of positive and negative words in one of three conditions: (1) the words describe them as another person might think of them; (2) the words describe how they think about themselves; (3) the words describe someone else. In a further condition, the prospect of giving a public speech was used to manipulate levels of anxiety. In a subsequent recall task, highly socially anxious participants recalled more negative than positive target words, but this trend was found only for words that described them from another perspective and only in the highly anxious condition (when they anticipated having to speak in public).

The 'cognitive revolution' in psychology also influenced the kinds of explanation of behaviour that were framed. Earlier explanations were based on the conditioning model of learning, where the features of a situation acted as stimuli to evoke responses that had become established through a process of stimulus–response association. Thus a person's recognition that a social situation involved new people might provide the stimulus for an avoidant response to be made. According to behaviourist models, processes of stimulus generalisation and discrimination learning could result in a range of different situations becoming equivalent in their capacity to elicit this kind of response. In terms of the output of behaviour, a range of alternative types of response might also be equivalent – avoiding the situation, escaping from it, keeping in the background, being reticent or replying to questions in ways intended to discourage further interaction. These reactions to social situations could occur directly without conscious intent. In any case, behaviourists argued that people's conscious awareness of what they were doing would not provide the explanation for their behaviour; thinking about the situation or their predicament would not cause them to withdraw, but was merely another form of non-overt response elicited by the circumstances of the situation.

Cognitive–behavioural explanations argue that what is learnt is not just stimulus–response contingencies but also expectations about what can happen in social situations. Bandura (1986; see also Chapter 2 of this volume) argues that these expectations mediate between stimulus and response. The individual finds meaning in the situation and chooses a response in the pursuit of particular goals that are appropriate to the situation as it has been interpreted. Social anxiety is associated with specific cognitions. One is a fear of being negatively evaluated by other people. Most people experience this fear at some time or other, but it can be pervasive in some individuals. Research has consistently demonstrated a significant correlation between measures of social anxiety and fear of negative evaluation.

Another belief is that the individual lacks the ability to make a desired impression on other people. Again, research has shown that not only do social phobics have a low opinion of their social abilities, they also underestimate their abilities in comparison with other people's assessments of their performance. Stopa and Clark (1993) show that this bias in perception is specific to social phobia and not simply a characteristic of generalised anxiety. This perception is reinforced by explanations of the causes of outcomes where the individual believes that his or her failure to attain desired goals is due to entrenched personal inadequacies and cannot readily be changed. This leads the shy person to discount any positive outcomes that may occur, believing that they must be due to factors beyond his or her control. Rewarding experiences do not lead to an increase in the subjective probability of being successful in the next social situation. On the other hand, failures only confirm these negative expectations, and therefore the individual sees no use in seeking out alternative explanations, either in terms of the characteristics of social situations or of the difficulties that other people might have with similar situations. Furthermore a social encounter is, by definition, an endeavour that is shared with others, and gaining satisfaction from it requires an active participant who contributes to the situation in appropriate ways and helps to sustain the interaction and make it rewarding for the other people involved. Beliefs about lack of efficacy, which lead to the adoption of forms of behaviour that are defensive and fail to contribute to the interaction, can produce outcomes that only serve to reinforce the individual's lack of confidence in him- or herself. Such beliefs can function as self-fulfilling prophecies.

It can also be the case that individuals who are high in social anxiety find their self-presentation goals very difficult to attain because the standards they set for themselves are unrealistically high. It is impossible to be liked, admired or even feared by everyone; making a *faux pas* or saying something foolish can never be avoided completely unless one adopts such a self-protective, reticent style that nothing at all is ventured. Studies of anxiety have shown that high frequencies of worrying can be associated with perfectionism, the setting of rigid and unrealistic standards, and catastrophic thinking, fearing that the worst possible outcome is likely to occur.

Clark (1999) has identified a number of processes that help to maintain the cognitions central to anxiety.

Safety behaviours

The individual takes some action that he or she believes will fend off a feared event. When the event fails to happen, this is attributed to the action that was taken, the 'safety behaviour', and consequently this action is repeated whenever a threat is detected. For example an individual might be afraid of blushing and will take steps to try to reduce body temperature, apply cosmetics such as a blusher or green foundation cream to mask the blush, or offer an alternative explanation for the redness of the face (hurrying, the hot weather and so on). These behaviours can be irrational, in that they can be unconnected to the outcome and can even make the feared outcome more likely to occur (by making their blush conspicuous or by acting in a strange way so that attention is drawn to them). They also result in the individual failing to identify and cope with the causes of the anxiety. The safety behaviour offers some temporary relief but it does nothing to help the person to become less anxious in the future. Uncovering and challenging safety behaviours plays a key role in the cognitive approach to the treatment of social phobia developed by Clark and Wells (1995).

Attention bias

We have already noted that anxious individuals are prone to detect threats in the environment and even innocuous events can provide cues for a threat. In general the appraisal of threat is not commensurate with the objective danger. Clark also suggests that there is evidence of a bias in attention *away* from threat cues. Priming studies have shown that socially anxious individuals pay less attention to faces if they are provided with the choice of looking at either a face or a household object. This may be associated with a tendency to minimise social contact by avoiding eye contact.

Selective memory processes

Patients with social phobia selectively recall negative information about past experiences in ways that confirm their negative image of themselves.

High frequency of spontaneously occurring images

A higher frequency of these images is found among patients with a range of phobias, and this is also the case with social phobia. Hackman and Clark (1998, cited in Clark, 1999) have found that these images are of high frequency, are repetitive and can often be traced to past traumatic social events.

Erroneous inferences about how one is seen by others

As we have noted, patients with social phobia believe that they appear more anxious to others than is actually the case. This bias seems to be due to extrapolating from their negative self-image and using feedback from their body sensations to make erroneous inferences about how they appear to others – if my heart is pounding I must appear anxious to everybody else.

Cognitive therapies

These aim to modify the thinking processes that maintain high levels of anxiety. Beck (1989) suggests that there are three kinds of approach that can be taken. The 'intellectual' approach aims to identify and expose the patient's misconceptions, to challenge them by testing their validity and to replace them with more appropriate lines of thought. Individuals who experience recurrent anxiety may not be aware of their automatic thoughts or their implicit notions about what should be done, rules that must apply to the situation or the standards that have to be attained in social situations. These habits of thinking or 'self-statements' can be brought to light. Patients can be encouraged to observe closely the chain of events that lead up to an anxious reaction and 'fill in the blank' between eliciting circumstances and the reaction (ibid., p. 239). Exploration with a young man of the reasons why he had avoided spending a train journey in the company of a woman acquaintance he knew and liked, by pretending that he had not seen her, uncovered a series of thoughts: 'after the first few minutes I won't know what to say'; 'I can never hold up my end of a conversation'; 'she will realise I have nothing much to say and will wish she had sat somewhere else'; 'she only smiles at me because she doesn't really know me'. He could be challenged to examine the validity of his thoughts and to see that they *are* thoughts and not an objective picture of reality.

Another approach is 'experiential', where the individual is exposed to feared situations that have hitherto been avoided and the outcomes that are experienced are sufficient to highlight the individual's misconceptions about what would happen. This is obviously similar to the exposure method of behavioural treatment. The main difference seems to be the cognitive therapist's focus on the patient's thought processes with respect to the feared situation. However it is presumably often the case that behaviourist therapists also draw attention to salient features of the situation and the individual's reactions to them, and insofar as this occurs the treatments are similar. Nevertheless the orientation is different. Consider the case of a man who has an intense fear of eating and drinking in public. By avoiding such situations the ideas he has about them and about the consequences of the events he fears – other people noticing his clumsiness, being humiliated by making mistakes in public – are never tested. Of course if he does go for a meal in a busy restaurant or a works canteen he may well be clumsy because his self-focused attention and symptoms such as shaking affect his coordination, and others might notice this. However the experience can be explored. What happened that was so terrible? What consequences ensued? Has anyone changed their opinion of him? How calamitous was it that he embarrassed himself? What happened the next day? In an important sense, the lesson is not that things do not necessarily go wrong (because the situations feared by social phobics are often demanding, by any standards) but that how the situation is perceived by the individual and the fears that he has are distorted. This thinking is at the heart of his problems.

A third therapeutic method discussed by Beck is the behavioural approach where the individual practises techniques that will help him or her to deal with social situations. This is obviously close to the social skills technique, and indeed some approaches to therapy, for example assertiveness training, draw upon a combination of cognitive restructuring and social skills instruction. The two complement each other in that both can challenge a negative evaluation of the self as a social actor. Concentration on the investigation of thought processes can also counteract any tendency of the client to use social techniques as 'safety behaviours'. For example it is possible to apply a conversational gambit in an automatic or even 'superstitious' way as a prop to fend off catastrophe, rather than challenge the catastrophic thinking itself.

Implicit in this account is that several approaches can be taken to cognitive behaviour therapy but that there is a common emphasis on the role of the contents and processes of thinking in the maintenance of social anxiety. The individual is guilty of exaggerating the risks and costs inherent in social situations or is prone to assume responsibility over events that cannot be controlled. He or she makes erroneous inferences, or makes overgeneralisations from isolated events. The approach is systematic, and three stages can be identified (Meichenbaum and Cameron, 1982). In the first stage the therapist encourages the client to engage in careful self-observation with the aim of enhancing awareness of the circumstances in which anxiety is typically experienced and developing an appreciation that alternative and more helpful ways of construing the experience are possible. In the second stage, new thinking and behaviours are developed. The aims are to help the client to continue to construe the problems in a positive way, to ensure that he or she is able to execute the new ways of behaving that are acquired, to encourage the self-monitoring of thoughts and behaviours, and to enable the client to implement new ways of thinking and acting in social situations. These new ways should be practised in actual situations, where the success of behaviours can be gauged and the client can attribute successful outcomes to the self. In the third phase, progress should be consolidated and maintained, efforts should be made to extend the new skills to novel situations and self-attribution of the causes of improvements should be fostered.

Heimberg *et al.* (1995) provide a detailed account of the steps involved in a group form of cognitive behaviour therapy. A cognitive–behavioural explanation of social phobia is developed. Clients are trained to identify and confront distorted cognitions. They are exposed to simulations of the kinds of situation that they find difficult. Cognitive restructuring is used to modify distorted thinking prior to, during and after exposure to these situations. Homework exercises are set where clients practise what they have learnt in *in vivo* situations; clients are taught cognitive restructuring procedures that they can implement themselves.

A substantial amount of research has evaluated cognitive behaviour therapy (restructuring) and compared its effectiveness with social skills training techniques and exposure methods. Stravynski and Greenberg (1998) have reviewed ten studies comparing cognitive restructuring with exposure in controlled investigations. Although all the studies compared different treatment conditions, the actual treatments and the design of the studies varied. Duration of treatment ranged from nine hours to 24 hours, with a median of 16 hours. Follow-up assessments were carried out after an interval ranging from one month to 18 months, with one study assessing maintenance of improvement at five years. Treatment conditions produced greater improvement than waiting list control groups in those studies where these were included in the design, but there was no obvious superiority of cognitive restructuring over exposure.

Three studies examined social skills training, all of them involving group forms of treatment. One study compared this with individual and group exposure techniques (25 one-hour sessions in each condition), one compared it directly with cognitive restructuring (eight sessions of 2.5 hours), and one compared social skills training with and without cognitive restructuring (12 two-hour sessions) with a control group. Social skills training was not superior to the cognitive approach in any study, although the single study with a control condition reported that patients in both social skills treatment groups had improved relative to the control group and that this was maintained at six months.

Although such overviews of intervention research are valuable for identifying trends, it can be misleading to regard different studies as equivalent. Although overall improvement rates are reported, these are based on varied criteria, for example reductions in anxiety, changes in responses to self-report measures, improved effectiveness in social situations, greater likelihood of involvement in social activities and so on. Furthermore no effect sizes were computed, so that it is difficult to assess the extent of the superiority of treatment conditions over control or waiting list groups. It is encouraging that improvements have been demonstrated for various intervention techniques, particularly as the drop-out rates from the studies were relatively small (a median rate of 16 per cent in the 12 studies reviewed by Stravynski and Greenberg, 1998). Future research needs to provide a more systematic examination of the client and treatment factors associated with reductions in anxiety and improvements in performance.

We finish this section with brief consideration of the Palo Alto Shyness Clinic. As discussed in Chapter 1, Philip Zimbardo and his associates were among the first to study shyness from a social psychological perspective, and from the outset they were concerned to use the findings of their research to help individuals overcome the problems associated with their shyness. The clinic was established at Stanford University in the 1970s and is currently based at Palo Alto, California (web site http://www.shyness.com/). Although it is called a shyness clinic, the clients receive a thorough psychological assessment prior to treatment and the large majority of them meet *DSM-IV* criteria for generalised social phobia. A comorbidity study of 114 clients showed that 97 per cent met the criteria for generalised social phobia and 67 per cent met the criteria for avoidant personality disorder (Henderson and Zimbardo, 1999, p. 298).

Their current approach to treatment is based on a 'social fitness' model analogous to the concept of physical fitness. The goal is positive well-being rather than simply overcoming shyness. Just as few people become world-class athletes but large numbers gain enjoyment and fulfilment from participation in physical exercise, the goal of the therapy is to enhance enjoyment and fulfilment through social interaction processes and interpersonal relationships. Becoming an athlete requires the acquisition and refinement of skills, typically through the development of specific techniques with the help of coaching and, inevitably, many hours of practise. These activities can be encouraged and motivation maintained by means of sports clubs and group activities that bring together individuals who can learn from each without the need to compete, rather they seek improvements in their own performance and measure this against their past standards.

The clinic adopts an eclectic approach, drawing upon individual and group forms of treatment, and it implements all the techniques introduced here: exposure, progressive relaxation, social skills training, assertiveness training and cognitive restructuring. After the initial assessment, treatment begins with 26 weeks of cognitive behavioural group therapy, with the group meeting for two hours each week. The first half of the course is devoted to role-play of feared situations accompanied by cognitive restructuring and social skills instruction. Between the weekly sessions the participants carry out homework assignments, including *in vivo* exposure, where specific target behaviours have to be accomplished, such as making a request, seeking advice or conversing for a specified period of time with a stranger in a public place. The second half of the course is devoted to training in verbal and non-verbal communication, using modelling of appropriate behaviour and rehearsal. Attention is also paid to assertiveness training and the development of intimate relationships.

Outcome data collected at the clinic show that the treatment package is effective in reducing anxiety and producing gain scores in measures of shyness and fear of negative evaluation. No controlled studies have been undertaken to compare its effectiveness with other forms of treatment. Of course the approach there is different from that taken in controlled research studies; instead of contrasting different treatments to discover which is most effective, the clinic draws upon a range of approaches. The only meaningful comparisons would therefore be with pharmacological treatments or waiting list control groups. We shall now consider pharmacological interventions.

The pharmacological approach

> 'The pill that makes a shrinking violet expand' – 'Sufferers of crippling shyness could soon be transformed into the life and soul of the party, thanks to a new discovery' (*Daily Mail*, 23 July 1998, p. 25).

Neurotransmitters and anxiety

We begin this section with a consideration of neurotransmitters in the brain, which are the target of several pharmacological treatments for social anxiety. Each brain cell has connections with a large number of other cells. The cells are separated from one another by a gap, or synapse, and the electrical impulses that carry messages between cells bridge this gap by means of chemical transmitters (see Figure 6.2). These are synthesised within specialised cells called neurons and are stored until they are released into the synapse when the neuron is stimulated. When a message is being sent an electrical impulse travels along an axon (or nerve fibre) of the presynaptic neuron. When it

Figure 6.2 Neurotransmitters and the transmission of information between nerve cells

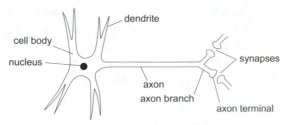

(a)
The dendrites and the cell body receive inputs to the nerve cell (neuron). The output from the neuron is sent down the axon (or nerve fibre). Information is transmitted along the axon, by means of electrical impulses called action potentials. The end of the axon swells to form the terminal.

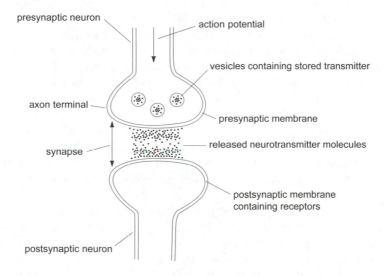

(b)
When the impulse reaches the axon terminal it releases a chemical (a neurotransmitter) that has been synthesised by the neuron and stored in vesicles. The neurotransmitter molecules cross the synapse (the gap separating the neurons) and bind to specific receptor molecules in the postsynaptic neuron. These alter shape and this change produces excitation or inhibition in the action potential within the postsynaptic neuron.

Pharmacological treatments of social phobia are designed to affect transmission at synapses. For example, increasing levels of serotonin within the synapse can be brought about by drugs that inhibit its reuptake or by drugs that inhibit the metabolic process whereby serotonin is converted into an inactive form.

reaches the terminal of the axon the chemical transmitter is released and travels across the synapse. This transmitter binds to receptors in the receiving (postsynaptic) neuron and the consequent change in the receptors generates the electrical impulse that carries the message onwards. After it has fulfilled this function, the transmitter is either broken down by enzymes or is taken back into the nerve ending of the presynaptic neuron, a process known as reuptake. Within the presynaptic cell an enzyme, monoamine oxidase (MAO), breaks down catecholamines and serotonin. Increasing the availability of transmitters is therefore a function of several processes: increased presynaptic synthesis, inhibition of the metabolic activity of MAO, increased release rate and inhibition of reuptake.

A number of neurotransmitters have been identified and their role in the regulation of emotion investigated. Three major categories are biogenic amines, amino acids and peptides. The biogenic amines include acetylcholine (ACh), serotonin (5-hydroxytryptamine, or 5-HT) and the catecholamines, a group comprising dopamine, norepinephrine and epinephrine. Amino acids include glutamate and GABA (gamma-amino-butyric-acid). Peptide neurotransmitters include leu-enkelaphin, met-enkelaphin and beta-endorphin, which belong to a class of peptides known as opioids. These are involved in the sensation of pain and in autonomic nervous system (ANS) activity. Peptides have neuromodular functions in that they affect large numbers of neurons simultaneously and modify (or modulate) their potential for activation by transmitters. This can have an adaptive function, for example in increasing the likelihood of transmission.

Norepinephrine is involved in arousal, alertness and sensitivity to sensory stimulation. Many of the final synapses of the sympathetic ANS use norepinephrine, thus it is involved in the control of heart rate and blood pressure. Not surprisingly the amygdala (in the medial temporal lobe) has an important role in this, both as an instigator of reactions and as a target. When it is activated by threat cues, the central and medial areas of the amygdala trigger activity in the paraventricular nucleus of the hypothalamus, which sends corticotropin releasing hormone (CRH) to the pituitary gland, causing it to release adrenocorticotropic hormone (ACTH) into the bloodstream. This acts on the adrenal cortex, producing epinephrine (which is involved in the regulation of body temperature, respiration and blood pressure) and cortisol. CRH also targets the locus coerulus, producing norepinephrine. The amygdala projects onto the lateral hypothalamus, which controls activity in the sympathetic ANS. It also projects onto the locus coerulus, which releases norepinephrine across a wide area of the forebrain and causes excitation of the amygdala and hippocampus, with consequent effects on sensitivity to environmental cues.

The neurotransmitter GABA, an amino acid, has inhibitory effects in a variety of brain areas, including the basolateral area of the amygdala, and can influence activity in the central nucleus, serving to reduce anxiety. A class of anxiety-reducing drugs, the benzodiazepines (including valium and librium), work by binding GABA to specific receptors in the nervous system.

Serotonin is a transmitter most frequently found in the central nervous system and is concentrated in the mid-brain raphe nuclei. These nuclei have widespread projections, including into the cerebral cortex and forebrain structures. They project into the amygdala, septum, hippocampus, thalamus, hypothalamus and periaqueductal grey. Serotonin is involved in behavioural arousal and vigilance. Spoont (1992) argues that it is involved in stabilising or 'fine tuning' the flow of information through the neural system, as it modifies the effects of signals across a range of responses. It seems to be involved in the flight/fight system, which is mediated by the amygdala, hypothalamus, septum and periaqueductal grey. Thus, for example, a decrease in the level of serotonin makes aggressive behaviour and suicide more likely. Stimulation of the periaqueductal grey elicits a fear response, but this response is modified by serotonin. A decrease in serotonin promotes sexual behaviour, whereas an increase reduces it. More generally, a depletion of serotonin results in either overreaction or oversensitivity to stimulation.

Different neurotransmitters have marked and specific effects on emotion, but it would be misleading to assume that they act in isolation of one another. Rather they interact with one another, and their eventual effects on the ANS and behaviour are the product of a balancing of excitatory and inhibitory effects. For example there are opposing effects between norepinephrine and GABA: serotonin constrains the transmission of dopamine and facilitates the transmission of GABA (Baumgarten and Grozdanovic, 1998).

Pharmacological treatments

Drug treatments for social phobia have attracted considerable media attention in recent years and remain highly controversial.

Much of the coverage lacks depth, and it has been argued that some of the attention has been orchestrated by the marketing departments of pharmaceutical companies, which have a commercial interest in the wider use of medication, but the extent of media attention is a significant phenomenon in itself. Clearly this approach to intervention is at the centre of disputes about the notion that shyness or social phobia is an 'illness' and therefore amenable to medication. Nevertheless, as we shall see, the most common pharmaceutical interventions for social phobia have drawn upon drugs developed for and established in the treatment of depression and anxiety disorders. No new forms of medication have been developed specifically for social phobia.

This section provides a brief overview of some of the research into the efficacy of different forms of treatment. We shall concentrate on reports in scholarly journals of controlled evaluations of medication. Well-controlled studies assign volunteer patients at random into one of two groups: one receiving the treatment drug and the other a placebo. While someone on the team of researchers knows which patient has been assigned to which group, those who rate the patients for their post-treatment condition are unaware of (are blind to) this. A design incorporating all these features is described as a double-blind, placebo-controlled study. Extensions of this design include testing more than one drug treatment against a placebo group, or comparing a behavioural approach such as *in vivo* exposure, social skills training or cognitive–behavioural therapy with a drug treatment and a placebo group. It is also important to precede the experiment with a period during which all medication is withheld, so that the effects of the treatment can be properly evaluated. Finally, it is important to provide a meaningful test of the efficacy of the treatment, including a follow-up assessment some time after the trial has finished and an evaluation of the patients' effectiveness and feelings of anxiety in *actual* social situations. It is also important to establish the consequences of discontinuing the pharmacological treatment.

Such studies are expensive to run, and in the early stages of drug testing open clinical trials may be run instead, where the above controls are absent. The research tests the potential of the drug and examines the effects of different dosages (for example a recent trial of a new application of a serotonergic drug, nefazodone, is reported by Van Ameringen *et al.*, 1999b). All this research is undertaken under the supervision of psychiatrists and is obliged to follow strict

Table 6.1   Types of drug used in the treatment of social phobia, with references to selected research studies

Drug type	Examples	Selected studies
MAOIs	Phenelzine	Gelernter *et al.* (1991)
	Tranylcypromine	Versiani *et al.* (1989)
	Brofaromine*	Van Vliet *et al.* (1992)
	Moclobemide*	Versiani *et al.* (1992)
SSRIs	Fluoxetine	Black and Uhde (1994)
	Fluvoxamine	Van Vliet *et al.* (1994)
	Paroxetine	Stein *et al.* (1998)
	Sertraline	Katzelnick *et al.* (1995)
	Nefazodone	Van Ameringen *et al.* (1999b)
	(SSRI related)	
Beta-blockers	Atenolol	Liebowitz *et al.* (1992)
	Propranolol	Falloon *et al.* (1981)
Benzodiazepines	Alprazolam	Gelernter *et al.* (1991)
	Clonazepam	Davidson *et al.* (1993)
	Diazepam	Gorenstein *et al.* (1995)
Nonbenzodiazepine Anxiolytics	Buspirone	Van Vliet *et al.* (1994)

* RIMA: reversible inhibitors of monoamine oxidase-A.

ethical guidelines. The findings are subject to peer review before publication and they also enter the public domain, being accessible in libraries and so on. Obviously, not all research that is carried out under strict guidelines enters the public domain. This includes studies undertaken on behalf of pharmaceutical companies, and individual psychiatrists will have their own experience of the efficacy of various treatments for individual patients. Our task here is to consider the implications of this approach to treatment for the understanding of social phobia. Readers who are interested in obtaining help for their own problems or on behalf of someone they know are advised to seek specialist medical advice, since all pharmaceutical treatment must be based on careful medical consideration of the circumstances surrounding each individual case and there is a risk of harmful side effects.

Four approaches to pharmaceutical intervention can be identified. Two of these involve drugs that have been primarily used in the treatment of depression: the MAOIs (monoamine oxidase inhibitors) and the SSRIs (selective serotonin reuptake inhibitors).

The other two approaches have applied beta-blockers and benzodi-azepines for the treatment of anxiety disorders. Table 6.1 provides a summary of the four types of drug that have been used in research into the treatment of social phobia.

MAOIs

Monoamine oxidase is an enzyme found in the presynaptic cell. It is involved in breaking down monoamine neurotransmitters such as dopamine, noradrenalin and serotonin. As the name monoamine oxidase inhibitor suggests, it acts to inhibit the activity of monoamine oxidase, and hence to increase the level of these neuro-transmitters in the synapse. High levels of monoamines have been shown to be associated with positive mood and low levels with negative mood, and MAOIs have been found to be effective in the treatment of depression. However there has been concern about serious side effects, particularly when the drug is taken with some forms of food, and patients taking these drugs have to be vigilant about their diet. This is because the monoamine tyramine is present in many foods, for example dairy products and wine, as well as in some cough and cold cure medicines that can be bought over the counter. Because MAOIs inhibit the breakdown of monoamines the overall level can become dangerously high. In an attempt to reduce some of the risk, a class of reversible MAOIs (RIMAs) has been developed.

Three carefully controlled studies have examined the effective-ness of MAOIs in the treatment of social phobia. Gelernter *et al.* (1991) compared the results obtained with phenelzine with those obtained with a benzodiazepine (alprazolam), group cognitive-behaviour therapy and a placebo. The participants were diagnosed on the basis of a clinical interview and those with a comorbid con-dition such as depression or substance abuse were excluded. The drugs were administered for a period of 12 weeks. A number of out-come measures were recorded immediately after discontinuation of treatment, including clinical ratings and self-report questionnaires, and these were repeated two months later. All four groups showed an improvement after the 12-week period, but the phenelzine patients and the cognitive-behaviour therapy group maintained their improved condition over the two-month period to a greater degree than the alprazolam and placebo groups. Nevertheless the overall differences among the four groups were slight.

Liebowitz *et al.* (1992) compared the results obtained with phenelzine with those obtained with atenolol (a beta blocker) and a placebo in a sample of 107 patients (data were collected for 74 of these). Social phobia was defined in terms of *DSM-III* criteria and the participants were free of depression. Drug treatment lasted for eight weeks, followed by another eight weeks of treatment and then a further period of four weeks when those taking phenelzine or atenolol were randomly assigned to further treatment or to a placebo condition. The outcome measures included a clinical rating of improvement and scores in clinician-report and self-report social anxiety questionnaires. At the end of eight weeks the clinician ratings showed that 64 per cent of the phenelzine group (16 out of 25 patients) were either very much or much improved compared with 30 per cent of the beta blocker group and 23 per cent of the control group. There were no significant differences in the self-report measures. At the end of a further period of eight weeks, during which the treatment was continued, 52 per cent of the phenelzine group showed improvement, higher than the placebo group (19 per cent) but not significantly higher than the beta blocker group (43 per cent).

Versiani *et al.* (1992) compared the results obtained with phenelzine with those obtained with moclobemide, a reversible inhibitor of monoamine oxidase (RIMA), and a placebo. Social phobia was defined in terms of *DSM-III–R* criteria and most of the patients (72 per cent) suffered from the generalised subtype. The design was similar to that implemented by Liebowitz *et al.* (1992): an eight-week treatment phase was followed by an eight-week maintenance phase and then an eight-week double-blind discontinuation phase. Outcome measures included ratings by clinicians and self-reports. At the end of 16 weeks, 90 per cent of the phenelzine group (73 per cent of those who had originally begun treatment) showed improvements in the clinician ratings. This compared with 82 per cent (54 per cent) of the moclobemide group and 43 per cent (12 per cent) of the placebo group. Patients in both drug groups experienced adverse side effects throughout the treatment, although those on moclobemide showed fewer effects, particularly during the second phase of the treatment.

These studies suggest that some improvements follow from the administration of MAOIs and that side effects can be reduced by the use of RIMAs. Other studies have investigated RIMAs, including brofaromine (a drug that has been withdrawn from the market) and additional studies of moclobemide. Van Ameringen *et al.* (1999a, 1999c) provide evaluative reviews of these studies but conclude that there are inconsistent findings and that the effectiveness of MAOIs has not been convincingly demonstrated.

SSRIs

The neurotransmitter serotonin (or 5-hydroxytryptamine) is active in a small number of neurons in the brainstem that have a large number of target neurons. These neurons have a coordinating and modulatory role and variations in the level of serotonin have multiple effects, associated with quality of mood, self-esteem and levels of arousal and vigilance. Serotonin seems to have an overall inhibitory effect and low levels result in the individual being less able to cope with stress, less effective in social behaviour and more prone to impulsive aggression. A low level of circulating serotonin, as measured by the level of 5-H acids, has been linked with increased irritability, mood change, increased risk-taking and a tendency towards suicidal behaviour. SSRIs are an established treatment for depression, and have also been used for obsessive-compulsive disorder, bulimia nervosa and panic attacks. SSRIs work by preventing the reuptake of serotonin, hence it remains longer in the synapse and facilitates the transmission of subsequent messages across the synapse.

Several studies have examined their effectiveness in the treatment of social phobia. Van Ameringen *et al.* (1999c) review five published reports of controlled studies that administered fluvoxamine, sertraline or paroxetine and compared them with a placebo condition. Van Vliet *et al.* (1994) reported the effectiveness of fluvoxamine over a 12-week treatment period in a double-blind study. The principal outcome measure, taken at the end of the treatment period, was the Liebowitz social anxiety scale (LSAS). This questionnaire was completed by clinicians and rated the degree of the patients' fear and avoidance in respect of 24 items on social and performance situations.

Stein *et al.* (1999) also assessed fluvoxamine in a double-blind, placebo-controlled study with a sample of 92 patients with generalised social phobia. The treatment lasted 12 weeks and outcome measures included clinician ratings of overall improvement and scores on the LSAS. On the clinician measures, 43 per cent of the patients were identified as improved compared with 23 per cent of the placebo group.

Two studies have tested sertraline. The first, by Katzelnick *et al.* (1995), involved only 12 patients who participated in both the active drug and the placebo conditions in a crossover design. Significant improvements were reported after the administration of sertraline. In a larger study with 206 patients (Van Ameringen *et al.*, 1998, cited in Van Ameringen *et al.*, 1999c) the treatment lasted 20 weeks, once more using a double-blind, placebo-controlled experimental design. Clinician ratings of overall improvement showed that 53 per cent of participants in the sertraline condition and 29 per cent in the placebo condition had improved.

Stein *et al.* (1998) examined the effectiveness of paroxetine over a period of 12 weeks. The participants, 187 patients who met *DSM-IV* criteria for generalised social phobia, were assigned at random to the active drug or the placebo condition. Once again the clinical rating of general improvement was the principal outcome measure; 53 per cent of the paroxetine group showed improvement compared with 23 per cent of the control group.

Since this review, three additional studies have been published (Van Ameringen *et al.*, 1999a). Two of these were conducted on behalf of the pharmaceutical company SmithKline Beecham, which manufactures Seroxat, a brand of paroxetine. A third study (Allgulander, 1998, cited in Van Ameringen *et al.* (1999a), carried out a placebo-controlled study with 29 social phobics. All three studies reported positive outcomes for paroxetine.

Black and Uhde (1994), using a placebo-controlled design, have tested the effectiveness of fluoxetine for the treatment of selective mutism. Six children received the drug over a period of twelve weeks. The findings were inconclusive and additional research will have to be undertaken with a larger sample and a longer trial period before the effectiveness of a pharmacological approach to this condition can be fully assessed.

These studies generally report benefits arising over the treatment period for those patients prescribed the SSRI relative to those who have received the placebo. Van Ameringen *et al.* (1999c, p. 314) suggest that this form of pharmacological intervention will become the 'new gold standard' for treatment. Nevertheless some words of caution are necessary. First, this research is in its infancy and further studies need to be undertaken to assess the effectiveness of these medications. Pharmaceutical companies have been involved in some of the recent investigations, and while there is nothing to suggest they have not been carried out as rigorously as other studies, the controversy over the use of pharmacological interventions for shyness and social phobia suggests that the case would be strengthened if the research base was larger than would be required if the issue was less tendentious. Second, the studies are short term in nature, with the assessment of outcomes being made after weeks rather than months, often immediately after the end of the treatment regime. While the difficulties of undertaking double-blind studies should not be underestimated, what is lacking is a sense of how medication would fit into a programme of treatment that would produce long-term improvements in social effectiveness. It is possible that any reduction in anxiety will be short-lived and social phobia will remain a chronic problem. Furthermore, assessments of improvements are based on therapist ratings and self-report questionnaires. While it is encouraging to know that patients do feel significantly less anxious after the pharmacological intervention, we do not know how they feel or behave in the kinds of situation that elicit intense anxiety.

Finally, it is not clear how these interventions produce their effects, particularly as they have been developed for depressive disorders where the contribution of elevated levels of serotonin is more readily understood. How do increased serotonin levels reduce phobic reactions? One possible explanation is that depression has a high prevalence of comorbidity with social phobia so that the improvements may follow a reduction in depression. Alternatively the more positive mood quality induced by the medication may make patients feel better about themselves and change their attitude towards their problem, at least in the short term. The arguments against this interpretation of the findings are, first, that participants are typically screened for the presence of comorbid conditions including depression and, second, that drugs to ameliorate depression that are not based on SSRIs, for example the tricyclic antidepressants, have not been shown to be effective (Sutherland and Davidson, 1995, p. 324).

Beta blockers and benzodiazepines

Given that social phobia involves heightened anxiety in the kinds of situation that are feared, it would be reasonable to assume that pharmacological treatments for anxiety disorders would be beneficial in this case too. Beta blockers inhibit the activity of adrenalin and noradrenalin, which produce faster heart rate, sweating and subjective components of anxiety. However there has been little research on their effectiveness for social phobia. A number of studies, including double-blind and placebo-controlled designs, have examined their ability to remedy performance anxiety, particularly as it affects professional musicians. There have been some positive results (reviewed by Sutherland and Davidson, 1995), but although stagefright and performing in front of others are prominent situations in social phobia checklists, participants have not been clinically assessed for the condition. There have been some investigations of their application to social phobia. We have already summarised the study by Liebowitz *et al.* (1992), which compared a beta blocker, atenolol, with an MAOI, phenelzine, and found the treatments to be comparable at the end of the continuation phase of the research. Turner *et al.* (1994) compared atenolol with *in vivo* exposure in a placebo-controlled study lasting eight weeks. The beta blocker was no more effective than the placebo and was inferior to the behavioural approach. Falloon *et al.* (1981) found no difference between a group who received social skills training in combination with treatment with propranolol and a group who received skills training with a placebo.

Benzodiazepines affect arousal by enhancing the activity of GABA, which is the major neurotransmitter in the inhibitory synapses of the central nervous system. High levels of GABA are associated with drowsiness and low levels with anxiety and excitement. Benzodiazepines have anticonvulsant and muscle-relaxant properties. They are widely used to treat anxiety disorders. Sutherland and Davidson (1995) review six open trials and case studies using clonazepam and alprazolam that have shown evidence of improvement. A further study of clonazepam (Davidson *et al.*, 1993) utilised a double-blind, placebo-controlled design, with 75 patients diagnosed according to *DSM-III–R* criteria. The treatment lasted 10 weeks, after which 78 per cent of the active drug group and 20 per cent of the placebo group were classified as improved. We have also referred to the study by Gelernter *et al.* (1991), which compared alprazolam with an MAOI (phenelzine), as well as incorporating a group cognitive–behavioural therapy condition and a placebo condition. The differences among the groups were small, and the alprazolam administration was less effective than the other treatments.

There are major reservations about the use of benzodiazepines because of their side effects on memory and concentration, particularly if their use is sustained over the long term, and about the potential abuse of tranquillisers such as Valium (diazepam). The combination of alcohol and benzodiazepines can be dangerous, for example it can impair driving or skilled performance at work (Sutherland and Davidson, 1995, p. 342). It has been found that individuals with social phobia are at greater risk of alcohol and other substance abuse. Of course it is possible that an improvement in their condition will reduce this risk, as alcohol is frequently used by social phobics and shy people (and many others as well) to cope with the anxiety aroused by potentially difficult social situations.

Pharmacological interventions have been shown to be effective in bringing about at least a short-term improvement in patients diagnosed with social phobia. In contrast with evaluation studies of interventions based on psychological models, disappointingly few studies have incorporated a follow-up assessment in their design (Stravynski and Greenberg, 1998). Little attention has been paid to the effects of discontinuing the medication. Three studies reviewed by Stravynski and Greenberg (ibid.) compared psychological with pharmacological interventions (a fourth study looked at professional musicians over a short treatment period and is not considered here). We have already referred to these studies. Gelernter *et al* (1991) reported few differences among subjects assigned to cognitive behaviour therapy, phenelzine, alprazolam or a placebo condition. Turner *et al*. (1994) found that the beta blocker atenolol was no more effective than the placebo and was inferior to the exposure approach. Falloon *et al*. (1981) found that adding the beta blocker propranolol to social skills training was not superior to social skills training alone. This is too small a research base to provide any conclusive evidence. The effectiveness of pharmacological treatment in reducing anxiety suggests that it might have a role in combination with behavioural methods, but this has yet to be evaluated in a systematic way.

The treatment of blushing problems

Blushing is a concern of some 50 per cent of patients diagnosed with social phobia (Stein and Bouwer, 1997), which is to be expected given that it is a sign of embarrassment and that fear of embarrass ment is central to social phobia as it is currently defined. The fear of blushing (erythophobia) is itself a common presenting problem among socially anxious individuals. Approaches to help people cope with their blushing problems are similar to the approaches to treating social anxiety more generally. Edelmann (1990c) outlines a self-help programme that draws upon cognitive restructuring, relaxation training and exercises designed to enhance self-confidence. Bögels *et al.* (1997) report that a programme based on reducing self-focused attention and directing attention towards the task led to reductions in the tendency to blush, the fear of blushing and thoughts about the negative consequences of blushing. Scholing and Emmelkamp (1996) carried out a series of studies that compared three treatments entailing different combinations of *in vivo* exposure and cognitive restructuring, with a waiting list control condition. The treatment conditions did not differ from each other but all were superior to the control condition in reducing scores in self-report measures of fear of blushing, sweating or trembling. The improvements were still evident at a follow-up session after 18 months.

A more radical surgical treatment has recently been developed to reduce blushing and sweating. A short operation interrupts the sympathetic ganglion nerve in the chest and this affects sympathetic signals to the blood vessels in the face. The procedure is carried out under a general anaesthetic and involves a keyhole (endoscopic) surgical technique where two small incisions are made in the area of the armpit. The technical term for this procedure is endoscopic thoracic sympathicotomy (ETS). Open trials have been reported in the literature. Teleranta (1998) carried out the procedure on 51 social phobic patients and reported significant improvements in blushing, tremor and anxiety, without any complications. Olsson-Rex *et al.* (1998) reported follow-up data, after intervals ranging from less than a year to three years, on 785 patients who had presented with a problem with hand sweating and 244 with a problem with blushing. The success rates, as assessed by the patients' ratings of their satisfaction with the outcome of the operation, were high. Where blushing was concerned, 96 per cent reported a positive outcome and 85 per cent were fully satisfied. Overall, complications were rare.

Although these are promising results this research is in its infancy. Individual patients must weigh up the benefits and costs in terms of the seriousness to them of their blushing problem and the potential

risks of surgery under general anaesthetic, as well as further complications. To a psychologist, one distinctive feature of this research
is its assumption that blushing is entirely a negative condition.
Although it can be regarded as a serious problem for individuals,
blushing also serves positive social functions, as discussed in
Chapter 5. Research has yet to explore whether blushing problems
can be addressed by cognitive–behavioural approaches, which have
proved effective in other areas of social anxiety and social phobia.
The fundamental question that Beck (1989) and others have posed is
whether it is the blush that is the problem or the individual's thinking about blushing.

Summary

Research into the overcoming of shyness has been dominated by
studies of the treatment of social phobia. The relevance of this
research to individuals who wish to seek help for problems they
attribute to their shyness is obscured by the problem of terminology.
The term shyness has been criticised because its use in everyday
language suggests that it is too imprecise to provide an adequate
basis for identifying and classifying problems in social behaviour or
designing intervention strategies. The term social phobia does not
share that problem, but it too is controversial. The concept of a phobia implies a specific target of the person's fear, but individuals with
high social anxiety tend to experience problems with a range of different social situations. The concept of generalised social phobia has
been proposed, but this is almost self-contradictory. There are problems too in distinguishing social phobia from avoidant personality
disorder.

A further difficulty is conceptualising the relationship between
the shyness that anyone can experience and the intense anxiety that
is associated with the condition of social phobia. One model of the
relationship is that there exists a continuum of social anxiety, with
social phobia located at one extreme of this (see Figure 6.1a). A second model is that there is a qualitative difference between shyness
and social phobia. A temperament or personality trait of shyness
might be one factor predisposing an individual to social phobia, but
there may be other factors as well, and these might work in tandem
with or in isolation from shyness (Figure 6.1b). A similar conceptual
problem is posed by depression. Is clinical depression qualitatively

different from grief or sadness, or is it a further step along a continuum of negative emotion? Such conceptual problems have practical
significance when the appropriateness of medical interventions for
these psychological conditions is considered. Despite advances in
the understanding of psychological conditions, and efforts to pro-
mote positive images of these in order to overcome the stigma
attached to them, there remains a lingering idea that they are not a
'real' illness, or that the individual is to some degree responsible for
his or her condition and the problem can be overcome with an effort
of will.

There is no doubt that any psychological condition has to be
understood in its cultural dimension as well as in psychological or
physiological terms. All cultures have norms in respect of what
forms of behaviour are appropriate and valued, and these influence
child-rearing and socialisation practices. Parents have attitudes
towards their children's temperamental qualities and typical behaviours and these are reflected in their practices and the labels they
attach to their children's characteristics. In turn these influence the
children's self-esteem and expectations of the outcomes of social
interactions and relationships. Nevertheless the problems which
individuals face are real and they can be helped to deal with them.

The evidence we have reviewed in this chapter does suggest
optimism with regard to helping individuals with the self-consciousness, low self-esteem, anxiety symptoms and difficulty in
behaving appropriately in social situations that characterise social
anxiety in its different forms. However, the potential contribution
of pharmacological treatments is uncertain. While they have had
some success in tackling symptoms and enhancing self-image (as
reflected in client self-reports), there has been no controlled
research into long-term benefits or whether any improvements survive the discontinuation of medication. Our analysis of shyness as
a complex phenomenon with cognitive, somatic and behavioural
components implies that pharmacological treatment will not be
effective in isolation, although it might be so in combination with
cognitive-behavioural intervention.

Chapter 7

Epilogue

When Ben was introduced to his great aunt he looked down at the ground and would not answer her questions. 'He's very shy', she said. 'He's not always like this', his mother replied. When it was time to begin play group he cried when his mother left him and it took a long time for the leaders to comfort him. He preferred to play on his own and when other children commandeered his toys or took his place in the sandpit he gave in without a fuss. He was silent when it was his turn to tell his news in the circle. 'He'll grow out of it', the leader assured his parents. When he started school he was very conscientious and was liked by the teachers and his classmates. He never volunteered answers to questions but when he was pressed he always had something interesting to say. He was very quiet in class and liked nothing better than to work on his own, colouring or reading. In the playground he hovered at the fringes of all the games. 'He's very quiet', said the teachers when his parents came to the open evening. 'Not at home', said his parents.

Ben's career at school was uneventful. He worked hard but kept to himself. He was never popular and tended to be passed over when children were picked to make teams, but nobody disliked him, and if pressed they would say he was a nice person. If he was asked to help with homework he was patient and kind. He had one or two close friends with whom he liked to go around, but he went home after school and declined their invitations to go out to play. He liked computer games and collecting things. When he was asked about these he could become very animated and talk without pausing. Teachers liked him, but they never felt they got to know him very well. He gave the out-of-school clubs a miss and did not go to parties.

But how did Ben feel about this? He always wanted to join in the social activities but did not feel able to. He could often think of something funny to say or had an answer to a teacher's question, but he was afraid that it would sound stupid. In any case he never managed to break into a conversation and the opportunity to speak passed. He could never think what to say to anybody and he dreaded being on his own with a teacher or even another child because there would inevitably be long silences and he knew that they could not think of anything to say to him either. Whenever he was in company he remained quiet, but his mind was racing. He rehearsed things he might say or a joke to make, but he could never bring himself to come out with any of these. Worse still, if he did find the courage to do so it never came out as he wished and often led to a silence or his contribution being ignored. Everyone teased each other and seemed prepared to make fools of themselves, but he was hurt if he was ever at the receiving end of this banter. He was reluctant to express an opinion in case it attracted ridicule. He had begun to think of himself as shy.

He became attracted to a girl whom he met at a dancing class. She was lively and very good looking and he found he could talk easily to her, but he believed that she would never reciprocate his feelings because, when she got to know him, she would discover he was shy. His first date was with a girl from school but he was intensely self-conscious and felt everyone was looking at them. He was intimidated that she seemed so 'grown-up' in her fashionable clothes and high heels. He felt stiff and awkward holding her hand and was too shy to kiss her at the end of the evening. His shyness was now a salient part of his personality.

What have we learned about the shyness of people like Ben? First, that his concerns are widespread. Shy people are tempted to think that they are unique in finding social situations problematic or in thinking that their problems are caused by their own personality. The Stanford survey and subsequent research has established that large numbers in the population experience these difficulties, they feel self-conscious, nervous and reluctant to join in conversations, and they see themselves as responsible for their difficulties. Not everyone is shy in the same way, of course; for some, shyness is reticence and an inability to know what to say (to quote 'Iorath', 'I am naturally shy and unable to make conversation'). For others, it is being self-conscious, or blushing too easily, or having symptoms of anxiety.

Psychological research into personality has been dominated by an emphasis on traits as stable attributes of a person. These attributes make an individual's behaviour consistent from one situation to another, and help distinguish the behaviour of one individual from another. These attributes can be measured, for example by means of questionnaires and rating scales, and these measures can be used to predict how people will behave in a given situation. This is an example of a realist conception of personality. According to this perspective, Ben's shyness is not simply a matter of his beliefs about himself, his assimilation of attitudes that others hold about him or his interpretation of the predictable course that particular recurring social situations seem to follow. The reasons for his shyness are to be found in his personality.

A trait perspective is not the only approach that can be taken to understand and explain consistencies or individual differences in shyness. The Stanford shyness survey offers an example of an approach that begins with individuals' own conceptions of their shyness and its implications for their social encounters and personal relationships. Although it gave an impetus to research (and most of the concerns expressed by its shy participants have found empirical support in laboratory studies of cognitions, feelings and behaviour) and it remains a valuable source of information about shyness, it has not provided a model for research into shyness. Another tradition of personality research is the ideographic method. This undertakes close examination of the circumstances of individual cases and has proved effective in other areas of enquiry where the case study method has been applied to the study of rare individuals, for example those identified as highly creative or those with specific conditions such as amnesia, language disorders or the effects of brain injury. This approach has seldom been taken to the study of shyness.

The trait approach has produced a substantial body of research into shyness. Several questionnaire measures have been constructed (Chapter 1). Individuals identified as shy or socially anxious on the basis of their scores on these measures differ from less shy or anxious peers in a number of ways. They are self-conscious, they are preoccupied with how poorly they perform and they are quick to identify a situation as potentially threatening to their esteem. They do not believe that they can reach the standards other people expect of them. In comparison with the less shy, they report more symptoms of anxiety and appear more anxious to those who interact with them. Several studies have examined peripheral measures of sympathetic nervous system activity or have made EEG recordings of brain activity. There are inconsistencies in the findings but several studies show that shy children and adults have a higher and more stable heart rate. They also have an elevated level of activity in the right frontal hemisphere, an area of the brain that has been identified as involved in fear and in the processing of threatening information. Shy children and adults are reticent and slow to enter conversations and to break silences, particularly when they are in the company of strangers or unfamiliar people. Research has also shown that shyness is more likely if people feel that they are likely to be evaluated by others or if they have to perform in front of an audience.

What are the origins of Ben's shyness? Individual differences in distress and reluctance to embrace new situations can be detected in the first two years of life and a substantial body of research has provided support for the notion that inhibition is a temperament with specific neurobiological correlates. There is also evidence of continuity between this temperament and shyness in later childhood. A small number of longitudinal studies suggest that the effects of inhibition extend into adulthood and influence long-term social relationships and work patterns (Chapter 3).

Nevertheless there remain several unresolved issues. Although Ben might well have been an inhibited infant, it seems likely that many shy children and adults were not inhibited in the early years. Important changes in self-awareness and self-evaluation take place from the second year onwards and these might contribute to shyness, given the roles that self-consciousness and beliefs about inadequate social performance play in shyness. The relationship between parent and child may also be involved. Insecure attachments might shape a child's expectations about social encounters. Alternatively the absence of adult models with poised or effective social behaviour might influence his or her self-confidence. Finally, temperament might interact with these relationships in complex ways. More evidence is needed.

Although shyness research is permeated with the assumption that it is a form of anxiety, theories of the 'self-conscious' emotions have regarded shyness as closer to embarrassment and shame. It is argued that these emotions are also aspects of social anxiety, but they do seem distinctive in terms of emotional displays and the greater involvement of parasympathetic nervous system activity. My own view is that a more rigorous conceptualisation of self-consciousness would clarify many of these issues.

What are the prospects for those who wish to overcome their shyness? Chapter 6 examined some of the clinical approaches that have

been developed to help people with social anxiety problems. It concentrated on these studies because this approach has attracted most
research. Moreover clinical intervention is an important topic since
many people suffer from severe problems. Nevertheless this should
not obscure the fact that many shy individuals find ways for themselves to interact with people more rewardingly. In part, this is associated with changes in the self-concept and with gains in self-confidence. Significant life changes can also make individuals less shy, in
part because these affect their self-concept, but also because they
can provide the individual with clearly defined roles. A woman
who is anxious about meeting other people socially can find that a
new role as mother, caregiver or career woman provides her with a
means of meeting others, a shared experience to form the basis of
conversations and friendships, and fresh personal goals. When Ben
does embark on a satisfying relationship many of his anxieties will
become redundant.

Social relationships grow between people who share interests and
values and find each other's company rewarding. It can take individuals some time to meet people to fill these roles. Difficulties with
social relationships may turn out to be ephemeral, but they do not
seem like that at the time. They are experienced against a cultural
background where social success and popularity are seen as the
norm, and these are attained by possession of the personal qualities
of poise, gregariousness and attractiveness. Yet this is a culture-
bound view of social relations, one that emphasises individualism
and pays little attention to the concepts of role, status and manners.
These concepts refer to principles of social organisation that have
always formed the basis of a mutually satisfying public life.
However there are costs involved in deviating from social norms,
rules or standards, for example disgrace, dishonour or exclusion,
and these can be experienced at the individual level as embarrassment, shame or humiliation. The fear expressed by those who are
shy, that they lack what it takes to contribute effectively to social
encounters and consequently will fall short of the standards, surely
relates to these emotions.

Shyness was a neglected topic in psychology for many years but
it has attracted increasing interest in recent years. This volume has
aimed to provide an overview of that research. Considerable
progress has been made, nevertheless many issues remain to be
resolved in terms of understanding shyness and facilitating change
in those who seek it.

References

Abe, J. A. and Izard, C. E. (1999) 'The developmental functions of emotions: An analysis in terms of Differential Emotions Theory', *Cognition and Emotion* **13**, 523–49.

Achenbach, T. M., McConaughy, S. H. and Howell, C. T. (1987) 'Child/adolescent behavioral/emotional problems: Implications of cross-informant correlations for situational specificity', *Psychological Bulletin* **101**, 213–32.

Aikawa, A. (1991) 'A study on the reliability and validity of a scale to measure shyness as a trait', *Japanese Journal of Psychology* **62**, 149–55.

Ainsworth, M. D. S., Blehar, M. C., Waters, E. and Wall, S. (1978) *Patterns of Attachment: A Psychological Study of the Strange Situation* (Hillsdale, NJ: Erlbaum).

Alluglander, C. (1998) 'Efficacy of paroxetine in social phobia: A single-center double-blind study of 96 symptomatic volunteers randomized to treatment with paroxetine 20–50mg or placebo for 3 months', *European Neuropsychopharmacology* **8** (2), S255.

American Psychiatric Association (1994) *Diagnostic and Statistical Manual of Mental Disorders, 4th edn* (Washington, DC: American Psychiatric Association).

Amsterdam, B. K. and Levitt, M. (1980) 'Consciousness of self and painful self-consciousness', *Psychoanalytic Study of the Child*, **35**, 67–83.

Arcus, D. and Kagan, J. (1995) 'Temperament and craniofacial variation in the first two years', *Child Development* **66**, 1529–40.

Arkin, R. M. (1981) 'Self-presentational styles', in J. T. Tedeschi (ed.), *Impression Management Theory and Social Psychological Research* (New York: Academic Press), 311–33.

Asendorpf, J. B. (1987) *A Longitudinal Study on the Development of Social Competence No. 3: Results of Wave One* (Munich: Max Planck Institute for Psychological Research).

Asendorpf, J. B. (1989) 'Shyness as a final common pathway for two different kinds of inhibition', *Journal of Personality and Social Psychology* **57**, 481–92.

229

Asendorpf, J. B. (1990a) 'The expression of shyness and embarrassment', in W. R. Crozier (ed.), *Shyness and Embarrassment: Perspectives from Social Psychology* (New York: Cambridge University Press), 87–118.

Asendorpf, J. B. (1990b) 'The development of inhibition during childhood: Evidence for situational specificity and a two-factor model', *Developmental Psychology* **26**, 721–30.

Asendorpf, J. B. (1991) 'Development of inhibited children's coping with unfamiliarity', *Child Development* **62**, 1460–74.

Asendorpf, J. B. (1993) 'Abnormal shyness in children', *Journal of Child Psychology and Psychiatry* **34**, 1069–81.

Asendorpf, J. B. and Meier, G. (1993) 'Personality effects on children's speech in everyday life: Sociability-mediated exposure and shyness-mediated reactivity to social situations', *Journal of Personality and Social Psychology* **64**, 1072–83.

Asendorpf, J. B. and Wilpers, S. (1998) 'Personality effects on social relationships', *Journal of Personality and Social Psychology* **74**, 1531–44.

Babcock, M. K. (1988) 'Embarrassment: A window on the self', *Journal for the Theory of Social Behaviour* **18**, 459–83.

Bandura, A. (1986) *Social Foundations of Thought and Action: A Social Cognitive Theory* (Englewood Cliffs, NJ: Prentice-Hall).

Baumgarten, H. G, and Grozdanovic, Z. (1998) 'Role of serotonin in obsessive-compulsive disorder', *British Journal of Psychiatry* **173** (Supplement 35), 13–20.

Beck, A. T. (1989) *Cognitive Therapy and the Emotional Disorders* (London: Penguin).

Beidel, D. C. and Turner, S. M. (1998) *Shy Children, Phobic Adults: Nature and Treatment of Social Phobia* (Washington, DC: American Psychological Association).

Bell, I. R., Amend, D., Kaszniak, A., Schwartz, G. E., Peterson, J. M., Stini, W. A., Miller, J. W. and Selhub, J. (1995) 'Trait shyness in the elderly: Evidence for an association between Parkinson's Disease in family members and biochemical correlates', *Journal of Geriatric Psychiatry and Neurology* **8**, 16–22.

Bell, I. R., Jasnoski, M. L., Kagan, J. and King, D. S. (1990) 'Is allergic rhinitis more frequent in young adults with extreme shyness? A preliminary survey', *Psychosomatic Medicine* **52**, 517–25.

Bell, I. R., Schwartz, G. E., Bootzin, R. R., Hau, V. and Davis, T. P. (1997) 'Elevation of plasma beta-endorphin levels of shy elderly in response to novel laboratory experiences', *Behavioral Medicine* **22**, 168–73.

Bennett, A. (1912) *Buried Alive* (London: Methuen).

Bertenthal, B. I. and Fischer, K. W. (1978) 'Development of self-recognition in the infant', *Developmental Psychology* **14**, 44–50.

Bieling, P. J. and Alden, L. E. (1997) 'The consequences of perfectionism for patients with social phobia', *British Journal of Clinical Psychology* **36**, 387–95.

Birmbaumer, N., Grodd, W., Diedrich, O., Klose, U., Erb, M., Lotze, M., Schneider, F., Weiss, U. and Flor, H. (1998) 'fMRI reveals amygdala activation to human faces in social phobics', *Neuroreport* **9**, 1223–6.

Black, B. and Uhde, T. W. (1992) 'Elective mutism as a variant of social phobia', *Journal of the American Academy of Child and Adolescent Psychiatry* **31**, 1090–4.

Black, B. and Uhde, T. W. (1994) 'Fluoxetine treatment of elective mutism: A double-blind, placebo-controlled study', *Journal of the American Academy of Child and Adolescent Psychiatry* **33**, 1000–6.

Blankstein, K. R., Toner, B. B. and Flett, G. L. (1989) 'Test anxiety and the contents of consciousness: Thought-listing and endorsement measures', *Journal of Research in Personality* **23**, 269–86.

Boer, F. and Westenberg, P. M. (1994) 'Factor structure of the Buss and Plomin EAS Temperament Survey (Parental ratings) in a Dutch sample of elementary school children', *Journal of Personality Assessment* **62**, 537–51.

Bögels, S. M., Alberts, M. and de Jong, P. J. (1996) 'Self-consciousness, self-focused attention, blushing propensity and fear of blushing', *Personality and Individual Differences* **21**, 573–81.

Bögels, S. M., Mulkens, S. and DeJong, P. J. (1997) 'Task concentration training and fear of blushing', *Clinical Psychology and Psychotherapy* **4**, 251–8.

Boomsma, D. I. and Plomin, R. (1986) 'Heart rate and behavior of twins', *Merrill-Palmer Quarterly* **32**, 141–51.

Bowlby, J. (1988) *A Secure Base* (London: Routledge).

Bradbury, M. (1978) *Eating People is Wrong* (London: Arrow Books).

Breck, B. E. and Smith, S. H. (1983) 'Selective recall of self-descriptive traits by socially anxious and nonanxious females', *Social Behavior and Personality* **11**, 71–6.

Briggs, S. R. (1988) 'Shyness: Introversion or neuroticism?', *Journal of Research in Personality* **22**, 290–307.

Briggs, S. R. and Smith, T. G. (1986) 'The measurement of shyness', in W. H. Jones, J. M. Cheek and S. R. Briggs (eds), *Shyness: Perspectives on Research and Treatment* (New York: Plenum Press), 47–60.

Brooks-Gunn, J. and Lewis, M. (1984) 'The development of visual self-recognition', *Developmental Review* **4**, 2151–239.

Bruce, C. S. (1997) 'Craig's Shyness Resource Page. Notes on niceness', WWW document. http://www.cyberus.ca/~csbruce/shyness/nice.html. Accessed 18 November 1999.

Bruch, M. A., Giordano, S. and Pearl, L. (1986) 'Differences between fearful and self-conscious shy subtypes in background and current adjustment', *Journal of Research in Personality* **20**, 172–86.

Bruch, M. A., Gorsky, J. M., Collins, T. M. and Berger, P. A. (1989) 'Shyness and sociability reexamined: A multicomponent analysis', *Journal of Personality and Social Psychology* **57**, 904–15.

Bruch, M. A., Hamer, R. J. and Heimberg, R. A. (1995) 'Shyness and public self-consciousness: Additive or interactive relation with social interaction?', *Journal of Personality* **63**, 47–63.

Buss, A. H. (1980) *Self-consciousness and Social Anxiety* (San Francisco: Freeman).

Buss, A. H. (1986) 'A theory of shyness', in W. H. Jones, J. M. Cheek and S. R. Briggs (eds), *Shyness: Perspectives on Research and Treatment* (New York: Plenum Press), 39–46.

Buss, A. H. and Plomin, R. (1984) *Temperament: Early Developing Personality Traits* (Hillsdale, NJ: Erlbaum).

Butterworth, G. and Jarrett, N. (1991) 'What minds have in common is space: Spatial mechanisms serving joint attention in infancy. Structure of the mind in human infancy', *British Journal of Developmental Psychology* **9**, 55–72.

Cacioppo, J. T., Glass, C. R. and Merluzzi, T. V. (1979) 'Self-statements and social evaluation: A cognitive response analysis of heterosocial anxiety', *Cognitive Therapy and Research* **3**, 259–62.

Calkins, S. D. and Fox, N. A. (1992) 'The relations among infant temperament, security of attachment, and behavioral inhibition at twenty-four months', *Child Development* **63**, 1456–72.

Calkins, S. D., Fox, N. A. and Marshall, T. R. (1996) 'Behavioral and physiological antecedents of inhibited and uninhibited behavior', *Child Development* **67**, 523–40.

Carducci, B. J. and Clark, D. L. (1999) 'The personal and situational pervasiveness of shyness: A replication and extension of the Stanford Survey on shyness 20 years later', unpublished paper, Indiana University Southeast Shyness Institute.

Carducci, B. J. and Webber, A. W. (1979) 'Shyness as a determinant of interpersonal distance', *Psychological Reports* **44**, 1075–8.

Carducci, B. J. and Zimbardo, P. G. (1995) 'Are you shy?', *Psychology Today* **28** (6), 34–41, 65–70, 78–9.

Carver, C. S. and Scheier, M. F. (1987) 'The blind men and the elephant: Selective examination of the public-private literature gives rise to a faulty perception', *Journal of Personality* **55**, 525–40.

Caspi, A. (1998) 'Personality development across the life course', in N. Eisenberg (ed.), *Handbook of Child Development*, 5th edn, vol. 3 (New York: Wiley), 311–88.

Caspi, A., Elder, G. H., Jr. and Bem, D. J. (1988) 'Moving away from the world: Life-course patterns of shy children', *Developmental Psychology* **24**, 824–31.

Castelfranchi, C. and Poggi, I. (1990) 'Blushing as a discourse: Was Darwin wrong?', in W. R. Crozier (ed.), *Shyness and Embarrassment: Perspectives from Social Psychology* (New York: Cambridge University Press), 230–51.

Cattell, R. B. (1973) *Personality and Mood by Questionnaire* (San Francisco: Jossey-Bass).

Cattell, R. B., Eber, H. W. and Tatsuoka, M. M. (1970) *Handbook for the Sixteen Personality Factor Questionnaire (16 PF)* (Champaign, IL: Institute for Personality and Ability Testing).

Cheek, J. M. and Briggs, S. R. (1990) 'Shyness as a personality trait', in W. R. Crozier (ed.), *Shyness and Embarrassment: Perspectives from Social Psychology* (New York: Cambridge University Press), 315–37.

Cheek, J. M. and Buss, A. H. (1981) 'Shyness and sociability', *Journal of Personality and Social Psychology* **41**, 330–9.

Cheek, J. M. and Krasnoperova, E. N. (1999) 'Varieties of shyness in adolescence and adulthood', in L. A. Schmidt and J. Schulkin (eds), *Extreme*

Fear, Shyness, and Social Phobia: Origins, Biological Mechanisms, and Clinical Outcomes (New York: Oxford University Press), 224–50.

Cheek, J. M. and Melchior, L. A. (1990) 'Shyness, self-esteem, and self-consciousness', in H. Leitenberg (ed.), *Handbook of Social and Evaluation Anxiety* (New York: Plenum), 47–82.

Cheek, J. M., Melchior, L. A. and Carpentieri, A. M. (1986) 'Shyness and self-concept', in L.M. Hartman and K. R. Blankstein (eds), *Perception of Self in Emotional Disorder and Psychotherapy* (New York: Plenum Press), 113–31.

Cheek, J. M. and Watson, A. K. (1989) 'The definition of shyness: Psychological imperialism or construct validity?', *Journal of Social Behavior and Personality* **4**, 85–95.

Chess, S. and Thomas, A. (1986) *Temperament in Clinical Practice* (New York: Guilford).

Chung, J. and Evans, M. A. (1994) 'Health complaints in young children: Exploring the association between shyness and illness', paper presented at the Annual Meeting of the Canadian Psychological Association, Penticton, BC.

Clark, D. M. (1999) 'Anxiety disorders: Why they persist and how to treat them', *Behaviour Research and Therapy* **37**, S5-S27.

Clark, D. M. and Wells, A. (1995) 'A cognitive model of social phobia', in R. Heimberg, M. Liebowitz, D. A. Hope and F. R. Schneier (eds), *Social Phobia: Diagnosis, Assessment and Treatment* (New York: Guilford Press), 69–93.

Constant, B. (1816/1964) *Adolphe*, transl. by L. W. Tancock (London: Penguin).

Coplan, R. J., Coleman, B. J. and Rubin, K. H. (1998) 'Shyness and Little Boy Blue: Iris pigmentation, gender, and social wariness in preschoolers', *Developmental Psychobiology* **32**, 37–44.

Costa, P. and McCrae, R. R. (1995) 'Solid ground in the wetlands of personality: A reply to Block', *Psychological Bulletin* **117**, 216–20.

Cottle, M. (1999) 'Selling shyness', *The New Republic* **221**, (5), 24–9.

Crozier, W. R. (1979) 'Shyness as a dimension of personality', *British Journal of Clinical Psychology* **18**, 121–8.

Crozier, W. R. (1981) 'Shyness and self-esteem', *British Journal of Social Psychology* **20**, 220–2.

Crozier, W. R. (1990) 'Social psychological perspectives on shyness, embarrassment, and shame', in W.R. Crozier (ed.), *Shyness and Embarrassment: Perspectives from Social Psychology* (New York: Cambridge University Press), 19–58.

Crozier, W. R. (1995) 'Shyness and self-esteem in middle childhood', *British Journal of Educational Psychology* **65**, 85–95.

Crozier, W. R. (1999) 'Individual differences in childhood shyness: Distinguishing fearful and self-conscious shyness', in L. A. Schmidt and J. Schulkin (eds), *Extreme Fear, Shyness, and Social Phobia* (New York: Oxford University Press), 14–29.

Crozier, W. R. and Burnham, M. (1990) 'Age-related differences in children's understanding of shyness', *British Journal of Developmental Psychology* **8**, 179–85.

Crozier, W. R. and Garbert-Jones, A. (1996) 'Finding a voice: Shyness in mature students' experience of university', *Adults Learning* **7**, 195–8.

Crozier, W. R., Rees, V., Morris-Beattie, A. and Bellin, W. (1999) 'Streaming, self-esteem and friendships within a comprehensive school', *Educational Psychology in Practice* **15**, 128–34.

Crozier, W. R. and Russell, D. (1992) 'Blushing, embarrassability and self-consciousness', *British Journal of Developmental Psychology* **8**, 179–85.

Cupach, W. R. and Metts, S. (1990) 'Remedial processes in embarrassing predicaments', in J. Anderson (ed.), *Communication Yearbook* (Newbury Park, CA: Sage), 323–52.

Cutlip II, W. D. and Leary, M. R. (1993) 'Anatomic and physiological bases of social blushing: Speculations from neurology and psychology', *Behavioural Neurology* **6**, 181–5.

Darwin, C. (1872/1965) *The Expression of the Emotions in Man and Animals* (London: John Murray, 1965 edition, Chicago, IL.: University of Chicago Press).

Davidson, J. R. T., Potts, N. S., Richichi, E., Krishnan, R., Ford, S. M., Smith, R. D. and Wilson, W. H. (1993) 'Treatment of social phobia with clonazepam and placebo', *Journal of Clinical Psychopharmacology* **13**, 423–8.

Davidson, R. J. and Irwin, W. (1999) 'The functional anatomy of emotion and affective style', *Trends in Cognitive Sciences* **3**, 11–21.

Davidson, R. J, Saron, C. D., Senulis, J. A., Ekman, P. and Friesen, W. V. (1990) 'Approach–withdrawal and cerebral asymmetry: Emotional expression and brain physiology 1', *Journal of Personality and Social Psychology* **58**, 330–41.

DeWit, D. J., Ogborne, A., Offord, D. R. and Macdonald, K. (1999) 'Antecedents of the risk of recovery from DSM-III-R social phobia', *Psychological Medicine* **29**, 569–82.

Dow, S. P., Sonies, B. C., Scheib, D., Moss, S. E. and Leonard, H. L. (1995) 'Practical guidelines for the assessment and treatment of selective mutism', *Journal of the American Academy of Child and Adolescent Psychiatry* **34**, 836–46.

Drummond, P. D. (1989) 'Mechanism of emotional blushing', in N. W. Bond and D. A. T. Siddle (eds), *Psychobiology: Issues and Applications* (Amsterdam: North-Holland), 363–70.

Drummond, P. D. (1997) 'The effect of adrenergic blockade on blushing and facial flushing', *Psychophysiology* **34**, 163–8.

Duggan, E. S. and Brennan, K. A. (1994) 'Social avoidance and its relation to Bartholomew's adult attachment typology', *Journal of Social and Personal Relationships* **11**, 147–53.

Edelmann, R. J. (1985) 'Individual differences in embarrassment: Self-consciousness, self-monitoring and embarrassibility', *Personality and Individual Differences* **6**, 223–30.

Edelmann, R. J. (1987) *The Psychology of Embarrassment* (Chichester, Sussex: Wiley).

Edelmann, R. J. (1990a) 'Embarrassment and blushing: A component-process model, some initial descriptive and cross-cultural data', in W. R. Crozier (ed.), *Shyness and Embarrassment: Perspectives from Social Psychology* (New York: Cambridge University Press), 205–29.

Edelmann, R. J. (1990b) 'Chronic blushing, self-consciousness and social anxiety', *Journal of Psychopathology and Behavioral Assessment* **12**, 119–27.

Edelmann, R. J. (1990c) *Coping With Blushing* (London: Sheldon Press).

Edelmann, R. J. (1991) 'Correlates of chronic blushing', *British Journal of Clinical Psychology* **30**, 177–8.

Edelmann, R. J. (1995) 'Individual differences in embarrassment: Self-consciousness, self-monitoring and embarrassability', *Personality and Individual Differences* **6**, 223–30.

Edelmann, R. J. and Hampson, S. E. (1979) 'Changes in non-verbal behaviour during embarrassment', *British Journal of Social and Clinical Psychology* **18**, 385–90.

Eisenberg, N., Fabes, R. A. and Murphy, B. C. (1995) 'Relations of shyness and low sociability to regulation and emotionality', *Journal of Personality and Social Psychology* **68**, 505–17.

Eisenberg, N., Shepard, S. A., Fabes, R. A., Murphy, B. C. and Guthrie, I. K. (1998) 'Shyness and children's emotionality, regulation, and coping: Contemporaneous, longitudinal, and across-context relations', *Child Development* **69**, 767–90.

Ekman, P. and Friesen, W. V. (1978) *Facial Action Coding System: A Technique for the Measurement of Facial Movement* (Palo Alto, CA: Consulting Psychologists Press).

Emde, R. N., Plomin, R., Robinson, J., Corley, R., De Fries, J., Fulker, D. W., Reznick, J. S., Campos, J., Kagan, J. and Zahn-Waxler, C. (1992) 'Temperament, emotion and cognition at fourteen months: The MacArthur Longitudinal Twin Study', *Child Development* **63**, 1437–55.

Erikson, E. (1968) *Identity, Youth and Crisis* (New York: Norton).

Evans, M. A. (1987) 'Discourse characteristics of reticent children', *Applied Psycholinguistics* **8**, 171–84.

Evans, M. A. (1993) 'Communication competence as a dimension of shyness', in K. H. Rubin and J. B. Asendorpf (eds), *Social Withdrawal, Inhibition, and Shyness in Childhood* (Hillsdale, NJ: Erlbaum) 189–212.

Evans, M. A. and Bienert, H. (1992) 'Control and paradox in teacher conversations with shy children', *Canadian Journal of Behavioural Sciences* **24**, 502–16.

Eysenck, H. J. (1956) 'The questionnaire measurement of neuroticism and extraversion', *Revista de Psicologia* **50**, 113–40.

Eysenck, H. J. (1970) *Structure of Human Personality* (London: Methuen).

Eysenck, H. J. (1982) 'Neobehavioristic (S-R) theory', in G. T. Wilson and C. M. Franks (eds), *Contemporary Behavior Therapy* (New York: Guilford Press) 205–76.

Eysenck, H. J. (1995) *Genius: The Natural History of Creativity* (Cambridge: Cambridge University Press).

Eysenck, M. W. (1992) *Anxiety: The Cognitive Perspective* (Hove, Sussex: Erlbaum).

Falloon, I. R., Lloyd, G. G. and Harpin, R. (1981) 'The treatment of social phobia: Real-life rehearsal with non-professional therapists', *Journal of Nervous and Mental Disease* **169**, 180–4.

Feist, G. J. (1998) 'A meta-analysis of personality in scientific and artistic creativity', *Personality and Social Psychology Review* **2**, 290–309.

Fenigstein, A., Scheier, M. F. and Buss, A. H. (1975) 'Public and private self-consciousness: Assessment and theory', *Journal of Consulting and Clinical Psychology* **43**, 522–7.

Fergusson, D. M. and Horwood, L. J. (1987) 'The trait and method components of ratings of conduct disorder – Part I. Maternal and teacher evaluations of conduct disorder in young children', *Journal of Child Psychology and Psychiatry* **28**, 249–60.

Fox, N. A., Coplan, R. J., Rubin, K. H. Porges, S. W., Calkins, S. D., Long, J. M., Marshall, T. R. and Stewart, S. (1995) 'Frontal activation asymmetry and social competence at four years of age', *Child Development* **66**, 1770–84.

Fox, N. A. and Davidson, R. J. (1987) 'Electroencephalogram asymmetry in response to the approach of a stranger and maternal separation in 10-month-old infants', *Developmental Psychology* **23**, 233–40.

Froming, W. J., Corley, E. B. and Rinker, L. (1990) 'The influence of public self-consciousness and the audience's characteristics on withdrawal from embarrassing situations', *Journal of Personality* **58**, 603–22.

Garcia-Coll, C., Kagan, J. and Reznick, J. S. (1984) 'Behavioral inhibition in young children', *Child Development* **55**, 1005–19.

Gaskell, E. (1967) *Ruth* (London: Dent). First published 1853.

Gelernter, C. S., Uhde, T. W., Cimbolic, P., Arnkoff, D. B., Vittone, B. J., Tancer, M. E. and Bartko, J. J. (1991) 'Cognitive-behavioral and pharmacological treatments of social phobia: A controlled study', *Archives of General Psychiatry* **48**, 938–45.

Gilbert, P. and Trower, P. (1990) 'The evolution and manifestation of social anxiety', in W. R. Crozier (ed.), *Shyness and Embarrassment: Perspectives from Social Psychology* (New York: Cambridge University Press), 144–77.

Glass, C. R., Merluzzi, T. V., Biever, J. L. and Larsen, K. H. (1982) 'Cognitive assessment of social anxiety: Development and validation of a self-statement questionnaire', *Cognitive Therapy and Research* **6**, 37–55.

Goffman, E. (1956) 'Embarrassment and social organization', *American Journal of Sociology* **62**, 264–74.

Goldsmith, H. H., Buss, K. A. and Lemery, K. S. (1997) 'Toddler and childhood temperament: Expanded content, stronger genetic evidence, new evidence for the importance of environment', *Developmental Psychology* **33**, 891–905.

Goldsmith, H. H., Lemery, K. S., Buss, K. A. and Campos, J. J. (1999) 'Genetic analyses of focal aspects of infant temperament', *Developmental Psychology* **35**, 972–85.

Gorenstein, C., Bernik, M. A., Pompeia, S. and Marcourakis, T. (1995) 'Impairment of performance associated with long-term use of benzodiazepines', *Journal of Psychopharmacology* **9**, 313–8.

Gortmaker, S. L., Kagan, J., Caspi, A. and Silva, P. A. (1997) 'Daylength during pregnancy and shyness in children: Results from northern and southern hemispheres', *Developmental Psychobiology* **31**, 107–14.

Gray, J. A. (1987) *The Psychology of Fear and Stress* 2nd edn (Cambridge: Cambridge University Press).

Gross, E. and Stone, G. P. (1964) 'Embarrassment and the analysis of role requirements', *American Journal of Sociology* **70**, 1–15.

Hackmann, A. and Clark, D. M. (1998) 'Images and memories in social phobia', paper presented at European Association of Behavioural and Cognitive Therapies, Cork, Ireland, September 9–12.

Harris, P. R. (1984) 'Shyness and Psychological Imperialism; on the dangers of ignoring the ordinary language roots of the terms we deal with', *European Journal of Social Psychology* **14**, 169–81.

Harris, P. R. (1990) 'Shyness and embarrassment in psychological theory and ordinary language', in W.R. Crozier (ed.), *Shyness and Embarrassment: Perspectives from Social Psychology* (New York: Cambridge University Press), 59–86.

Harter, S. (1990) 'Causes, correlates and the functional role of global self-worth: A life-span perspective', in J. Kolligian and R. J. Sternberg (eds), *Perceptions of Competence and Incompetence across the Life-span* (New Haven, CT: Yale University Press), 67–98.

Hass, R. G. (1984) 'Perspective-taking and self-awareness: Drawing an E on your forehead', *Journal of Personality and Social Psychology* **46**, 788–98.

Hazen, A. L. and Stein, M. B. (1995) 'Clinical phenomenology and comorbidity', in M. B. Stein (ed.), *Social Phobia: Clinical and Research Perspectives* (Washington, DC: American Psychiatric Press), 3–41.

Heider, F. (1958) *The Psychology of Interpersonal Relations* (Hillsdale, NJ: Erlbaum).

Heimberg, R. G., Juster, H. R., Hope, D. A. and Mattia, J. (1995) 'Cognitive-behavioral group treatment: Description, case presentation, and empirical support', in M. B. Stein (ed.), *Social Phobia: Clinical and Research Perspectives* (Washington, DC: American Psychiatric Press), 293–321.

Henderson, L. and Zimbardo, P. G. (1999) 'Commentary: Developmental outcomes and clinical perspectives', in L. A. Schmidt and J. Schulkin (eds), *Extreme Fear, Shyness, and Social Phobia* (New York: Oxford University Press), 294–305.

Higgins, E. T. (1987) 'Self-discrepancy: A theory relating self and affect', *Psychological Review* **94**, 319–40.

Hill, G. J. (1989) 'An unwillingness to act: Behavioral appropriateness, situational constraint, and self-efficacy in shyness', *Journal of Personality* **57**, 871–89.

Hirschfeld, D. R., Rosenbaum, J. F., Biederman, J., Bolduc, A. A., Faraone, S. V., Snidman, N., Reznick, J. S. and Kagan, J. (1992) 'Stable behavioral inhibition and its association with anxiety disorder', *Journal of the American Academy of Child and Adolescent Psychiatry* **31**, 103–11.

Holmes, T. H., Treuting, T. and Wolff, H. G. (1951) 'Life situations, emotions, and nasal disease', *Psychosomatic Medicine* **13**, 71–82.

Hope, D. A. and Heimberg, R. G. (1988) 'Public and private self-consciousness and social phobia', *Journal of Personality Assessment* **52**, 629–39.

Hymel, S., Woody, E. and Bowker, A. (1993) 'Social withdrawal in childhood: Considering the child's perspective', in K. H. Rubin and J. B. Asendorpf (eds), *Social Withdrawal, Inhibition and Shyness in Childhood* (Hillsdale, NJ: Erlbaum), 237–62.

Jackson, T., Towson, S. and Narduzzi, K. (1997) 'Predictors of shyness: A test of variables associated with self-presentational models', *Social Behavior and Personality* **25**, 149–54.

Jennings, J. R. and McKnight, J. D. (1994) 'Inferring vagal tone from heart rate variability', *Psychosomatic Medicine* **56**, 194–6.

Jones, W. H. and Russell, D. (1982) 'The Social Reticence Scale: An objective instrument to measure shyness', *Journal of Personality Assessment* **46**, 629–31.

Kagan, J. (1981) *The Second Year* (Cambridge, MA: Harvard University Press).

Kagan, J. (1994) *Galen's Prophecy: Temperament in Human Nature* (London: Free Association Books).

Kagan, J. (1998) 'Biology and the child', in N. Eisenberg (ed.), *Handbook of Child Psychology. Volume 3. Social, Emotional and Personality Development* (New York: Wiley), 177–235.

Kagan, J., Reznick, J. S., Clark, C. and Snidman, N. (1984) 'Behavioral inhibition to the unfamiliar', *Child Development* **55**, 2212–25.

Kagan, J., Reznick, J. S. and Snidman, N. (1987) 'The physiology and psychology of behavioral inhibition in children', *Child Development* **58**, 1459–73.

Kagan, J., Reznick, J. S., Snidman, N., Gibbons, J. and Johnson, M. O. (1988) 'Childhood derivatives of inhibition and lack of inhibition to the unfamiliar', *Child Development* **59**, 1580–9.

Kagan, J., Snidman, N. and Arcus, D. (1993) 'On the temperamental categories of inhibited and uninhibited children', in K. H. Rubin and J. B. Asendorpf (eds), *Social Withdrawal, Inhibition, and Shyness in Childhood* (Hillsdale, NJ: Erlbaum), 19–28.

Kagan, J., Snidman, N., Julia-Sellers, M. and Johnson, M. O. (1991) 'Temperament and allergic symptoms', *Psychosomatic Medicine* **53**, 332–40.

Karafa, J. A. and Cozzarelli, C. (1997) 'Shyness and reduced sexual arousal in males: The transference of cognitive interference', *Basic and Applied Social Psychology* **19**, 329–44.

Katzelnick, D. J., Kobak, K. A., Greist, J. H., *et al.* (1995) 'Sertraline for social phobia: A double-blind, placebo-controlled crossover study', *American Journal of Psychiatry* **152**, 1368–71.

Keltner, D. (1995) 'The signs of appeasement: Evidence for the distinct displays of embarrassment, amusement, and shame', *Journal of Personality and Social Psychology* **68**, 441–54.

Keltner, D. and Buswell, B. N. (1997) 'Embarrassment: Its distinct form and appeasement functions', *Psychological Bulletin* **122**, 250–70.

Keltner, D. and L. A. Harker (1998) 'The forms and functions of the nonverbal signal of shame', in P. Gilbert and B. Andrews (eds), *Shame* (New York: Oxford University Press), 78–98.

Kemple, K. M. (1995) 'Shyness and self-esteem in early childhood', *Journal of Humanistic Education and Development* **33**, 173–82.

Kerr, M., Lambert, W. W. and Bem, D. J. (1996) 'Life course sequelae of childhood shyness in Sweden: Comparison with the United States', *Developmental Psychology* **32**, 1100–5.

Kerr, M., Lambert, W. W., Stattin, H. and Klackenberg-Larsson, I. (1994) 'Stability of inhibition in a Swedish longitudinal sample', *Child Development* **65**, 138–46.

Kerr, M., Tremblay, R. E., Pagani, L. and Vitaro, F. (1997) 'Boys' behavioral inhibition and the risk of later delinquency', *Archives of General Psychiatry* **54**, 809–16.

Kessler, R. C., McGonagle, K. A., Zhao, S., Nelson, C. B., Hughes, M., Eshleman, S., Wittchen, H.-U. and Kendler, K. S. (1994) 'Lifetime and 12-month prevalence of DSM-III-R psychiatric disorders in the United States', *Archives of General Psychiatry* **51**, 8–19.

Kessler, R. C., Stang, P., Wittchen, H.-U. and Walters, E. E. (1999) 'Lifetime comorbidities between social phobia and mood disorders in the US National Comorbidity Survey', *Psychological Medicine* **29**, 555–67.

Kowalski, R. M. and Leary, M. (1990) 'Strategic self-presentation and the avoidance of aversive events: Antecedents and consequences of self-enhancement and self-depreciation', *Journal of Experimental Social Psychology* **26**, 322–36.

Kretchmer, E. (1925) *Physique and Character*, 2nd edn, transl. W. J. H. Sprott (New York: Harcourt Brace).

Leary, M. R. (1983) *Understanding Social Anxiety* (Beverly Hills, CA: Sage).

Leary, M. R. and Downs, D. L. (1995) 'Interpersonal functions of the self-esteem motive: The self-system as a sociometer', in M. Kernis (ed.), *Efficacy, Agency, and Self-esteem* (New York: Plenum), 123–44.

Leary, M. R. and Kowalski, R. M. (1995) *Social Anxiety* (New York: Guilford Press).

Leary, M. R. and Meadows, S. (1991) 'Predictors, elicitors, and concomitants of social blushing', *Journal of Personality and Social Psychology* **60**, 254–62.

LeDoux, J. E. (1998) *The Emotional Brain* (London: Weidenfeld and Nicolson).

Lewinsky, H. (1941) 'The nature of shyness', *British Journal of Psychology* **32**, 105–13.

Lewis, M. (1995) 'Embarrassment: The emotion of self-exposure and evaluation', in J. P. Tangney and K. W. Fischer (eds), *Self-conscious Emotions* (New York: Guilford), 198–218.

Lewis, M., Alessandri, S. M. and Sullivan, M. W. (1992) 'Differences in shame and pride as a function of children's gender and task difficulty', *Child Development* **63**, 630–8.

Lewis, M. and Brooks-Gunn, J. (1979) *Social Cognition and the Acquisition of Self* (New York: Plenum Press).

Lewis, M., Sullivan, M. W., Stanger, C. and Weiss, M. (1989) 'Self-development and self-conscious emotions', *Child Development* **60**, 146–56.

Liebowitz, M. R., Schneier, P., Campeas, R., Hollander, E., Hatterer, J., Fyer, A., Gorman, J., Papp, L., Davies, S., Gully, R. and Klein, D. F. (1992) 'Phenelzine vs atenolol in social phobia: A placebo controlled trial', *Archives of General Psychiatry* **49**, 290–300.

Lykken, D. T., McGue, M., Tellegen, A. and Bouchard, T. J. (1992) 'Emergenesis: Genetic traits that may not run in families', *American Psychologist* **47**, 1565–77.

Marcus, D. K. and Miller, R. S. (1999) 'The perception of "live" embarrassment: A social relations analysis of class presentations', *Cognition and Emotion* **13**, 105–17.

Marshall, P. (1989) 'Attention deficit disorder and allergy: A neurochemical model of the relation between the illnesses', *Psychological Bulletin* **106**, 434–46.

Marshall, P. J. and Stevenson-Hinde, J. (1998) 'Behavioral inhibition, heart period, and respiratory sinus arrhythmia in young children', *Developmental Psychobiology* **33**, 283–92.

Matheny, Jr, A.P. (1989) 'Children's behavioral inhibition over age and across situations: Genetic similarity for a trait during change', *Journal of Personality* **57**, 215–35.

Matthews, G. and Gilliland, K. (1999) 'The personality theories of H. J. Eysenck and J. A. Gray: A comparative review', *Personality and Individual Differences* **26**, 583–626.

McCroskey, J. C. (1970) 'Measures of communication-bound anxiety', *Speech Monographs 37*, 269–77.

McCroskey, J. C., Anderson, J. F., Richmond, V. P. and Wheeless, L. R. (1981) 'Communication apprehension of elementary and secondary school students and their teachers', *Communication Education* **30**, 122–32.

McCroskey, J. C. and Beatty, M. J. (1986) 'Oral communication apprehension', in W. H. Jones, J. M. Cheek and S. R. Briggs (eds), *Shyness: Perspectives on Research and Treatment* (New York: Plenum), 279–93.

McLeod, C. (1996) 'Anxiety and cognitive processes', in I. G. Sarason, G. R. Pierce and B. R. Sarason (eds), *Cognitive Interference* (Mahwah, NJ: Erlbaum), 47–76.

Meichenbaum, D. and Cameron, R. (1982) 'Cognitive-behavior therapy', in G. T. Wilson and C. M. Franks (eds), *Contemporary Behavior Therapy* (New York: Guilford Press), 310–38.

Melchior, L. A. and Cheek, J. (1990) 'Shyness and anxious self-preoccupation during a social interaction', *Journal of Social Behavior and Personality* **5**, 117–30.

Miller, R. S. (1987) 'Empathic embarrassment: Situational and personal determinants of reactions to the embarrassment of another', *Journal of Personality and Social Psychology* **53**, 1061–9.

Miller, R. S. (1992) 'The nature and severity of self-reported embarrassing circumstances', *Personality and Social Psychology Bulletin* **18**, 190–8.

Miller, R. S. (1995) 'On the nature of embarrassability: Shyness, social evaluation, and social skill', *Journal of Personality* **63**, 315–39.

Miller, R. S. (1996) *Embarrassment: Poise and Peril in Everyday Life* (New York: Guilford Press).

Mills, R. S. L. and Rubin, K. H. (1993) 'Socialization factors in the development of social withdrawal', in K. H. Rubin and J. B. Asendorpf (eds), *Social Withdrawal, Inhibition, and Shyness in Childhood* (Hillsdale, NJ: Erlbaum), 117–48.

Mischel, W. (1968) *Personality and Assessment* (New York: Wiley).

Modigliani, A. (1968) 'Embarrassment and embarrassability', *Sociometry 31*, 313–26.

Modigliani, A. (1971) 'Embarrassment, facework, and eye contact: Testing a theory of embarrassment', *Journal of Personality and Social Psychology 17*, 15–24.

Morris, C. G. (1982) 'Assessment of shyness', unpublished manuscript, University of Michigan.

Mosher, D. L. and White, B. B. (1981) 'On differentiating shame and shyness', *Motivation and Emotion* **5**, 61–74.

Mueller, C. M. and Dweck, C. S. (1998) 'Praise for intelligence can undermine children's motivation and performance', *Journal of Personality and Social Psychology* **75**, 33–52.

Ohman, A. and Dimberg, U. (1978) 'Facial expressions as conditioned stimuli for electrodermal responses: A case of "preparedness"?' *Journal of Personality and Social Psychology* **36**, 1251–8.

Ohman, A., Dimberg, U. and Ost, L. G. (1985) 'Animal and social phobias: Biological constraints on learned fear responses', in S. Reiss and R. R. Bootzin (eds), *Theoretical Issues in Behavior Therapy* (New York: Academic Press), 123–75.

Olsson-Rex, L., Drott, C., Claes, G., Gothberg, G. and Dalman, P. (1998) 'The Boras experience of endoscopic thoracic sympathicotomy for palmar, axillary, facial hyperhidrosis and facial blushing', *European Journal of Surgery* **164**, S580, 23–6.

Ortony, A., Clore, G. L. and Collins, A. (1988) *The Cognitive Structure of Emotions* (Cambridge: Cambridge University Press).

Parrott, W. G., Sabini, J. and Silver, M. (1988) 'The roles of self-esteem and social interaction in embarrassment', *Personality and Social Psychology Bulletin* **14**, 191–202.

Parrott, W. G. and Smith, S. F. (1991) 'Embarrassment: Actual vs. typical cases, classical vs. prototypical representations', *Cognition and Emotion* **5**, 467–88.

Patterson, F. G. P. and Cohn, R. H. (1994) 'Self-recognition and self-awareness in lowland gorillas', in S. T. Parker, R. W. Mitchell and M. L. Boccia (eds), *Self-awareness in Animals and Humans* (Cambridge: Cambridge University Press), 273–90.

Paulhus, D. L. and Morgan, K. L. (1997) 'Perceptions of intelligence in leaderless groups: The dynamic effects of shyness and acquaintance', *Journal of Personality and Social Psychology* **72**, 581–91.

Pilkonis, P. A. (1977a) 'Shyness, public and private, and its relationship to other measures of social behavior', *Journal of Personality* **45**, 585–95.

Pilkonis, P. A. (1977b) 'The behavioral consequences of shyness', *Journal of Personality* **45**, 596–611.

Pilkonis, P. A. and Zimbardo, P. G. (1979) 'The personal and social dynamics of shyness', in C.E. Izard (ed.), *Emotions in Personality and Psychopathology* (New York: Plenum), 133–60.

Plomin, R. and Daniels, D. (1987) 'Why are children in the same family so different from each other?', *The Behavioral and Brain Sciences* **10**, 1–16.

Porges, S. W., Doussard-Roosevelt, J. A. and Maiti, A. K. (1994) 'Vagal tone and the physiological regulation of emotion', *Monographs of the Society for Research in Child Development* **59**, 167–86.

Reddy, V. (2000) 'Coyness in early infancy', *Developmental Science* **3**, 186–92.

Reimer, M. S. (1996) '"Sinking into the ground": The development and consequences of shame in adolescence', *Developmental Review* **16**, 321–63.

Reznick, J. S., Kagan, J., Snidman, N., Gersten, M., Baak, K. and Rosenberg, A. (1986) 'Inhibited and uninhibited children: A follow-up study', *Child Development* **57**, 660–80.

Rodgers, J. L., Rowe, D. C. and Li, C. (1994) 'Beyond nature versus nurture: DF analysis of nonshared influences on problem behaviors', *Developmental Psychology* **30**, 374–84.

Rothbart, M. K. and Bates, J. E. (1998) 'Temperament', in N. Eisenberg (ed.), *Handbook of Child Psychology. Volume 3. Social, Emotional and Personality Development* (New York: Wiley), 105–76.

Rowe, D. C. and Plomin, R. (1977) 'Temperament in early childhood', *Journal of Personality Assessment* **41**, 150–6.

Rubin, K. H. (1993) 'The Waterloo Longitudinal Project: Correlates and consequences of social withdrawal from childhood to adolescence', in K. H. Rubin and J. B. Asendorpf (eds), *Social Withdrawal, Inhibition, and Shyness in Childhood* (Hillsdale, NJ: Erlbaum), 291–314.

Russell, D., Cutrona, C. and Jones, W. H. (1986) 'A trait-situational analysis of shyness', in W. H. Jones, J. M. Cheek and S. R. Briggs (eds), *Shyness: Perspectives on Research and Treatment* (New York: Plenum Press), 239–49.

Rutter, M. (1989) 'Pathways from childhood to adult life', *Journal of Child Psychology and Psychiatry* **30**, 25–51.

Scherer, K. R. (1984) 'On the nature and function of emotion: A component process approach', in K. R. Scherer and P. Ekman (eds), *Approaches to Emotion* (Hillsdale, NJ: Erlbaum), 293–318.

Schlenker, B. R. and Leary, M. R. (1982) 'Social anxiety and self-presentation: A conceptualization and model', *Psychological Bulletin* **92**, 641–69.

Schlette, P., Brandstrom, S., Eisemann, M., Sigvardsson, S., Nylander, P.-O., Adolfsson, R. and Peris, C. (1998) 'Perceived parental rearing behaviours and temperament and character in healthy adults', *Personality and Individual Differences* **24**, 661–8.

Schmidt, L. A. and Fox, N. A. (1994) 'Patterns of cortical electrophysiology and autonomic activity in adults' shyness and sociability', *Biological Psychology* **38**, 183–98.

Schmidt, L. A. and Fox, N. A. (1996) 'Left-frontal EEG activation in the development of toddlers' sociability', *Brain and Cognition* **32**, 243–6.

Schmidt, L. A. and Fox, N. A. (1999) 'Conceptual, biological, and behavioral distinctions among different categories of shy children', in L. A. Schmidt and J. Schulkin (eds), *Extreme Fear, Shyness, and Social Phobia* (New York: Oxford University Press), 47–66.

Schmidt, L. A., Fox, N. A., Rubin, K. H., Sternberg, E. M., Gold, P. W., Smith, C. C. and Schulkin, J. (1997) 'Behavioral and neuroendocrine responses in shy children', *Developmental Psychobiology* **30**, 127–40.

Schmidt, L. A., Fox, N. A., Sternberg, E., Gold, P. W., Smith, C. C. and Schulkin, J. (1999) 'Adrenocortical reactivity and social competence in seven year-olds', *Personality and Individual Differences* **26**, 977–85.

Schmidt, L. A. and Robinson, Jr., T. N. (1992) 'Low self-esteem in differentiating fearful and self-conscious forms of shyness', *Psychological Reports* **70**, 255–7.

Schneier, F. R., Johnson, J., Horning, C. D., Liebowitz, M. R. and Weissman, M. M. (1992) 'Social phobia: Comorbidity and morbidity in an epidemiologic sample', *Archives of General Psychiatry* **49**, 282–8.

Scholing, A. and Emmelkamp, P. M. G. (1996) 'Treatment of fear of blushing, sweating, or trembling: Results at long-term follow-up', *Behavior Modification* **20**, 338–56.

Schore, A. N. (1998) 'Early shame experiences and infant brain development', in P. Gilbert and B. Andrews (eds), *Shame* (New York: Oxford University Press), 57–77.

Seifer, R., Schillier, M., Sameroff, A. J., Resnick, S. and Riordan, K. (1996) 'Attachment, maternal sensitivity, and infant temperament during the first year of life', *Developmental Psychology* **32**, 12–25.

Seligman, M. E. P. (1971) 'Phobias and preparedness', *Behavior Therapy* **2**, 307–20.

Selman, R. (1980) *The Growth of Interpersonal Understanding: Development and Clinical Analysis* (New York: Academic Press).

Semin, G. R. and Manstead, A. S. R. (1981) 'The beholder beheld: a study of social emotionality', *European Journal of Social Psychology* **11**, 253–65.

Semin, G. R. and Manstead, A. S. R. (1982) 'The social implications of embarrassment displays and restitution behaviour', *European Journal of Social Psychology* **12**, 367–77.

Semin, G. R. and Manstead, A. S. R. (1983) *The Accountability of Conduct: A Social Psychological Analysis* (London: Academic Press).

Shearn, D., Bergman, E., Hill, K., Abel, A. and Hinds, L. (1990) 'Facial coloration and temperature responses in blushing', *Psychophysiology* **27**, 687–93.

Sheldon, W. H. (1940) *The Varieties of Human Physique* (New York: Harper).

Shepperd, J. A. and Arkin, R. M. (1990) 'Shyness and self-presentation', in W. R. Crozier (ed.), *Shyness and Embarrassment: Perspectives from Social Psychology* (New York: Cambridge University Press), 286–314.

Silver, M., Sabini, J. and Parrott, W. G. (1987) 'Embarrassment: A dramaturgic account', *Journal for the Theory of Social Behaviour* **17**, 47–61.

Simmons, R. G., Rosenberg, F. and Rosenberg, M. (1973) 'Disturbance in the self-image at adolescence', *American Sociological Review* **38**, 553–68.

Spinath, F. M. and Angleiter, A. (1998) 'Contrast effects in Buss and Plomin's EAS questionnaire: A behavioral-genetic study on early developing personality traits assessed through parental ratings', *Personality and Individual Differences* **25**, 947–63.

Spoont, M. R. (1992) 'Modulatory role of serotonin in neural information processing: Implications for human psychopathology', *Psychological Bulletin* **112**, 330–50.

Stein, D. J. and Bouwer, C. (1997) 'Blushing and social phobia: A neuroethological speculation', *Medical Hypotheses* **49**, 101–8.

Stein, M. B., Fyer, A. J., Davidson, J. R. T., Pollack, M. H. and Wiita, B. (1999) 'Fluvoxamine in the treatment of social phobia: A double-blind, placebo-controlled study', *American Journal of Psychiatry* **156**, 756–60.

Stein, M. B., Liebowitz, M., Lydiard, B., Pitts, C. D., Bushnell, W. and Gergel, I. (1998) 'Paroxetine treatment of generalized social phobia (social anxiety disorder)', *JAMA: Journal of the American Medical Association* **280**, 708–13.

Stein, M. D., Heuser, I. J., Juncos, J. L. and Uhde, T. W. (1990) 'Anxiety disorders in patients with Parkinson's disease', *American Journal of Psychiatry* **147**, 217–20.

Steins, G. and Wicklund, R. A. (1996) 'Perspective-taking, conflict, and press: Drawing an E on your forehead', *Basic and Applied Social Psychology* **18**, 319–46.

Stevenson-Hinde, J. and Glover, A. (1996) 'Shy girls and boys: A new look', *Journal of Child Psychology and Psychiatry* **37**, 181–7.

Stevenson-Hinde, J. and Shouldice, A. (1993) 'Wariness to strangers: A behavior systems perspective revisited', in K. H. Rubin and J. B. Asendorpf (eds), *Social Withdrawal, Inhibition, and Shyness in Childhood* (Hillsdale, NJ: Erlbaum), 101–16.

Stipek, D. (1995) 'The development of pride and shame in toddlers', in J. P. Tangney and K. W. Fischer (eds), *Self-conscious Emotions* (New York: Guilford Press) 237–52.

Stopa, L. and Clark, D. M. (1993) 'Cognitive processes in social phobia', *Behaviour Research and Therapy* **31**, 255–67.

Stravynski, A. and Greenberg, D. (1998) 'The treatment of social phobia: A critical assessment', *Acta Psychiatrica Scandinavica* **98**, 171–81.

Sutherland, S. M. and Davidson, J. R. T. (1995) 'Beta-blockers and benzodiazepines in pharmacotherapy', in M. B. Stein (ed.), *Social Phobia* (Washington, DC: American Psychiatric Press), 323–46.

Szkrybalo, J. and Ruble, D. N. (1999) '"God made me a girl": Sex-category constancy judgments and explanations revisited', *Developmental Psychology* **35**, 392–402.

Tangney, J. P. and Fischer, K. W. (eds) (1995) *Self-conscious Emotions* (New York: Guilford).

Tangney, J. P., Miller, R. S., Flicker, L. and Barlow, D. H. (1996) 'Are shame, guilt, and embarrassment distinct emotions?', *Journal of Personality and Social Psychology* **70**, 1256–64.

Tannen, D. (1992) *You Just Don't Understand. Women and Men in Conversation* (London: Virago).

Taylor, G. (1985) *Pride, Shame, and Guilt: Emotions of Self Assessment* (Oxford: Clarendon Press).

Teleranta, T. (1998) 'Treatment of social phobia by endoscopic thoracic sympathicotomy', *European Journal of Surgery* **164**, S580, 27–32.

Tice, D. M., Buder, J. and Baumeister, R. F. (1985) 'Development of self-consciousness: At what age does audience pressure disrupt performance?', *Adolescence* **20**, 301–5.

Tomkins, S. S. (1963) *Affect, Imagery, Consciousness. Vol. 2: The Negative Affects* (New York: Springer).

Tomkins, S. S. (1995) 'The varieties of shame and its magnification', in E. V. Demos (ed.), *Exploring Affect: The Selected Writings of Silvan S. Tomkins* (Cambridge: Cambridge University Press), 397–410.

Turner, B. and Rennell, T. (1995) *When Daddy Came Home* (London: Hutchinson).

Turner, S. M., Beidel, D. C. and Jacob, R. G. (1994) 'Social phobia: A comparison of behavior therapy and atenolol', *Journal of Consulting and Clinical Psychology* **62**, 350–8.

Turner, S. M., Beidel, D. C. and Townsley, R. M. (1990) 'Social phobia: Relationship to shyness', *Behaviour Research and Therapy* **28**, 497–505.

Turner, S. M., Beidel, D. C. and Wolff, P. L. (1996) 'Is behavioral inhibition related to the anxiety disorders?', *Clinical Psychology Review* **16**, 157–72.

Updike, J. (1980) *Your Lover Just Called* (Harmondsworth: Penguin).

Van Ameringen, M., Mancini, C., Farvolden, P. and Oakman, J. M. (1999a) 'Pharmacotherapy for social phobia: What works, what might work and what doesn't work at all', *CNS Spectrums: The International Journal of Neuropsychiatric Medicine* **4** (11), 61–8.

Van Ameringen, M., Mancini, C. and Oakman, J. M. (1998) 'The relationship of behavioral inhibition and shyness to anxiety disorder', *Journal of Nervous and Mental Disease*, 186, 425–31.

Van Ameringen, M., Mancini, C. and Oakman, J. M. (1999b) 'Nefazodone in social phobia', *Journal of Clinical Psychiatry* **60**, 96–100.

Van Ameringen, M., Mancini, C., Oakman, J. M. and Farvolden, P. (1999c) 'Selective Serotonin Reuptake Inhibitors in the treatment of social phobia', *CNS Drugs* **11**, 307–15.

Van der Molen, H. (1990) 'A definition of shyness and its implications for clinical practice', in W. R. Crozier (ed.), *Shyness and Embarrassment: Perspectives from Social Psychology* (New York: Cambridge University Press), 255–85.

Van Vliet, I. M., Den Boer, J. A. and Westenberg, H. G. M. (1992) 'Psychopharmacological treatment of social phobia: Clinical and biochemical effects of brofaromine, a selective MAO-A inhibitor', *European Neuropsychopharmacology* **2**, 21–9.

Van Vliet, I. M., Den Boer, J. and Westenberg, H. G. M. (1994) 'Psychopharmacological treatment of social phobia: A double-blind placebo controlled study with fluvoxamine', *Psychopharmacology* **115**, 128–34.

Van Vliet, I. M., Den Boer, J. A., Westenberg, H. G. M. and Pian, K. L. H. (1997) 'Clinical effects of buspirone in social phobia: A double-blind placebo-controlled study', *Journal of Clinical Psychiatry* **58**, 164–8.

Versiani, M., Nardi, A. E. and Mundim, F. D. (1989) 'Fobia social/Social phobia', *Jornal Brasilerio de Psiquitria* **38**, 251–63.

Versiani, M., Nardi, A. E., Mundim, F. D., Alves, A. B., Liebowitz, M. R. and Amrein, R. (1992) 'Pharmacotherapy of social phobia: A controlled study with moclobemide and phenelzine', *British Journal of Psychiatry* **161**, 353–60.

Walker, J. R. and Stein, M. B. (1995) 'Epidemiology', in M. B. Stein (ed.), *Social Phobia* (Washington, DC: American Psychiatric Press), 43–75.

Watson, J. B. and Rayner, R. (1920) 'Conditioned emotional reactions', *Journal of Experimental Psychology* **3**, 319–24.

Wells, A., Clark, D. M., Salkovskis, P., Ludgate, J., Hackmann, A. and Gelder, M. G. (1995) 'Social phobia: The role of in-situation safety behaviors in maintaining anxiety and negative beliefs', *Behavior Therapy* **26**, 153–61.

Wimmer, H. and Perner, J. (1983) 'Beliefs about beliefs: Representation and constraining function of wrong beliefs in young children's understanding of deception', *Cognition* **13**, 103–28.

Woody, S. R., Chambless, D. L. and Glass, C. R. (1997) 'Self-focused attention in the treatment of social phobia', *Behaviour Research and Therapy* **35**, 117–29.

Younger, A. J. and Daniels, T. M. (1992) 'Children's reasons for nominating their peers as withdrawn: Passive withdrawal versus active isolation', *Developmental Psychology* **28**, 955–60.

Younger, A. J. and Piccinin, A. M. (1989) 'Children's recall of aggressive and withdrawn behaviors: Recognition memory and likability judgments', *Child Development* **60**, 580–90.

Zajonc, R. B. (1980) 'Feeling and thinking: Preferences need no inferences', *American Psychologist* **35**, 151–75.

Zimbardo, P. G. (1977) *Shyness* (Reading, MA: Addison-Wesley).

Zimbardo, P. G., Pilkonis, P. A. and Norwood, R. M. (1974) *The silent prison of shyness*, Office of Naval Research Technical Report Z–17, Stanford University.

Index